The NHL in t

(Above: Fred Perlini's Team)

Stuart Latham

The NHL in the UK

Stuart Latham

ISBN number: 978-1-8384609-8-3
Printed by CPI Group (UK) Ltd, Croydon, CR0 4YY
Published by: S & T Sales and Marketing Ltd, Sale, Cheshire M33 4QN
Contents are copyrighted by the photographers who took the photographs. No part of this book should be reproduced without their permission.

Other Books from Stuart Latham:
The History of Alloa Athletic – ISBN No: 978-1-8384609-9-0
Diary of a Season Swinton Lions 2021 – ISBN No: 978-1-8381165-8-3
Diary of a Season Swinton Lions 2022 – ISBN No: 978-1-915697-01-1
Ice Hockey in Solihull – ISBN No - 978-1-8384609-5-2
A Kick in the Grass – ISBN No: 9780953060801
A Love That Refused to Die – ISBN No: - 0-9530608-1-0
The History of Chalfont St Peter AFC – ISBN No:9780953060825
Roughriders – The City of London Yeomanry During the First World War. – ISBN No:9780953060849
The History of Ice Hockey in Peterborough ISBN No: 978-0-9530608-6-3
The History of the Swindon Wildcats 1986 – 2016 ISBN No: 978-0-9530608-7-0
The History of the Swindon Wildcats 1986 – 2012 ISBN No; 9780953060832
The History of the Bracknell Bees ISBN No 978-0-9530608-8-7
The City of London Yeomanry 1907-1918 ISBN: 978-0-9530608-5-6
March F1 – The Leyton House Years - 1987 – 1993 ISBN No: 978-0-9530608-9-4
Hadrian Bayley The Man Who Accepted the Surrender of Jerusalem ISBN: 978-1-8381165-1-4
60 Years of The Altrincham Aces ISBN No: 978-1-8381165-0-7
The Deeside Dragons ISBN No: 978-1-8381165-3-8
Ice Hockey in Bristol ISBN No: 978-1-8381165-2-1
The Manchester Storm ISBN No: 978-1-8381165-4-5
Chalfont St Peter AFC 1926-2020 ISBN No: 978-1-8381165-5-2
The Rise and Fall of the Manchester Phoenix ISBN No: 978-1-8381165-6-9
Always and Forever ISBN No: 978-1-8381165-7-6
The Cardiff Devils – ISBN No: 978-1-8381165-9-0
Ice Hockey Memories – ISBN No: 978-1-8383328-0-8
The Slough Jets – ISBN No 978-1-8383328-2-2
The City of London Yeomanry Through Old Photographs – ISBN No: 978-1-8383328-3-9
More Ice Hockey Memories – ISBN No: 978-1-8383328-4-6
Ice Hockey in Edinburgh – ISBN No: 978-1-8383328-5-3
An Alternative View of the World of Cricket – ISBN No 978-1-8383328-7-7
Into the Abyss – ISBN No 978-1-8383328-8-4
Stars Wars– Oxford City Stars – ISBN No: 978-1-8383328-9-1
Swindon Ice Hockey Statistically Speaking 1986-2021 – ISBN No: 978-1-8384609-0-7
In Their Own Words - Swindon Ice Hockey Memories – ISBN No: 978-1-8384609-1-4
The Royal Tournament – A Pictorial History – ISBN No: 978-1-8384609-2-1
Hockey in Haringey – ISBN No: 978-1-8384609-3-8
From Vikings to Devils - Ice Hockey on the Solent – ISBN No: 978-1-8384609-4-5

Further details available from: Stuartlatham65@sky.com

Contents

Introduction 5
Acknowledgements 8
Subscribers List 8
The NHL 9
The NHL Comes to the UK 16
    Teams Playing in the UK 16
The Early Days 36
    Gordie Poirer 39
    Farrand Gillie 41
The Post War Years 42
    The 1950's to the 1970's 42
    Bert Peer 48
    Tord Lundstrom 50
    Terry Clancy 53
    Ulf Sterner 55
    Mike Korney 59
    Rick McCann 60
    Bill McKenzie 61
    Thomas Mellor 68
    Rick Newell 70
    Nelson Pyatt 71
    Terry Richardson 72
    Murray Wing 74
The Resurgence of the Sport in the UK 75
    The 1980's and 1990's 75
    Ron Plumb 76
    Jamie Leach 78

Fred Perlini	85
Frank Pietrangelo	97
Kurt Kleinendorst	103
Tony Hand	108
Garry Unger	115
Rob Robinson	123
Daryl Evans	127
Paxton Schulte	129
Todd Bidner	134
Al Sims	137
Mark Pavelich	139
Jere Gillis	143
Doug Smail	147
Mike Ware	150
Darren Banks	153
Mike Blaisdell	157
The Present Day	160
2000 to Date	160
Jared Staal	160
Jared Aulin	163
Mike Torchia	169
Jay Rosehill	173
Sean McMorrow	177
Dody Wood	182
Justin Hodgman	186
CHRONOLOGICAL LIST	194

Introduction

Welcome to my latest offering on the world of ice hockey. Having written a lot about the game in the UK, it seemed only natural to expand the topic to cover those men from North America who came over the "pond" to ply their trade over here. In effect hockey players coming home to where it all started!

Lord Frederick Stanley, the 16th Earl of Derby was a distant blood relative of mine. The Lord Stanley of Preston (as he was known) between 1886 and 1893, was a Conservative Party politician in the United Kingdom who served as Colonial Secretary from 1885 to 1886 and Governor General of Canada from 1888 to 1893. An avid sportsman, he built Stanley House Stables in England and is famous in North America for presenting Canada with the Stanley Cup. Stanley was also one of the original inductees of the Hockey Hall of Fame.

Frederick Arthur Stanley

Stanley's sons became avid ice hockey players in Canada, playing in amateur leagues in Ottawa, and Lord and Lady Stanley became staunch hockey fans. In 1892, Stanley gave Canada a treasured national icon, the Stanley Cup, known originally as the Dominion Hockey Challenge Cup. He originally donated the trophy as a challenge cup for Canada's best amateur hockey club, but in 1909, it became contested by professional teams exclusively. Since 1926, only teams of the National Hockey League have competed for the trophy. This now-famous cup bears Stanley's name as a tribute to his encouragement and love of outdoor life and sport in Canada. In recognition of this, he was inducted into the Canadian Hockey Hall of Fame in 1945 in the "Honoured Builders" category. The original size of the Stanley Cup was 7 inches (180 mm) and is now around 36 inches (910 mm)

and weighs 35 pounds (16 kg). I visited the Ice Hockey Hall of Fame just over 10 years ago with my former partner and her children and was able to have my photo taken with this trophy.

I have visited the USA and Canada a few times and have family who live in Ontario, so do feel at home when I am around Toronto and have watched a few NHL games whilst visiting North America. My first trip to Los Angeles was to witness one of Wayne Gretzky's last games before he retired. I struggled through the game having been awake for over 24 hours thanks to turbulence on my flight, but to be sat in the old Great Western Forum witnessing Marc Messier and Wayne playing made it worthwhile. Although strangely enough I came away from that match a fan of Yanic Perreault who had an exceptional match for the Kings that evening. That was a memorable trip as during my time in LA I also ended up featuring as an extra in "Godzilla", a couple of seconds in front of a green screen, but I'm on the film as an American soldier having a water tower collapse on me!

I returned to LA a few months later staying on the Queen Mary and bringing my kids with me to watch Anaheim play at the "Duck Pond/ Honda Centre". My son was now also hooked on the sport, although for some reason he supported the Pittsburgh Penguins.

A few years later I returned but this time to Toronto, whilst my former partner was concentrating on visiting Niagara Falls and the lake I managed to get tickets for the Leafs v Buffalo Sabres at the Air Canada Centre. Stub Hub sold me the seats in a block of 3 together and one a couple of rows behind. On arrival though the 3 were together but the single ticket was on the other side of the rink. It was wonderful, I got to drink beer whilst watching the game without being moaned at!

Back in the UK I started writing books on UK teams and have had 42 books published in total so far. Most have been widely accepted and enjoyed and I have a following now of fans waiting for the next instalment. The only issue I have ever had was after writing a book on the Telford Tigers, the club owners refused to allow me to publish claiming copyright on their logo and images. That's a one off as the other clubs all saw the publication as a positive move and good publicity for the product they were producing on the ice. It got "Bums on Seats" as the books created interest amongst the public so it was good for the clubs!

So as I wrote the books I got in contact with players past and present and obtained their viewpoints on the sport. This started off as a simple task but I quickly found out that hockey players can talk a lot, but getting them to write something was a totally different matter. This developed into a new hobby known as "Hassle a Hockey Player". A couple wrote articles, some said yes then disappeared when I reapproached them, others asked for questions which they answered and most seemed to have an issue typing so I had to call them and that's where they came into their own. I spent over 3 hours chatting with Garry Ungar before my phone battery ran out! Living in Sale, just outside of Manchester, the Storm were my local senior team, so as a result a few former Manchester Storm players were approached. A couple disappeared, but the others were more than happy to assist in the writing of this book. I am grateful to all that have helped me compile this book and hope that you enjoy reading their thoughts on playing in both the NHL and the UK.

Stuart Latham   January 2023

Acknowledgements

I would like to thank the following for their help in compiling this book:

Elite Prospects website for their statistics
Mark Ferriss for his photography skills

Jay Rosehill	Fred Perlini	Jared Aulin
Garry Ungar	Kurt Kleinendorst	Frank Pietrangelo
Tony Hand	Paxton Schulte	Francis Page
Jamie Leach	Sean McMorrow	Mike Torchia
Dody Wood	Rob Robinson	Justin Hodgman

Paul Breeze for listing the players in the Chronological list
The late Peter Collins for his interviews with Frank Pietrangelo and Kurt Kleinendorst.
Martin Harris and the British Ice Hockey Hall of Fame
WWW.TheLeafsnation.com   Wikipedia
Photographs kindly supplied by Getty Images Bruce Bennett
Kevin Paul Dupont and his article: https://www.boston.com/sports/bruins-blog/2010/10/02/bruins_vs_belfa/
Nathaniel Oliver   WWW.Theguardian.com   WWW.UPI.Com
Media Guides for Colorado Rockies; Kansas City Scouts; Detroit Red Wings
Chic Cottrell regarding Fife quotes
Francis Page

Subscribers List

I would like to thank the following subscribers to the book:

Mark Ferriss	Jay Rosehill
Fred Perlini	Nadya Familnova
Victoria Salomon	Mick Chambers
Paul Breeze	Gary Lee
Mark Cull	Richard Evans
Paxton Schulte	Jack Cooper
Chic Cottrell	Mike Torchia
Nicole Brigstocke-Lockyer	Paule Mayoh
Andy Brindle	Rob Hutchinson
Lee McBride	James Ashton
Jared Aulin	Jamie Leach
Fred Perlini	Sean McMorrow
Dody Wood	

The NHL

The National Hockey League (NHL; French: *Ligue nationale de hockey—LNH*, French pronunciation: [liɡ nasjɔnal də ɔkɛ]) is a professional ice hockey league in North America comprising 32 teams—25 in the United States and 7 in Canada. It is considered to be the top ranked professional ice hockey league in the world, and is one of the four major professional sports leagues in the United States and Canada. The Stanley Cup, the oldest professional sports trophy in North America, is awarded annually to the league playoff champion at the end of each season. The NHL is the fifth-wealthiest professional sport league in the world by revenue, after the National Football League (NFL), Major League Baseball (MLB), the National Basketball Association (NBA), and the English Premier League (EPL).

The National Hockey League was organized at the Windsor Hotel in Montreal on November 26, 1917, after the suspension of operations of its predecessor organization, the National Hockey Association (NHA), which had been founded in 1909 in Renfrew, Ontario. The NHL immediately took the NHA's place as one of the leagues that contested for the Stanley Cup in an annual interleague competition before a series of league mergers and folding's left the NHL as the only league left competing for the Stanley Cup in 1926.

At its inception, the NHL had four teams, all in Canada, thus the adjective "National" in the league's name. The league expanded to the United States in 1924, when the Boston Bruins joined, and has since consisted of both American and Canadian teams. From 1942 to 1967, the league had only six teams, collectively (if not contemporaneously) nicknamed the "Original Six". The NHL added six new teams to double its size at the 1967 NHL expansion. The league then increased to 18 teams by 1974 and 21 teams in 1979. Between 1991 and 2000 the NHL further expanded to 30 teams. It added its 31st and 32nd teams in 2017 and 2021, respectively.

The league's headquarters have been in Midtown Manhattan since 1989, when the head office moved from Montreal. There have been four league-wide work stoppages in NHL history, all occurring after 1992. The International Ice Hockey Federation (IIHF) considers the Stanley Cup to be one of the "most important championships available to the sport".The NHL draws many highly skilled players from all over the world and currently has players from approximately 20 countries.[12] Canadians have historically constituted the majority of the players in the league, with an increasing percentage of American and European players in recent seasons.

The Montreal Canadiens have the most NHL titles with 24 (including 23 Stanley Cup championships since entering the league). Entering the 2022–23 season, the Colorado Avalanche, who defeated the Tampa Bay Lightning 4–2 in the 2022 Stanley Cup Finals, are the reigning league champions.

Early years
The National Hockey League was established in 1917 as the successor to the National Hockey Association (NHA). Founded in 1909, the NHA began play in 1910 with seven teams in Ontario and Quebec, and was one of the first major leagues in professional ice hockey. However, by its eighth season, a series of disputes with Toronto Blueshirts owner Eddie Livingstone led team owners of the Montreal Canadiens, the Montreal Wanderers, the Ottawa Senators, and the Quebec Bulldogs to hold a meeting to discuss the league's future. Realizing the NHA constitution left them unable to force Livingstone out, the four teams voted instead to suspend the NHA, and on November 26, 1917, formed the National Hockey League. Frank Calder was chosen as the NHL's first president, serving until his death in 1943.

The Bulldogs were unable to play in the NHL, and the remaining owners founded the Toronto Arenas to compete with the Canadiens, Wanderers and Senators. The first games were played on December 19, 1917. The Montreal Arena burned down in January 1918, causing the Wanderers to cease operations, and the NHL continued on as a three-team league until the Bulldogs returned in 1919.

The Stanley Cup in 1930, several years after it became the *de facto* championship trophy for the NHL

The NHL replaced the NHA as one of the leagues that competed for the Stanley Cup, an interleague competition at the time. Toronto won the first NHL title, and then defeated the Vancouver Millionaires of the Pacific Coast Hockey Association (PCHA) for the 1918 Stanley Cup. The Canadiens won the league title in 1919, but the series in the Stanley Cup Finals against the PCHA's Seattle Metropolitans was abandoned due to the Spanish Flu epidemic. In 1924, Montreal won their first Stanley Cup as a member of the NHL. The Hamilton Tigers won the regular season title in 1924–25, but refused to play in the championship series unless they were given a C$200 bonus. The league refused and declared the Canadiens the league champion after they defeated the Toronto St. Patricks (formerly the Arenas) in the semi-final. Montreal was then defeated by the Victoria Cougars of the Western Canada Hockey League (WCHL) in 1925. It was the last time a non-NHL team won the trophy, as the Stanley Cup became the *de facto* NHL championship in 1926, after the WCHL ceased operation.

The National Hockey League embarked on a rapid expansion in the 1920s, adding the Montreal Maroons and the Boston Bruins in 1924, the latter being the first American team to join the league. The New York Americans began play in 1925 after purchasing the assets of the Hamilton Tigers, and were joined by the Pittsburgh Pirates. The New York Rangers were added in 1926, and the Chicago Black Hawks and Detroit Cougars (later the Red Wings) were added after the league purchased the assets of the defunct WCHL. A group purchased the Toronto St. Patricks in 1927 and immediately renamed them the Toronto Maple Leafs.

Original Six era
In 1934, the first NHL All-Star Game was held to benefit Ace Bailey, whose career ended on a vicious hit by Eddie Shore. The second was held in 1937 in support of Howie Morenz's family when he died of a coronary embolism after breaking his leg during a game.

The Great Depression and the onset of World War II took a toll on the league. The Pirates became the Philadelphia Quakers in 1930, then folded a year later. The Senators likewise became the St. Louis Eagles in 1934, also lasting only a year. The Maroons did not survive, as they suspended operations in 1938. The Americans were suspended in 1942 due to a lack of available players, and were never reactivated.

A game between the Montreal Canadiens and the New York Rangers in 1962
For the 1942–43 season, the NHL was reduced to six teams: the Boston Bruins, the Chicago Black Hawks, the Detroit Red Wings, the Montreal Canadiens, the New York Rangers, and the Toronto Maple Leafs, a line-up, often referred to as the "Original Six", which would remain constant for the next 25 years. In 1947, the league reached an agreement with the Stanley Cup trustees to take full control of the trophy, allowing it to reject challenges from other leagues that wished to play for the Cup.

In 1945, Maurice "Rocket" Richard became the first player to score 50 goals, doing so in a 50-game season. Richard later led the Canadiens to five consecutive titles between 1956 and 1960, a record no team has matched.

On March 13, 1948, Asian Canadian Larry Kwong became the first non-white player in the NHL and broke the league's colour barrier by playing for the New York Rangers. On January 18, 1958, Willie O'Ree became the first Black player in the league's history when he made his debut with the Boston Bruins.

Expansion era
By the mid-1960s, the desire for a network television contract in the United States, coupled with concerns that the Western Hockey League was planning to declare itself a major league and challenge for the Stanley Cup, spurred the NHL to undertake its first expansion since the 1920s. The league doubled in size to 12 teams for the 1967–68 season, adding the Los Angeles Kings, the Minnesota North Stars, the Philadelphia Flyers, the Pittsburgh Penguins, the California Seals, and the St. Louis Blues. However, Canadian fans were outraged that all six teams were placed in the United States, so the league responded by adding the Vancouver Canucks in 1970, along with the Buffalo Sabres, both located on the Canada–United States border. Two years later, the emergence of the newly founded World Hockey Association (WHA) led the league to add the New York Islanders and the Atlanta Flames to keep the rival league out of those markets. In 1974, the Washington Capitals and the Kansas City Scouts were added, bringing the league up to 18 teams.

The NHL fought the WHA for players, losing 67 to the new league in its first season of 1972–73, including the Chicago Black Hawks' Bobby Hull, who signed a ten-year, $2.5 million contract with the Winnipeg Jets, then the largest in hockey history. The league attempted to block the defections in court, but a counter-suit by the WHA led to a Philadelphia judge ruling the NHL's reserve clause to be illegal, thus eliminating the elder league's monopoly over the players. Seven years of battling for players and markets financially damaged both leagues, leading to a merger agreement in 1979 that saw the WHA cease operations while the NHL absorbed the Winnipeg Jets, the Edmonton Oilers, the Hartford Whalers, and the Quebec Nordiques. The owners initially rejected this merger agreement by one vote, but a massive boycott of Molson Brewery products by Canadian fans resulted in the Montreal Canadiens, which was owned by Molson, reversing its position, along with the Vancouver Canucks. In a second vote, the plan was approved.

Wayne Gretzky played one season in the WHA for the Indianapolis Racers (eight games) and the Edmonton Oilers (72 games) before the Oilers joined the NHL for the 1979–80 season. Gretzky went on to lead the Oilers to win four Stanley Cup championships in 1984, 1985, 1987, and 1988, and set single season records for goals (92 in 1981–82), assists (163 in 1985–86) and points (215 in 1985–86), as well as career records for goals (894), assists (1,963) and points (2,857). In 1988, he was traded to the Los Angeles Kings in a deal that dramatically improved the league's popularity in the United States. By the turn of the century, nine more teams were added to the NHL: the San Jose Sharks, the Tampa Bay Lightning, the Ottawa Senators, the Mighty Ducks of Anaheim, the Florida Panthers, the Nashville Predators, the Atlanta Thrashers (now the Winnipeg Jets), and in 2000, the Minnesota Wild and the Columbus Blue Jackets. On July 21, 2015, the NHL confirmed that it had received applications from prospective ownership groups in Quebec City and Las Vegas for possible expansion teams, and on June 22, 2016, NHL Commissioner Gary Bettman announced the addition of a 31st franchise, based in Las Vegas and later named the Vegas Golden Knights, into the NHL for the 2017–18 season. On December 4, 2018, the league announced a 32nd franchise in Seattle, later named the Seattle Kraken who joined in the 2021–22 season.

Labour issues
There have been four league-wide work stoppages in NHL history, all occurring after 1992. The first was a strike by the National Hockey League Players' Association in April 1992, which lasted for ten days but was settled quickly with all affected games rescheduled.

A lockout at the start of the 1994–95 season forced the league to reduce the schedule from 84 games to 48, with the teams playing only intra-conference games during the reduced season. The resulting collective bargaining agreement (CBA) was set for renegotiation in 1998, and extended to September 15, 2004.

With no new agreement in hand when the contract expired, league commissioner Gary Bettman announced a lockout of the players union and closed the league's head office for the 2004–05 season. The league vowed to install what it dubbed "cost certainty" for its teams, but the Players' Association countered that the move was little more than a euphemism for a salary cap, which the union initially said it would not accept. The lockout shut down the league for 310 days, making it the longest in sports history, as the NHL became the first professional sports league to lose an entire season. A new collective bargaining agreement was eventually ratified in July 2005, including a salary cap. The agreement had a term of six years with an option of extending the collective bargaining agreement for an additional year at the end of the term, allowing the league to resume as of the 2005–06 season.

On October 5, 2005, the first post-lockout season took to the ice with all 30 teams. The NHL received record attendance in the 2005–06 season, with an average of 16,955 per game. However, its television audience was slower to rebound due to American cable broadcaster ESPN's decision to drop its NHL coverage. The league's post-lockout agreement with NBC gave the league a share of revenue from each game's advertising sales, rather than the usual lump sum paid up front for game rights. The league's annual revenues were estimated at $2.27 billion.

On September 16, 2012, the labour pact expired, and the league again locked out the players. The owners proposed reducing the players' share of hockey-related revenues from 57 percent to 47 percent. All games were cancelled up to January 14, 2013, along with the 2013 NHL Winter Classic and the 2013 NHL All-Star Weekend. On January 6, a tentative agreement was reached on a ten-year deal. On January 12, the league and the Players' Association signed a memorandum of understanding on the new deal, allowing teams to begin their training camps the next day, with a shortened 48-game season schedule that began on January 19.

Player safety issues
Player safety has become a major issue in the NHL, with concussions resulting from a hard hit to the head being the primary concern. Recent studies have shown how the consequences of concussions can last beyond player retirement. This has significant effects on the league, as elite players have suffered from the aftereffects of concussions (such as Sidney Crosby being side-lined for approximately ten and a half months), which adversely affects the league's marketability. In December 2009, Brendan Shanahan was hired to replace Colin Campbell, and was given the role of senior vice-president of player safety. Shanahan began to hand out suspensions on high-profile perpetrators responsible for dangerous hits, such as Raffi Torres receiving 25 games for his hit on Marian Hossa. To aid with removing high-speed collisions on icing, which had led to several potential career-ending injuries such as Hurricanes' defenceman Joni

Pitkanen, the league mandated hybrid no-touch icing for the 2013–14 NHL season.

On November 25, 2013, ten former NHL players (Gary Leeman, Rick Vaive, Brad Aitken, Darren Banks, Curt Bennett, Richie Dunn, Warren Holmes, Bob Manno, Blair Stewart, and Morris Titanic) sued the league for negligence in protecting players from concussions. The suit came three months after the National Football League agreed to pay former players US$765 million due to a player safety lawsuit.

Women in the NHL
From 1952 to 1955, Marguerite Norris served as president of the Detroit Red Wings, being the first female NHL executive and the first woman to have her name engraved on the Stanley Cup. In 1992, Manon Rhéaume became the first woman to play a game in any of the major professional North American sports leagues, as a goaltender for the Tampa Bay Lightning in a pre-season game against the St. Louis Blues, stopping seven of nine shots. In 2016, Dawn Braid was hired as the Arizona Coyotes' skating coach, making her the first female full-time coach in the NHL. The first female referees in the NHL were hired in a test-run during the league's preseason prospect tournaments in September 2019.

In 2016, the NHL hosted the 2016 Outdoor Women's Classic, an exhibition game between the Boston Pride of the National Women's Hockey League and the Les Canadiennes of the Canadian Women's Hockey League, as part of the 2016 NHL Winter Classic weekend festivities. In 2019, the NHL invited four women from the US and Canadian Olympic teams to demonstrate the events in All-Star skills competition before the All-Star Game. Due to Nathan MacKinnon choosing not to participate following a bruised ankle, Team USA's Kendall Coyne Schofield competed in the Fastest Skater competition in his place becoming the first woman to officially compete in the NHL's All-Star festivities. The attention led the NHL to include a 3-on-3 women's game before the 2020 All-Star Game.[79] Rheaume returned to perform as a goaltender for the 2022 NHL All-Star Game's Breakaway Challenge.

The NHL Comes to the UK

Teams Playing in the UK

1938 Detroit Red Wings–Montreal Canadiens European tour

In 1938, for the first time in NHL history two of the league's teams, the Detroit Red Wings and the Montreal Canadiens, went on a tour of Europe with a nine-game series in England and France. The Canadiens won the series with a record of 5–3–1.

Date	City	Arena	Team	Team	Score
April 21	London, United Kingdom	Empress Hall, Earl's Court	Detroit Red Wings	Montreal Canadiens	5–4 (OT)
April 23	Brighton, United Kingdom	Sports Stadium Brighton	Detroit Red Wings	Montreal Canadiens	5–5
April 25	Paris, France		Detroit Red Wings	Montreal Canadiens	10–8
April 27	Paris, France		Detroit Red Wings	Montreal Canadiens	4–3
April 29			Detroit Red Wings	Montreal Canadiens	7–5
May 5	London, United Kingdom	Empress Hall, Earl's Court	Detroit Red Wings	Montreal Canadiens	6–3
May 7	Brighton, United Kingdom	Sports Stadium Brighton	Detroit Red Wings	Montreal Canadiens	10–5
May 10	London, United Kingdom	Empress Hall, Earl's Court	Detroit Red Wings	Montreal Canadiens	5–4
May 14	Brighton, United Kingdom	Sports Stadium Brighton	Detroit Red Wings	Montreal Canadiens	5–2

Unsuccessful attempts

The idea of NHL teams playing exhibition games in Europe goes back to 1924. Frank Patrick, the head coach of the Vancouver Maroons (PCHA), wanted the Montreal Canadiens to join his team in London for exhibition games during the British Empire Exhibition which was to take place in April–October 1924. Those plans did not materialize. Later, in 1932, when Lester Patrick, Frank's brother and head coach of the New York Rangers, had a deal to have his team play exhibition games in London and other European cities, he too asked the Canadiens to join him on the tour. This also failed to come to fruition. The main cause both times was lack of proper hockey rinks. Yet another plan arose three years later, when Leo Dandurand, the general manager of the Canadiens, announced on February 8, 1935, that his team is "virtually certain" to undertake an eight-game tour of London, Paris, Berlin, and Milan, playing two games in each city.

The Boston Bruins or the New York Rangers were suggested as possibly joining the Canadiens. Negotiations seemed to go smoothly, and on March 5 it was announced that arrangements had been made for the Canadiens and likely the Rangers to undertake a trip to Europe for five games in London, as well as games in Vienna and Budapest, and possibly other cities. However, Armand Vincent, Montreal sports promoter who had championed a European tour by NHL teams, announced on March 25 that he was unable to finalize the deal to have the Canadiens and the Rangers tour Europe. Two days later Vincent announced that arrangements finally were completed for the Canadiens to tour Europe in 1936 for fifteen games: in London for three games, in Berlin, Munich, Garmisch, Prague, and Vienna for two games, and a game in Budapest and Zurich. Once again, that plan never got off the ground.

Final negotiations
After the Detroit Red Wings won the 1937 Stanley Cup, their second in a row, they failed to make the 1938 playoffs, placing last in the American Division and second-to-last overall. Meanwhile, the Montreal Canadiens made the 1938 playoffs, but lost to the Chicago Black Hawks in the first round. After the Canadiens were eliminated from the playoffs on March 26, Cecil Hart, Montreal's head coach, announced tentative plans for a trip to London and Paris. On March 29, Armand Vincent announced that the arrangements had been made for a European tour for Detroit and Montreal. This took Hart by surprise. He said: "That's funny. They announce over there that the trip is all set, and we don't know anything about it over here." On March 31, Hart received agreement of the British Ice Hockey Association to have the European tour, and the agreement of the French Ice Hockey Federation followed shortly. Both organizations deposited $2,500 in order to stage the games. The tour was officially announced by Hart on April 1, yet as late as two days prior to departure, Hart stated that the $2,500 sum had not yet been deposited, nor a contract had been signed by the British. In addition to games in England and France, preliminary plans also called for games in Belgium, Germany, and Scotland, but that did not come into fruition. Nor did the initial plan for the NHL teams to play local amateur teams.

Pre-tour games
On April 5, Detroit travelled to Montreal, and then both teams travelled to Sydney, Nova Scotia. Prior to departing on the RMS Ausonia for Europe on April 9 from Halifax, Nova Scotia, the teams played three exhibition games: in Sydney on April 7, and in Halifax on April 8 and 9.
Montreal's Paul Haynes scored all three goals in the 3–2 win in Sydney. The next day, at the Halifax Forum, Montreal again beat Detroit, winning in

overtime 6–5 in front of 5,000 spectators, with Toe Blake scoring the overtime winner for the Canadiens. The following day, the Red Wings came back, winning 7–2. The teams were also asked to play a game in Moncton, but scheduling did not allow for it.

Date	City	Arena	Winning team	Losing team	Score
April 7	Sydney		**Montreal Canadiens**	Detroit Red Wings	3–2
April 8	Halifax	Halifax Forum	**Montreal Canadiens**	Detroit Red Wings	6–5 OT
April 9	Halifax	Halifax Forum	**Detroit Red Wings**	Montreal Canadiens	7–2

The Tour
England (April 21–23)
The two teams arrived in London, England, on April 19 and were met with high interest and heavy ticket sales. The first game of the tour took place at Empress Hall, Earls Court, a suburb of London on April 21 in front of 8,000 spectators. Jack Adams, Detroit's head coach, addressed the crowd at various points during the game, explaining the differences between NHL rules and those of the English amateur league. Montreal's goaltender Wilf Cude, a native of Wales, was presented with a wreath of leeks and received an ovation. The teams were tied after regulation, and Montreal forward Toe Blake scored in overtime to win the game 5–4. Next, the teams travelled to Brighton, and played their second game of the tour on April 23. The game featured two fights: the first between Marty Barry and Red Goupille; the second between Toe Blake and Peter Bessone. Montreal's Johnny Gagnon scored three goals, and Detroit rallied twice from behind putting continuous pressure on the Canadiens in the third to force overtime, which went scoreless and the game ended in a 5–5 tie.

France (April 25–29)
After two games in England, the teams travelled to France for three games in Paris. The first game, on April 25, the first professional hockey game in France, was a fast and exciting 10–8 affair with Detroit's Hec Kilrea and Montreal's Johnny Gagnon each scoring three goals. The second game in

Paris took place on April 27 in front of a raving crowd, and the Red Wings won 4–3, coming back with three goals in the third period, after being down 3–1. The third and final game in Paris was played on April 29, and Montreal defeated Detroit 7–5.

England (May 5–14)

The games resumed back in Earls Court on May 5, with the Canadiens winning 6–3 in front of 8,500 fans. It was a rough game featuring two fights, and Hec Kilrea also received a major penalty for arguing with a referee. Paul Haynes scored twice in the third period to secure the win for Montreal. Next, the teams once again travelled to Brighton where Detroit won its second game of the tour on May 7 by a score of 10–5, the largest margin of victory of the entire tour. Detroit's Doug Young, Carl Liscombe, and Mud Bruneteau each scored twice in front of a crowd of 8,500. Moving back to Earls Court, Montreal won the next game on May 10 by a score of 5–4. Montreal's Toe Blake scored three goals, including the game-winner. Trailing at the end of the third period, Detroit head coach Jack Adams pulled his goaltender Normie Smith for an extra attacker, but the Red Wings failed to get the tying goal. For the final game of the tour, the two teams once again travelled to Brighton and played the concluding game on May 14. Detroit won their third game in the series by a score of 5–2. Mud Bruneteau and Marty Barry of the Red Wings each tallied two goals. After the game, Montreal's head coach Cecil Hart said: "We've had a successful and enjoyable trip. The boys played wonderful hockey and I'm sure they've sold the professional game in a big way to British and French fans". The teams travelled to Southampton where they embarked on their journey back to North America.

Post-tour

The Montreal Canadiens and the Detroit Red Wings returned home on May 23 on the RMS Aurania. The overall reception of the tour was very enthusiastic despite poor publicity, although reportedly the English fans were disappointed that the games did not feature as much body-checking as they were hoping for. The head coaches of both teams agreed the tour was wonderful and a success, and the players proclaimed it was the greatest experience of their lives. Each player earned $250 for the tour. Speaking about the European tour, Cecil Hart said: "It was wonderful; simply marvellous, I can't get over it. Yes, I believe pro hockey is still five years off over there; they haven't got the rinks yet. But think of the opportunities with no traveling expenses and such thickly-populated areas. We packed them in everywhere. The last game we played over there, we turned away between 3,000 and 4,000 fans. And that with very little publicity." During the tour there was an offer to play a three-game series in Switzerland, but the offer had to be turned down as it came just a day prior to departure, and there was discussion of another such exhibition tour. Nothing came of those plans at the time.

Attempted second tour in 1953

Fifteen years later, in early March 1953, the Montreal Canadiens announced plans for a tour of Europe, visiting England, France, Germany, Italy, Switzerland, Scotland, and possibly other countries. Originally Montreal was to again play the Detroit Red Wings, but Detroit could not complete all necessary arrangements, so the Chicago Black Hawks were supposed to go instead. However, on March 25 Montreal's general manager Frank Selke said that Chicago players did not want to make the trip and so the tour was in jeopardy. On March 30 it was officially announced that the tour was cancelled. According to Bill Tobin, Chicago's president, the scheduling did not work out, and the teams were only left with the proposition of playing ten games in England. Selke said: "I'm not going to ask another team for the series. I asked the Hawks because I like them and the way they play. I guess it's all off".

1959 Boston Bruins–New York Rangers European Tour

In 1959, the Boston Bruins and the New York Rangers (aided by Bobby Hull, Ed Litzenberger, Eric Nesterenko, and Pierre Pilote of the Chicago Black Hawks) went on a 23-game tour of Europe, visiting England, Switzerland, France, Belgium, West Germany, and Austria. The Rangers won the series with a record of 11–9–3.

The first game in Geneva was attended by a sell-out crowd of 11,000, the attendance for the Zürich games was 4500 and 2000.[3] In Berlin, only 600 people went to see the first game.

Date	City	Arena	Team	Team	Score	Attendance
April 29	London, United Kingdom	Empire Pool, Wembley[6]	Boston Bruins	New York Rangers	7–5	
April 30			Boston Bruins	New York Rangers	4–3	
May 2	Geneva, Switzerland	Patinoire des Vernets	Boston Bruins	New York Rangers	4–3	11,000
May 3			Boston Bruins	New York Rangers	12–4	

Date	Location	Venue	Team 1	Team 2	Score	Attendance
May 4	Boulogne-Billancourt, France	Patinoire de Boulogne-Billancourt[7][8]	Boston Bruins	New York Rangers	6–2	
May 5			Boston Bruins	New York Rangers	6–4	
May 6			Boston Bruins	New York Rangers	6–3	
May 7	Antwerp, Belgium	Sportpaleis[9]			6–3	
May 8			Boston Bruins	New York Rangers	8–4	
May 9	Zürich, Switzerland	Hallenstadion			7–6	4,500
May 10			Boston Bruins	New York Rangers	4–2	2,000
May 12	Dortmund, West Germany		Boston Bruins	New York Rangers	4–2	
May 13			Boston Bruins	New York Rangers	6–4	
May 14	Essen, West Germany				6–4	
May 15					4–3	
May 16	Krefeld, West Germany	Rheinlandhalle[10]	Boston Bruins	New York Rangers	8–0	
May 17					7–2	
May 19			Boston Bruins	New York Rangers	6–6	600
May 20	West Berlin, West Germany	Sportpalast	Boston Bruins	New York Rangers	3–2	
May 21			Boston Bruins	New York Rangers	8–2	
May 22	Vienna, Austria		Boston Bruins	New York Rangers	2–2	

Date				Team	Team	Score	
May 23				Boston Bruins	New York Rangers	5–3	
May 24				Boston Bruins	New York Rangers	4–4	

In 1992, the Chicago Blackhawks and the Montreal Canadiens played a two-game series in England. Each team won one game.

Date	City	Arena	Team	Team	Score
September 12	London, United Kingdom	Wembley Arena	Chicago Blackhawks	Montreal Canadiens	2–3
September 13			Chicago Blackhawks	Montreal Canadiens	5–4 (OT)

In 1993, the New York Rangers and the Toronto Maple Leafs played a two-game series in England. The Rangers won both games.

Date	City	Arena	Team	Team	Score
September 11	London, United Kingdom	Wembley Arena	Toronto Maple Leafs	New York Rangers	3–5
September 12			New York Rangers	Toronto Maple Leafs	3–1

1992 Chicago Blackhawks v Montreal Canadiens
WEMBLEY, LONDON, UK. (SEPTEMBER 12, 1992)
MONTREAL CANADIENS 3 CHICAGO BLACKHAWKS 2
1. BENOIT BRUNET (22) SCORES FOR CANADIENS 1-0
2. EQUALISER FOR BLACKHAWKS BY JEREMY ROENIK AFTER PROLONGED ATTACK 1-1
3. STEPHAN LEBEAU (47) SCORES AFTER SCRAPPY ATTACK 2-1
4. CONFRONTATION INVOLVING STU GRIMSON (23) AND EWAN
5. LEBEAU (47) SCORES EARLY IN SECOND PERIOD 3-1
6. BLACKHAWKS SCORE (BRENT SUTTER) 3-2

WEMBLEY, LONDON, UK. (SEPTEMBER 13, 1992)
MONTREAL CANADIENS V CHICAGO BLACKHAWKS
1. BENOIT BRUNET (22) SCORES FOR MONTREAL, 1-0
2. DENIS SAVARD (18) SCORES FOR MONTREAL, 2-0
3. STEVE LARMER (28) SCORES FOR CHICAGO, 2-1
4. BRIAN NOONAN (10) SCORES FOR CHICAGO, 2-2
5. GILBERT DIONNE (45) SCORES FOR MONTREAL, 3-2
6. MIKE HUDSON (20) SCORES FOR CHICAGO, 3-3
7. CHRISTIAN RUUTTU (22) SCORES FOR CHICAGO, 3-4

8. PATRICK KJELLBERG (27) SCORES FOR MONTREAL, 4-4
9. DIONNE PENALTY SAVED BY JIMMY WAITE,
CHICAGO WIN THE TOURNAMENT

The Chicago Blackhawks captured the first trophy of the NHL season, winning a double shootout to beat the Montreal Canadiens in the two-game Molson Challenge exhibition series at Wembley Arena.

The series, billed as a return by hockey to its spiritual roots, went the Blackhawks' way after they lost Saturday's opener 3-2 and then were tied 4-4 after regulation play and a five-minute overtime in Sunday's finale.

A shootout followed, and the Blackhawks won that 2-0 to capture the contest and tie the series at one game apiece.

Then a second shootout was employed to decide the series winner, and the Blackhawks won that 2-1.

In the first shootout, four Canadiens failed to beat Chicago goaltender Jimmy Waite, while Michel Goulet and Steve Larmer connected for the Blackhawks.

In the second, Canadiens goalie Patrick Roy stopped shots by Larmer and Christian Ruuttu, but allowed goals to Goulet and Roenick. Stephane Lebeau scored for Montreal, but four other Canadiens failed to beat Waite.

The formula to decide the trophy, although enjoyed by the near sellout crowd of 8,557, came under immediate criticism by officials and players.

'We won one game and tied the second, and still we lost the series,' complained Canadiens captain Guy Carbonneau. 'But we had our chances to decide the matter early in today's game.'

He was referring to the almost seven minutes that Montreal had a manpower advantage after Benoit Brunet had put them into an early lead on a power play.

At 7:43 of the first period, Chris Chelios was dealt a minor and a match penalty for starting a fight. The Canadiens upped the score to 2-0 while holding an advantage, but failed to score later when the Blackhawks were two men short.

The Blackhawks followed up with two power-play goals, by Larmer and Brian Noonan, with Larmer's coming just with two seconds left in the first period.
On another power-play goal, Gilbert Dionne put the Canadiens ahead early in the second. On the first equal strength goals of the game, Mike Hudson and Ruuttu turned the game around late in the second period for a 4-3 lead.

The Canadiens' Swedish rookie, Patric Kjellberg, forced the game into overtime when he slipped a rebound into the empty near corner at 1:58 of the third period.

The Canadiens dominated the late stages, including the overtime, but Waite came up with some numerous good saves, including one one a clean breakaway by Swedish rookie Patrick Carnback in overtime.

The first two periods were rather physical, with 88 penalty minutes called, 45 against the Blackhawks. Chelios was not the only player ejected as referee Andy van Hellemond threw out the Candiens' Mike Keane for attempting to injure Bryan Marchment after having been high-sticked by the Blackhawk defenseman.

The NHL billed the series as a return to hockey's spiritual roots because it is believed British soldiers stationed in Kingston Harbor, Ontario, in 1860, first substituted a puck for a round ball -- thus inventing the modern game. The series also gave the NHL a chance to test markets outside North America.

1993 New York Rangers v Toronto Maple Leafs
The Maple Leafs took on the Rangers in London, England, in a two-game exhibition series known as the French's Challenge.

Named in honour of America's favourite mustard, the weekend event was a joint venture between the NHL, the NHLPA, and, of course, French's. It provided hockey fans with just the second time in thirty years to take in an NHL game on British soil and give the league with the opportunity to raise the sport's profile internationally.

While the NHL was thrilled with chance to grow the game, French's was just as excited. In his welcome message for the commemorative programme, President Bill Carpenter said, "two of America's best loved pastimes – eating and ice hockey – have joined forces to bring you the first French's Challenge…So sit back, enjoy a taste of America and savour the action!"

Two of America's best loved pastimes. Image above was taken from the official commemorative programme of the French's Challenge. Courtesy of Martin Harris.

Even if you're old enough to remember the series, odds are you didn't get the chance to see it. While the Madison Square Garden Network- aired the games in the United States, they were never broadcasted in Canada due a scheduling conflict on TSN. Evidently, the weekend games in Wembley ran counter to the network's coverage of soccer and the Italian Grand Prix. According to the *Globe and Mail's* William Houston, "Soccer and motor racing do not have the general appeal of hockey, but TSN feels obliged to serve these special interest audiences."

It was quite the way to start the 1993-94 season for both teams. Leafs players found themselves strolling through England with more walking around money than usual. Apparently, their daily per diem for meals and expenses had been increased to 80$ (USD) to cover the increased costs they'd be incurring in London.

But besides having deeper pockets, Leafs players also had the opportunity to take in the sights and sounds of the United Kingdom. Before the games kicked off on the weekend, the team went on a cruise on the River Thames and had the chance to take in a soccer game on one of their free nights. Most of the players were reportedly very excited to catch a game of footy, especially the late Peter Zezel, who had quite the soccer resume himself. He even played in a few exhibition matches for the Toronto Blizzard of the North American Soccer League, before he joined the NHL.

Maple Leafs Head Coach Pat Burns was certainly no stranger to what- London had to offer. He was there just twelve months earlier when he was at the helm for the Canadians. That year, Montreal opened exhibition play at Wembley in a two game series against the Blackhawks. While it was reported that Burns was not very enthusiastic about his second trip across the pond, you would have to think that given how Montreal's season ended in 1992-93, starting it off again in England wouldn't necessarily be a bad thing.

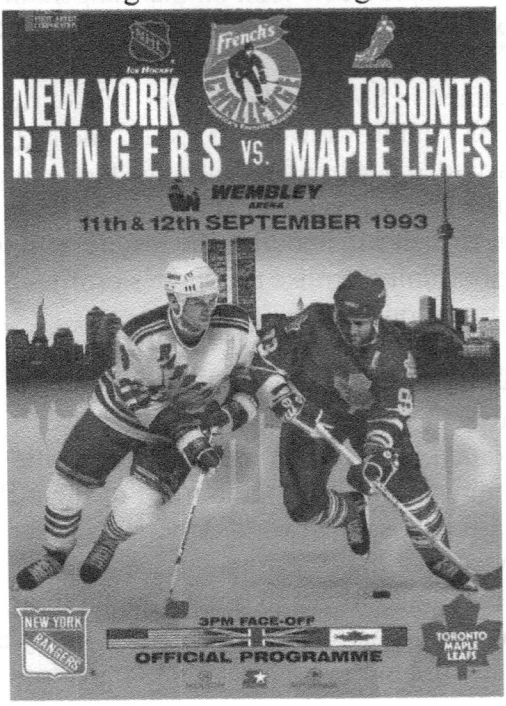

Game one started off with a bang. Literally. Before the puck dropped, players and fans were treated to a laser show, holographic images, and a fireworks display at Wembley Arena. There were even celebrities roaming the stands between play. Mickey Mouse was on hand to serve as Disney's ambassador for the Mighty Ducks of Anaheim, the NHL's newest expansion team who were ready to take flight in their inaugural season.

Although the games did not count in their standings, there was more than just pride on the line. To raise the stakes for the tournament, $50,000 was on the line. The winner of each game took home $12,500 and the club who won the series, presumably on aggregate, captured the remaining $25,000.

But things did not go the Maple Leafs' way. They dropped the first game to the Rangers 5-3 on Saturday afternoon. The action continued on Sunday with

New York hoping to add to their winnings, while Toronto was just looking to head back across the Atlantic with a victory. But it was not meant to be.

Although the Leafs kept the game tighter than the first contest, they were unable to convert on five power plays, which cost them dearly. Early into the second period, the Rangers' Mike Gartner buried a goal off a rebound to give the Blueshirts a 2-0 lead and put the game out of reach for the Leafs. Wendel Clark prevented Toronto from getting blanked when he scored the Leafs lone goal in the third period to cut the deficit to one. However, the Rangers sealed the deal when Adam Graves potted an empty-netter to give the team the win and secure the $50,000 purse.

The players certainly forged some unforgettable memories both on and off the ice. When it came to the games at Wembley, it was probably the one and only time that Mark Messier awaited his next shift from the comforts of a velvet-covered chair. According to reports, each team had two benches, one behind the other, but the bench closest to the boards was too short to accommodate the entire team. As a result, the arena staff had to appropriate some cushioned chairs to keep players as close to the ice as possible for their upcoming shifts.

After returning to North America, both teams had great regular season performances. Toronto finished second in the Central Division with a sterling record of 43-29-12 and in the postseason advanced as far as the

Conference Finals for the second year in a row. Meanwhile, the Rangers were a powerhouse, they went 52-24-8 en route to the second Presidents' Trophy in franchise history. Although they faltered in the 1992 playoffs after taking home the league's top honours, they exorcised their demons and ended the club's 54 year championship drought in the spring of 1994.

With New York hoisting Lord Stanley's silverware that season, it marked the second straight year where a team that opened preseason action in London went on to win it all. There would be no third, as the NHL and French's did not return to England the following September. In fact, it took another fourteen years before the league returned to London, when the Kings and Ducks played their first two regular season games there in 2007-08.

Given the success that the Canadians and Rangers went on to enjoy after starting out in Wembley, perhaps it's time for the Leafs to take a trip back across the pond to see if they can cut the mustard.

2007 NHL Premiere - *2007–08 NHL season*

In 2007, the NHL opened its regular season in Europe for the first time. The Anaheim Ducks and the Los Angeles Kings played a two-game series in England. Each team won one game. Prior to this, the Kings played a two-game series in Austria against the Austrian team Red Bull Salzburg and the Swedish team Färjestad Karlstad, winning both.

Date	City	Arena	Team	Team	Score
September 25	Salzburg, Austria	Eisarena Salzburg	Los Angeles Kings	Red Bull Salzburg	7–6
September 26				Färjestad Karlstad	3–2

September 29	London, United Kingdom	The O₂ Arena	Anaheim Ducks	Los Angeles Kings	1–4
September 30			Los Angeles Kings	Anaheim Ducks	1–4

Anaheim Ducks 4-1 LA Kings

NHL champions the Anaheim Ducks gained revenge for their season-opening defeat to the Los Angeles Kings with a 4-1 victory in the second game of the ground-breaking two-game Premiere Series at the O2 Arena in London.

More than 17,000 fans from all over the UK, Europe and North America piled into the old Millennium Dome for the second night running, though again there were logistical problems: on Saturday face-off had been delayed by nearly half an hour because the lights inside the arena would not come on after the national anthems, and last night many seats were still empty when the game started 15 minutes late because of delays on the London underground.

This is the first time the NHL has staged regular-season fixtures in Europe - games have been played in Japan on three occasions - and such teething problems need to be ironed out before ice-hockey returns to London, and indeed before the O2 Arena stages the gymnastics and basketball events during the 2012 Olympics.

Despite these issues, the players and coaches themselves seemed more than satisfied with the venue, which is owned by Anschutz Entertainment Group, the same organisation that owns the Kings. "I haven't heard any complaints from our players about the decision to come here," said Ducks coach Randy Carlyle. "Maybe it's because we gave them a day off to do something in London."

LA's Mike Cammalleri, who scored twice on Saturday and once last night, was equally effusive. "I love London, it's been good to us this weekend," he said. "It felt like a North American hockey crowd. There wasn't much difference - a couple of waves, like soccer, which was fun to watch."

The action on the ice was equally fun to watch. The Ducks, bringing the famous old Stanley Cup back to the country in which it was made by a London silversmith in the late 19th century, had been consistently thwarted by 19-year-old goaltender Jonathan Bernier in Saturday's 4-1 defeat, but found it easier to beat Jason Labarbera last night with four goals in the first 25 minutes from Corey Perry (twice), Chris Kunitz and Travis Moen.

Cammalleri scored a consolation for the Kings, but the biggest cheer of the evening was reserved for George Parros and Scott Thornton, whose 60-second fistfight brought a standing ovation from the crowd. To show the league isn ot all about big rugged brawlers, the fans were then treated to Kiss Cam, for which spectators were encouraged to embrace their near neighbours on the big screen.

The NHL is the first of three North American sports leagues to play in London this autumn - the NBA will be represented by the Minnesota Timberwolves and the Boston Celtics at the O2 Arena on October 10, while the Miami Dolphins and the New York Giants will contest the NFL's first game outside North America at Wembley on October 28 - and the players have certainly had to adjust their approach this week for the commercial benefit of their sport.

"I don't remember taking a boat up a river to get to a game very often," said Kings defenseman Rob Blake, when asked what he found different about playing by the Thames as opposed to southern California. Normality will be restored for both teams when they resume their schedule in the United States this week, but to judge by the number of smiles and replica shirts in the stands, there is little doubt their venture east has been a big success.

2010 NHL Premiere - *2010–11 NHL season*

In 2010, a record six NHL teams (the Boston Bruins, the Carolina Hurricanes, the Columbus Blue Jackets, the Minnesota Wild, the Phoenix Coyotes, and the San Jose Sharks) opened their regular seasons in Europe. The Hurricanes and the Wild played a two-game series in Finland, with the Hurricanes winning both games. The Blue Jackets and the Sharks played a two-game series in Sweden, with each team winning one game. The Bruins and the Coyotes played a two-game series in the Czech Republic, with each team winning one game. Prior to this, all six teams also played against various European teams (Adler Mannheim from Germany, Belfast Giants Selects from Northern Ireland (an all-star team of the EIHL), SKA Saint Petersburg from Russia, Ilves Tampere from Finland, HC Bílí Tygři Liberec from the Czech Republic, Malmö Redhawks from Sweden, and Dinamo Riga from Latvia). The NHL teams had a record of 6–1–0 against the European teams.

Date	City	Team	Team	Score
October 2	Mannheim, Germany	**San Jose Sharks**	Adler Mannheim	3–2 (SO)

	Belfast, United Kingdom	**Boston Bruins**	Belfast Giants Selects	5–1
October 4	Saint Petersburg, Russia	Carolina Hurricanes	**SKA Saint Petersburg**	3–5
	Tampere, Finland	**Minnesota Wild**	Ilves Tampere	5–1
October 5	Liberec, Czech Republic	**Boston Bruins**	HC Bílí Tygři Liberec	7–1
	Malmö, Sweden	**Columbus Blue Jackets**	Malmö Redhawks	4–1
October 6	Riga, Latvia	**Phoenix Coyotes**	Dinamo Riga	3–1
October 7	Helsinki, Finland	**Carolina Hurricanes**	Minnesota Wild	4–3
October 8		Minnesota Wild	**Carolina Hurricanes**	2–1 (SO)
	Stockholm, Sweden	**San Jose Sharks**	Columbus Blue Jackets	3–2
October 9	Prague, Czech Republic	**Phoenix Coyotes**	Boston Bruins	5–2

	Stockholm, Sweden	**Columbus Blue Jackets**	San Jose Sharks	3–2 (OT)
October 10	Prague, Czech Republic	**Boston Bruins**	Phoenix Coyotes	3–0

Boston Bruins 5 Belfast Giants 1
A pair of Tyler Seguin goals, one amid a three-goal outburst late in the second period, lifts the Bruins to a 5-1 exhibition win over the UK's best and brightest at Odyssey Arena.

Seguin also scores on penalty shot late in the third period against the Belfast Giant Select squad. The Bruins, after falling behind, 1-0, in the second period, also get strikes from Zdeno Chara, Brad Marchand and Milan Lucic.

A sell out of some 5,500 at Odyssey Arena. Bruins finish with a 42-23 shot advantage.

Second Period
The Selects break a 0-0 deadlock with 4:24 left in the period on a blistering wrister to the top right corner by Jade Galbraith. Locals love it, Giants play David role, taking down mighty B's.

But David doesn't keep the mojo going.

Seguin ties it 18:24 with a power play, getting help from point men Dennis Seidenberg and Matt Hunwick.

Only 21 seconds later, Zdeno Chara smacks home the go-ahead goal, 2-1, an even-strength strike aided by Strongman Shawn Thornton and newcomer Greg Campbell.

And with 50 seconds to go in the period, Brad Marchand caps off a three-goal spree with the 3-1 lead, all three goals coming in a span of 46 seconds. Shawn Thornton picks up a second helper and Chara is credited with second assist.

For the better part of the first two periods, the Bruins control the play but are unable to pot some prime chances, a number of them from close range.

First period
Neither side able to put the puck in the net.

The Bruins, who finish with an impressive 13-7 shot lead for the 20 minutes, can't solve Steady Steve Murphy in the Belfast cage.

Tuuka Rask barely tested by the pesky Giants, who clearly have a better feel for the big sheet (15 feet wider than NHL version). Good zip by the UK guys, but not enough finish.

Bartowski continues to impress
He's not in tonight's line-up, but rookie Matt Bartkowski, proud son of Pittsburgh, remains in the thick of the hunt for one of Boston's roster spots on the blue line.

Acquired along with Dennis Seidenberg in the swap with Florida that sent Byron Bitz to the Panthers, Bartkowski played the last two seasons for the Ohio State Buckeyes. He hadn't planned on bolting campus after two years, but the swap to Boston encouraged him to turn pro, although not necessarily with the thought that he'd make the Black-and-Gold's varsity roster right out of Division 1 NCAA hockey.

"But I definitely came in to camp setting my sights high," said the 22-year-old blueliner, who was chosen 190th overall in the '08 draft.

Coach Claude Julien, who opted to take a look here at Adam McQuaid in the line-up and also leave Johnny Boychuk side-lined, said Friday that he has been very impressed with Bartkowski, noting that he has been very quick to grasp defensive coverage.

Now, will Bartowski still be on the active roster when the club opens the NHL season next weekend with back-to-back games against the Coyotes in Prague? Julien won't give up that answer. However, he made a point of saying that if Bartkowski makes the team, it won't be as a seventh defenseman. If the kid sticks, he's in the top six pack. Otherwise, Julien and GM Peter Chiarelli want him getting 20 minutes a more or night with the Providence WannaBs.

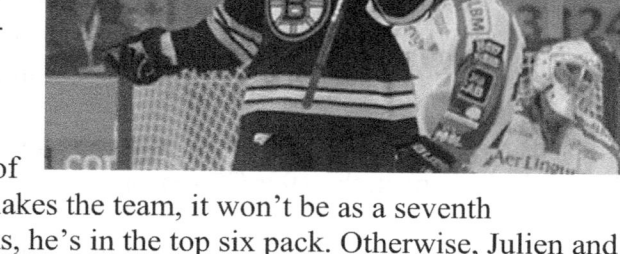

The line-up:
Forwards
Mark Recchi–Patrice Bergeron–Jordan Caron
Milan Lucic–David Krejci–Nathan Horton
Blake Wheeler-Tyler Seguin-Michael Ryder
Brad Marchand-Greg Campbell-Shawn Thornton
Defensemen
Zdeno Chara-Dennis Seidenberg
Mark Stuart-Matt Hunwick
Andrew Ference-Adam McQuaid
Goalies
Starter: Tuukka Rask
Backup: Tim Thomas

Scratches: Danny Paille and Brian McGrattan at forward; Matt Bartkowski and Johnny Boychuk on defence; Nolan Schaefer (G).

The Early Days

George Redding,   **Farrand Gillie**   **and Gordie Poirier**

James "Babe" Donnelley played 35 NHL league and playoff games for the Montreal Maroons in the 1926/27 season.

He played around the North American minor leagues and came to the UK as a player coach at Streatham in the 1935/36 season.

Bill Boucher played over 200 games in the NHL for the Montreal Canadiens, New York Americans and Boston Bruins during 1921 to 1928. He was a Stanley Cup winner with Montreal in 1924.

He also notched up some 190 games in minor leagues in Canada and the USA before he arrived at Brighton Tigers as head coach for the 1937/38 season.
The Tigers finished 5th in the English National League that season – their highest placing in the pre-war period. Boucher returned as coach for the 1938/39 season.

George Redding played 35 games in the NHL for the Boston Bruins from 1924 to 1926 and also played over 100 minor league games in a 10 year North American career.

Although he was left winger, he went in goal for 11 minutes in a Bruins game against Toronto St Patricks during the 1924/25 season after the regular netminder was injured. He conceded just 1 goal for an all-time netminder career GAA of 5.45.

The NHL in the UK

In the 1936/37 season, he played for the Richmond Hawks in the English League and in 1937/38 he was non playing head Coach of the Earls Court Rangers.

A not very good photo from the Illustrated Sporting and Dramatic News of Friday 17th April 1936 shows "Babe" Donnelly in action for Streatham against Wembley Lions in the final of the London-Paris Tournament – played at Streatham Ice Rink. Donnelly is the player dribbling the puck on the right of the photo (Photo by Console)

Farrand Gillie made 1 NHL appearance for the Detroit Cougars – as the Red Wings were originally known – during the 1928/29 season but otherwise played around the North American minor leagues.
In 1938 he joined Brighton Tigers as a player and coach for the 1938/39 English National League season.

The Brighton Tigers team of 1937/38 endorsing Coca Cola on a promotional postcard. Head coach Billy Boucher is right of centre on the front row.

Gordie Poirier had played three seasons for the Brighton Tigers in the pre-war English National League in the 1936/37, 37/38 and 38/39 seasons, scoring 69 goals and 47 assists in league, cup and tournament games.

He returned to his native Canada and made 10 appearances for the Montreal Canadiens in the NHL during the 1939/40 season, contributing 1 assist.

After 4 seasons in the QSHL playing for various teams around Ottawa, he returned to England and was a key member of the Brighton Tigers for three more seasons – 1946/47, 47/48 and 48/49, playing in 132 English National League games, scoring 89 goals, 109 assists and picking up 138 PIM.

The Tigers won the League, National Tournament and Autumn Cup treble in his first season back and retained the league crown the following season.

After a season's break, he played one season with the Harringay Racers in 1950/51, scoring 2+12 in 40 competitive matches.

Gordie Poirer

Gordie Poirer's citation to the Hall of Fame at the time of his induction read, "claimed by many as the most clever player in British puck history." The 1950 Ice Hockey World Annual continued further stating, "a good forward pre-war, he turned into a brilliant defenceman after the war, playing a big part in Brighton's two successive title wins."

Born October 27th, 1914 in Maple Creek Saskatchewan, Gordie Poirer as a teenager progressed to the 1931/32 Montreal Columbus team in the cities junior league, moving on to St.Francois Xavier. A year later, aged nineteen, the French Canadian broke into the Canadiens of the senior league, before he came to Europe for the 1933/34 season as coach to Diavolo Rosso Neri in Milan, Italy. Under Poirer, the Milanese club lifted the prestigious Spengler Cup. A season in Switzerland followed before returning to Canada to join representative team to tour the USA, before returning to Milan for the 1935/36 campaign as coach and captain.

The 5'10" left shooting centreman, weighing just 158lb (11¼ stone) joined the Brighton Tigers of the English National League in 1936 and very quickly incurred a serious chin injury, which turned so septic that the doctors attending him gave him barely five hours to live. Needless to say, he did survive and went on to stay with the south coast club until the outbreak of WW2, recording 66 goals and 47 assists for 113 points.

He returned to Canada and joined the St.Hyacinthe Gaulois of the Quebec PHL, playing 36 games and scoring 80 points, and also appeared in ten NHL games for the Montreal Canadiens. He joined the Canadian army in 1942 and attained the rank of captain. The following year, he scored the winning goal for the Ottawa Commandos in the Allan Cup Final and when the allies set about liberating Europe in 1944, he landed in France on D-Day plus 17.

With peacetime came a return to 'Civvy Street' and playing hockey, this time with the Ottawa Senators, before accepting an invitation to return to the Brighton Tigers for the first post-war campaign. Playing in a defensive position did little to reduce his offensive power as the Tigers won the English National League, the National Tournament and the inaugural Autumn Cup with Gordie Poirer finishing as the teams third highest scorer with 75 points and an All Star A-team selection. The following season, he again finished the Tigers third top scorer with 62 points (31+31) as the Tigers successfully defended their league crown. While the Tigers failed to win any silverware in the third post-war season, Poirer's last with them, he moved up to second top scorer before spending his final winter in Britain icing with the Harringay Racers in 1950, contributing 2 goals and 12 assists in 40 appearances.

His total post war British statistics read:- GP 180 Goals 102 Ass 120 Pts 222 PIM 163

An all-round athlete in his youth, as well as playing ice hockey, he was a scratch golfer and a champion canoeist. An electrical worker by trade, after retiring from hockey he became both a restaurant owner and import businessman back in Canada.

Gordie Poirer died in 1972 in Beaconsfield, a suburb of Montreal, Quebec.

Compiled with research, provided by Martin C.Harris – August 1999.

Welcome to The British Ice Hockey Hall of Fame

Since 1948 we have been inducting people in to the Hall of Fame, through our new website you can browse the histories of these great people who have built the sport in the UK to what it is today.

https://www.britishicehockeyhalloffame.com/index.php

Farrand Gillie

Farrand Douglas Gillie was born on May 11, 1905 and died on October 7, 1972. He was a Canadian professional ice hockey left winger who played in one National Hockey League game for the Detroit Cougars during the 1928–29 NHL season. After his lone game in the NHL, Gillie spent several years in the minor International Hockey League before moving to the United Kingdom for one season, finishing his career in the Quebec Senior Hockey League, retiring in 1942.

S	TEAM	LEAGUE	GP	G	A	TP	PIM	+/-	POST	GP	G	A	TP	PIM	+/-
1926-27	Cornwall Colts	LOVHL	-	-	-	-	-	-							
1927-28	Detroit Olympics	CPHL	10	0	0	0	0	-							
1928-29	Detroit Olympics	CPHL	41	5	4	9	31	-	Playoffs	7	0	0	0	8	-
1929-30	Detroit Olympics	IHL	42	9	7	16	38	-	Playoffs	3	0	0	0	0	-
1930-31	Detroit Olympics	IHL	46	19	6	25	36	-							
1931-32	Detroit Olympics	IHL	48	16	10	26	31	-	Playoffs	6	0	0	0	8	-
1932-33	London Tecumsehs	IHL	44	13	9	22	36	-	Playoffs	6	3	1	4	6	-
1933-34	London Tecumsehs	IHL	44	11	5	16	26	-	Playoffs	6	2	2	4	2	-
1934-35	Windsor Bulldogs	IHL	43	4	7	11	22	-							
1935-36	Windsor Bulldogs	IHL	11	0	0	0	4	-							
	Rochester Cardinals	IHL	38	5	9	14	10	-							
1936-37	Did not play														
1937-38	Cornwall Flyers	QSHL	24	8	9	17	18	-	Playoffs	6	3	1	4	8	-
1938-39	Brighton Tigers	English	-	11	6	17	-	-							
1939-40	Cornwall Flyers	LOVHL	28	4	2	6	20	-	Playoffs	5	2	3	5	7	-
1940-41	Cornwall Flyers	QSHL	34	7	21	28	8	-	Playoffs	4	0	2	2	2	-
1941-42	Cornwall Flyers	QSHL	1	0	0	0	0	-							
S	TEAM	LEAGUE	GP	G	A	TP	PIM	+/-	POST	GP	G	A	TP	PIM	+/-
1937-38	Cornwall Flyers	Allan Cup	11	4	5	9	22	-							
1938-39	Brighton Tigers	London Cup	-	2	0	2	-	-							

The Post War Years

The 1950's to the 1970's

The 1950's from a British perspective started well with 4th place going to the Great Britain team in the World Championships, but it was also to see the decline in the sport being played by British players and that unfortunately led to the demise of the sport in the UK as interest dwindled. What was served up though was a league that mostly contained professional Canadian hockey players including:

Joe Shack, who had also played for three seasons in England before the Second World War – for Harringay Greyhounds in 1936/37/, 37/38 and 38/39 and during the conflict he played 70 games in the NHL for the New York Rangers over two seasons from 1942 to 1945, along with 270 minor pro league games.

He returned to the UK and played 17 games for the Greyhounds in the 1947/48 season before switching to the Racers where he played for the next 6 seasons – two of them as captain.

Shack made 5 appearances for the Dunfermline Vikings the new British League in 1954/55 but then retired from playing and later went onto be head coach of the Swedish national team.

During World War, 2 Tony Licari served with the Canadian air force, playing with several air force teams and while posted in England, he played a few exhibition games.

Licari played 9 NHL games for the Detroit Red Wings in the 1946/47 season and accrued some 400 minor league appearances in North America before he arrived at Harringay Racers for the 1951/52 English National League season.

He remained with the Racers for three seasons and was a member of their Autumn Cup winning side of 1952.

Licari played 171 competitive games for Harringay (that we know of) and scored 134 goals and 178 assist with 108PIM.

London Lions

British ice hockey was very much in the doldrums in the early 1970s with no national league in place and separate competitions being played in the South and North. A lot of the former big hockey venues that had sprung up in the boom years of the 1930s had closed and many of the remaining rinks did not even allow ice hockey to be played. Of the ones that did, ice time was hard to get and training sessions and matches were often played at very unsociable hours.

In 1971, Detroit Red Wings NHL owner Bruce Norris came up with an idea to set up a pan-European professional league with teams playing in a regular season competition - and the top teams able to participate in the North American Stanley Cup play-offs.

The proposed league would start in the 1973/74 season and was to include the top club teams from Sweden, Russia and Czechoslovakia, with various NHL clubs operating "farm teams" in other European cities.

Along with a consortium of other useful people, Norris set up a team in London called the Lions who would play their home matches at the Empire Pool stadium (now known as the Wembley Arena), but there were a number of problems and the European League did not get started in 1973 as planned.

With the London Lions set-up already established, Norris decided to run the team anyway as an exhibition team, playing challenge games against all the top sides across Europe as a pre-cursor to running the European League the following season. They also played a number of games against regional "select" sides across the UK to fill out the schedule and help spread the word among the established hockey fraternity.

The Lions' first ever game – the only one they were to play outside the UK and Europe - came on 11th October 1973 when they played IHL side Toledo Hornets in Detroit, coming out 0-1 victors.

Between October 1973 and March 1974, the Lions played 72 games, winning 52, losing 13 and drawing 7 - with 448 goals for and 234 against.

Obviously, with the Detroit involvement in the club, most of the Lions players were either Red Wings signings who weren't currently playing in the NHL team - or were playing for Detroit affiliate teams in the minor North American leagues - supplemented by a few European sourced players. Several of the Lions team had already had experiences of playing in the NHL before they came to England – and a number of others went on to enjoy greater pro league success in later years.

The NHLers who turned out for the London Lions during the 1973/74 season were:

Right Winger Terry Clancy played 7 games for the California /Oakland Seals in the NHL in the 1967/68 season and then went on to play 86 times for the Toronto Maple Leafs between 1968 and 1973.

He made 35 appearances for the London Lions, scoring 6+13 with 22 PIM.

Defenceman Mike Korney played two games for Detroit Red Wings in the 1973/74 season and went on to play 31 games for the London Lions, scoring 15+10 with 33 PIM.

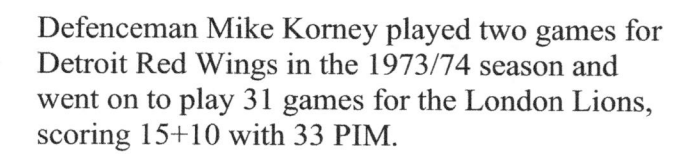

He went on to play 27 more times for Detroit and also had a season with the New York Rangers in 1978/79.

Tord Lundström had been a three time silver medal winner in the World Championships with Sweden and he joined the Detroit Red Wings for the 1973/74 season.

After injuring his shoulder, he broke his contract and left the NHL to join the London Lions for the rest of the season, playing 45 games and contributing 38+31 with 24 PIM.

After his year in London he returned to his native Sweden where he played out the rest of his career.

Centre ice Rick McCann had played 30 games for the Detroit Red Wings in the NHL from 1967 to 1972 before joining the London Lions.

He played in 70 games for the Wembley based side, scoring 25+55 with 29PIM.

He returned to the Red Wings for the following season and then enjoyed two seasons in the AHL.

Bill McKenzie was a netminder who played 13 games for the Detroit Red Wings in the NHL in the 1973/74 season before making two appearances in goal for the London Lions. In 120 minutes play he let in 6 goals for GAA of 3.00.

After his brief cameo with the Lions, McKenzie went on to play 78 more games in the NHL with Detroit, Kansas City Scouts and Colorado Rockies.

Defenceman Tom Mellor played 25 games for the Detroit Red Wings in the NHL during the 1973/74 season and also made 6 appearances for the London Lions, scoring 2+5 with 20PIM.

He played one more NHL game for Detroit the following season.

Defenceman Rick Newell played 7 games for the Detroit Red Wings from 1972-74 and then made 17 appearances for the London Lions, scoring 12+11 with 63 PIM.

He went on to play the 1974/75 season with the Phoenix Roadrunners in the World Hockey league which was a rival competition to the NHL that operated between 1972 and 1979.

Centre ice Nelson Pyatt played 5 games for the Detroit Red Wings in the 1973/74 season and then made 61 appearances for the London Lions, scoring 35+28 with 4 PIM.

He returned to the Red Wings for the 74/75 season making 9 NHL appearances and later played in the NHL the Washington Capitals and Colorado Rockies.

Terry Richardson was a Canadian netminder who, after being Detroit's first round pick in the 1973 NHL draft, never quite rose to expectations.

He played 9 games for the Red Wings in the 1973/74 season and then made 14 appearances for the London Lions, conceding 37 goals in 710 minutes for a GAA of 3.12.

He played 10 more NHL games for the Red Wings in subsequent seasons and also made 1 NHL appearance for the St Louis Blues in 1978/79.

Left wing Ulf Sterner played in nine world championship overall for Sweden, winning 1 gold, 5 silver and 1 bronze medal and he was the first ever European to play for an NHL team when he joined New York Rangers for the 1964/65 season.

He only played 4 games in the NHL and, unused to the physical side of the North American game, returned to Sweden after 2 seasons in the minors.

He resurfaced with the London Lions where he played 64 games, scoring 27+88 with 71 PIM. He finished up the highest points scorer for the Lions overall and also had the highest number of assists.

Defenceman Murray Wing played 1 game for Detroit Red Wings in the NHL in the 1973/74 season and then played in 71 games for London Lions, scoring 21+21 with 24 PIM.

Along with Brian McCutcheon, he played the higher number of games for the Lions. After his season London, he dropped to the minor pro leagues.

The proposed professional European League anticipated for the 1974/75 season never did get started up and the London Lions club was subsequently disbanded.

Europe had to wait several more decades before a fully-fledged pan-European league style competition finally came into being.

Bert Peer

The Ice Hockey World citation on Bert Peer's induction to the Hall of Fame stated, "possibly the greatest right winger in the history of senior amateur (sic) hockey…If he had taken his hockey more seriously in North America, there is no doubt he would have made the NHL."

Bert Peers was born in Port Credit, Ontario, on November 12th 1910. Peer played for the juvenile inter-church champions of the province, then the intermediate winners, joining the senior ranks in 1934 with the British Consuls of the Toronto League and the Oakville Villans of the OHA circuit.

The newly formed Harringay Racers in north London lured him across the Atlantic in 1936 and he made an immediate impact. As the Racers finished runners-up in the English National League, Peer finished as the third highest scorer with 60 points and an All Star A-team selection. Amazingly, Peer refused offers to turn professional in North America in order to return to Harringay for the 1937/38 campaign, where despite him missing several weeks through injury in the early part of the season, the Racers won the league and he was selected to the All Star B-team. Those two seasons saw him amass 107 points made up of 57 goals and 30 assists with 78 penalty minutes.

From 1938, the 5'11" winger, whose deceptive changes of pace and swerve mystified other players, plied his trade in North America. A season with the Valleyfield Braves in the Quebec PHL was followed by a winter split between the senior Ottawa Senators and the Omaha Knights of the American Hockey Association, sandwiching in one game in the National hockey League for the Detroit Red Wings.

Whilst with the Fort Worth Rangers in the AHA for the 1941/42 season, his 85 points gained him an All Star B-team ranking. The following season saw him serving with the Canadian Navy, but still find the time to ice ten games for their Toronto squad in the OHA Senior League. He returned full-time to the ice in 1945 for three more seasons, finishing his career in the OHA-SL with the Hamilton Tigers.

Compiled with research, provided by Martin C.Harris – July 1999

Bert's Stats

S	TEAM	LEAGUE	GP	G	A	TP	PIM	+/-	POST	GP	G	A	TP	PIM	+/-
1932-33	Toronto Bell Telephone	TMHL	11	4	1	5	10		Playoffs	4	1	1	2	4	
1933-34	Toronto Bell Telephone	TMHL	-	-	-	-	-								
1934-35	Toronto British Consols	TIHL	12	7	3	10	2		Playoffs	4	2	0	2	6	
	Oakville Villans	OHA-Sr.	14	9	3	12	20		Playoffs	2	0	2	2	0	
1935-36	Oakville Villans	OHA-Sr.	15	10	4	14	15		Playoffs	2	1	0	1	2	
	Toronto British Consols	TMHL	14	11	3	14	19		Playoffs	5	0	1	1	26	
1936-37	Harringay Racers	English	-	38	22	60	26								
1937-38	Harringay Racers	English	-	8	5	13	-								
1938-39	Valleyfield Braves	QPHL	36	25	24	49	61		Playoffs	11	5	6	11	8	
1939-40	Detroit Red Wings	NHL	1	0	0	0	0								
	Omaha Knights	AHA	34	14	17	31	14		Playoffs	9	1	7	8	19	
	Ottawa Senators	QSHL	8	0	2	2	0								
1940-41	Omaha Knights	AHA	32	8	14	22	13								
1941-42	Fort Worth Rangers	AHA	50	38	40	78	31		Playoffs	5	3	4	7	7	
1942-43	Toronto Navy	OHA-Sr.	10	3	15	18	4		Playoffs	10	7	9	16	8	
1943-44	Did not play														
1945-46	Tulsa Oilers	USHL Sr.	11	7	8	15	4		Playoffs	13	5	4	9	2	
	Valleyfield Braves	QSHL	16	6	9	15	4								
1946-47	Hamilton Tigers	OHA-Sr.	24	16	17	33	2		Playoffs	7	3	3	6	0	
1947-48	Hamilton Tigers	OHA-Sr.	35	6	13	19	10		Playoffs	10	0	2	2	6	

S	TEAM	LEAGUE	GP	G	A	TP	PIM	+/-	POST	GP	G	A	TP	PIM	+/-
1937-38	Harringay Racers	London Cup	-	5	1	6	-								
	Harringay Racers	Nat-Tmt	-	6	2	8	-								
1946-47	Hamilton Tigers	Allan Cup	9	5	3	8	6								
1947-48	Hamilton Tigers	Allan Cup	6	0	1	1	0								

Tord Lundstrom

Tord was born on March 4, 1945 and is a retired Swedish professional ice hockey player and coach. Lundström won the Swedish Championship nine times playing for Brynäs IF, he also played for the Detroit Red Wings of the National Hockey League (NHL).

In 2011, Lundstrom was inducted into the IIHF Hall of Fame. Growing up in Kiruna, Sweden, Lundström attributed his love of hockey began after watching Eilert Määttä win the 1957 World Cup. Although he played hockey, Lundström was also interested in football and wrestling.

At 18, Lundström played his last season for Kiruna AIF before moving to Brynäs. That same year, he made his national team debut in November 1963. In his national team career, Lundström played in 200 games, including nine IIHF World Championships and the Olympic Games. He competed as a member of the Sweden men's national ice hockey team at the 1968 and 1972 Winter Olympics. Lundström then moved to North America where he joined the Detroit Red Wings of the National Hockey League (NHL) for the 1973–94 season. During that season, he became the second Swedish forward to score an NHL goal. After injuring his shoulder, Lundström broke his contract and left the NHL to join the London Lions in England for the rest of the season. He subsequently returned to Brynäs IF for the 1974–1975 season.

After retiring as a player, Lundström turned to coaching before working as a property manager in 2010. In 2011, he was inducted into the IIHF Hall of Fame and later the Swedish Hockey Hall of Fame. His number was also retired by Brynäs IF.

The NHL in the UK

Tord's Stats

S	TEAM	LEAGUE	GP	G	A	TP	PIM	+/-	POST	GP	G	A	TP	PIM	+/-
1959-60	Kiruna AIF	Division 2	-	-	-	-	-	-							
1960-61	Kiruna AIF	Division 2	-	-	-	-	-	-							
1961-62	Kiruna AIF	Division 2	16	15	6	21	4	-							
1962-63	Kiruna AIF	Division 2	20	32	12	44	8	-							
1963-64	Brynäs IF	Division 1	21	17	13	30	19	-							
1964-65	Brynäs IF	Division 1	28	30	22	52	6	-							
	Sweden (all)	International	-	-	-	-	-	-							
	Sweden	WC	7	6	3	9	4	-							
1965-66	Brynäs IF	Division 1	21	17	14	31	10	-							
	Sweden	WC	6	0	1	1	4	-							
	Sweden (all)	International	-	-	-	-	-	-							
1966-67	Brynäs IF	Division 1	21	23	12	35	12	-	Playoffs	6	5	6	11	0	-
	Sweden B (all)	International	2	2	-	-	-	-							
1967-68	Brynäs IF	Division 1	21	21	21	42	16	-							
	Sweden	OG	7	2	3	5	6	-							
	Sweden (all)	International	-	-	-	-	-	-							
1968-69	Brynäs IF	Division 1	21	13	14	27	8	-							
	Sweden (all)	International	-	-	-	-	-	-							
	Sweden	WC	10	5	2	7	12	-							
1969-70	Brynäs IF	Division 1	28	27	16	43	14	-							
	Sweden	WC	10	5	5	10	0	-							
1970-71	Brynäs IF	Division 1	28	26	23	49	16	-							
	Sweden (all)	International	-	-	-	-	-	-							
	Sweden	WC	10	6	4	10	4	-							
1971-72	Brynäs IF	Division 1	28	17	15	32	8	-							
	Sweden	OG	6	3	2	5	2	-							
	Sweden "C"	WC	10	4	5	9	8	-							
1972-73	Brynäs IF	Division 1	28	26	15	41	10	-							
	Sweden	WC	10	3	2	5	0	-							
1973-74	Detroit Red Wings	NHL	11	1	1	2	0	-2							
	London Lions	International	45	38	31	69	24	-							
1974-75	Brynäs IF	Division 1	21	15	17	32	32	-							
	Sweden "C"	WC	10	11	5	16	2	-							
1975-76	Brynäs IF "C"	Elitserien	35	21	27	48	16	-	Playoffs	4	4	1	5	0	-
	Sweden	CC	5	1	3	4	6	-							
1976-77	Brynäs IF "C"	Elitserien	36	16	19	35	37	-	Playoffs	4	1	6	7	0	-
	Sweden (all)	International	5	1	1	2	-	-							
1977-78	Brynäs IF "C"	Elitserien	36	20	15	35	28	-	Playoffs	3	0	1	1	0	-
1978-79	Brynäs IF	Elitserien	36	12	15	27	29	-							
1979-80	Mörrums GoIS	Division 1	4	1	1	2	2	-							

TOURNAMENT STATISTICS

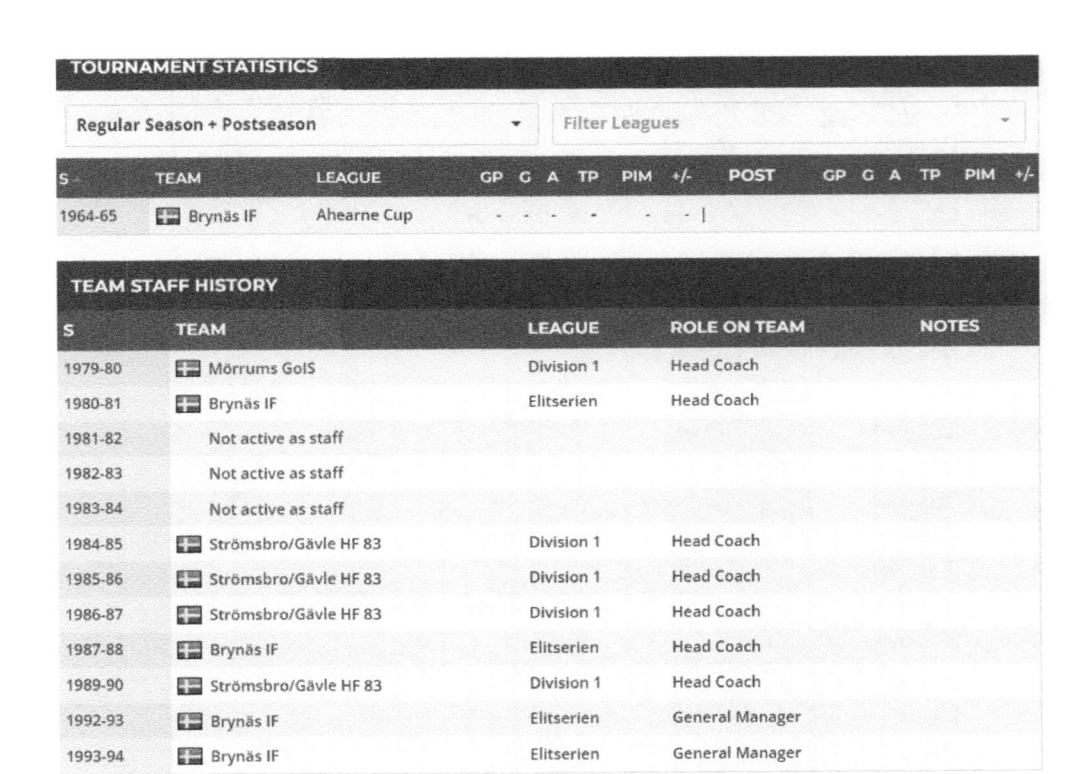

Regular Season + Postseason | Filter Leagues

S	TEAM	LEAGUE	GP	G	A	TP	PIM	+/-	POST	GP	G	A	TP	PIM	+/-
1964-65	🇸🇪 Brynäs IF	Ahearne Cup	-	-	-	-	-	-							

TEAM STAFF HISTORY

S	TEAM	LEAGUE	ROLE ON TEAM	NOTES
1979-80	🇸🇪 Mörrums GoIS	Division 1	Head Coach	
1980-81	🇸🇪 Brynäs IF	Elitserien	Head Coach	
1981-82	Not active as staff			
1982-83	Not active as staff			
1983-84	Not active as staff			
1984-85	🇸🇪 Strömsbro/Gävle HF 83	Division 1	Head Coach	
1985-86	🇸🇪 Strömsbro/Gävle HF 83	Division 1	Head Coach	
1986-87	🇸🇪 Strömsbro/Gävle HF 83	Division 1	Head Coach	
1987-88	🇸🇪 Brynäs IF	Elitserien	Head Coach	
1989-90	🇸🇪 Strömsbro/Gävle HF 83	Division 1	Head Coach	
1992-93	🇸🇪 Brynäs IF	Elitserien	General Manager	
1993-94	🇸🇪 Brynäs IF	Elitserien	General Manager	

Terry Clancy

Terrance John Clancy was born on April 2, 1943 and is a Canadian former professional ice hockey player who played 93 games in the National Hockey League between 1967 and 1973. He played with the Oakland Seals and the Toronto Maple Leafs. The rest of his career, which lasted from 1963 to 1975, was mainly spent in the minor leagues, as well as with an independent professional hockey team, the London Lions, during the 1973–74 season. He is the son of King Clancy, who played in the NHL between 1921 and 1937 and was elected to the Hockey Hall of Fame. Internationally Clancy played for Canada at the 1964 Winter Olympics.

Clancy played junior with the Toronto St. Michael's Majors of the Ontario Hockey Association. He helped St. Michael's win the 1961 Memorial Cup, the championship of junior hockey in Canada. After two seasons with St. Michael's Clancy moved to the Montreal Junior Canadiens for one season, followed by a stint with the Canadian national team. On his return from the 1964 Winter Olympics Clancy turned professional. playing 3 games with the Rochester Americans of the minor American Hockey League (AHL). Signed by the Toronto Maple Leafs of the National Hockey League (NHL) in October 1964, he stayed in the minor leagues and split 1964–65 between Rochester and the Tulsa Oilers of the Central Hockey League, and spent the 1965–66 season with Tulsa, but returned to Rochester and the AHL for 1966–67.

The NHL expanded in 1967, doubling in size, and Clancy was claimed by the newly-formed California/Oakland Seals (the team changed names midway through the season) in the expansion draft. He made his NHL debut in Seals first game, October 11, 1967 against the Philadelphia Flyers. He played seven games for the Seals that year, all at the start of the season. Reassigned to the minor leagues, Clancy spent the rest of the 1967–68 with the Vancouver Canucks of the minor Western Hockey League and the Buffalo Bisons of the AHL. After the season ended, on May 14, 1968, Clancy was traded back to Toronto.

Back with Tulsa for the 1968–69 season, Clancy played two games in the NHL with the Toronto Maple Leafs in December 1968. He played 52 games for the Maple Leafs in 1969–70, recording his first goal on December 6, 1969 against the Pittsburgh Penguins. Clancy finished with 6 goals and 11 points. The 1970–71 season saw Clancy spend time with both the Phoenix Roadrunners of the WHL and after being traded to the Montreal Canadiens on December 23, 1970, their AHL affiliate the Montreal Voyageurs of the AHL. He sitting out the 1971–72 season, and being traded back to Toronto on August 30, 1971, he played 32 games for Toronto in 1972–73, his final time in the NHL. On October 17, 1973 Clancy was traded once more, going to the Detroit Red Wings, though he spent the 1973–74 season split with the Albuquerque Six-Guns of the CHL and the London Lions, a British-based team that played across Europe that year. After a nine-game stint with the Virginia Wings of the AHL in 1974–75 Clancy retired from playing.

Clancy played for Canada in the 1964 Winter Olympics. He scored 1 goal and had 1 assist in 7 games played, but missed a medal as Canada finished in a 3-way tie and controversially ended up in 4th place.

Terry's Stats

S	TEAM	LEAGUE	GP	G	A	TP	PIM	+/-	POST	GP	G	A	TP	PIM	+/-
1960-61	Toronto St. Michael's Majors	OHA-Jr.	38	2	3	5	30	-	Playoffs	20	2	3	5	16	-
1961-62	Toronto St. Michael's Majors	MTJAHL	32	4	14	18	16	-	Playoffs	12	6	3	9	20	-
1962-63	Montréal Jr. Canadiens	OHA-Jr.	27	6	7	13	29	-	Playoffs	10	1	6	7	10	-
1963-64	Rochester Americans	AHL	3	0	0	0	0	-							
	Team Canada	International	-	-	-	-	-	-							
	Canada	OG	7	1	1	2	2	-							
1964-65	Rochester Americans	AHL	30	1	5	6	6	-							
	Tulsa Oilers	CPHL	33	10	10	20	18	-	Playoffs	12	4	1	5	14	-
1965-66	Tulsa Oilers	CPHL	70	15	18	33	74	-	Playoffs	11	3	5	8	5	-
1966-67	Rochester Americans	AHL	72	14	24	38	51	-	Playoffs	10	0	2	2	4	-
1967-68	Buffalo Bisons	AHL	14	4	1	5	4	-							
	Vancouver Canucks	WHL-Sr.	46	6	9	15	10	-							
	California/Oakland Seals	NHL	7	0	0	0	2	-4							
1968-69	Tulsa Oilers	CHL	47	5	13	18	24	-	Playoffs	5	1	0	1	2	-
	Toronto Maple Leafs	NHL	2	0	0	0	0	-1							
1969-70	Toronto Maple Leafs	NHL	52	6	5	11	31	4							
1970-71	Phoenix Roadrunners	WHL-Sr.	18	2	1	3	9	-							
	Montréal Voyageurs	AHL	33	5	3	8	6	-	Playoffs	3	0	0	0	0	-
1971-72	Did not play														
1972-73	Toronto Maple Leafs	NHL	32	0	1	1	6	-10							
1973-74	Albuquerque Six Guns	CHL	19	4	0	4	21	-							
	London Lions	International	35	6	13	19	22	-							
1974-75	Virginia Wings	AHL	9	0	0	0	0	-							

Ulf Sterner

Ulf Ivar Erik "Uffe" Sterner was born on 11 February 1941 and is a Swedish former professional ice hockey forward. He played in nine IIHF World Championships for Sweden, where the team won seven medals: one gold, five silver, and one bronze. He was also a member of the silver medal team at the 1964 Winter Olympics. Sterner played for Forshaga IF from 1956–61, Västra Frölunda IF from 1961–64, and for the New York Rangers in 1964–65, before returning to Sweden to play for Rögle BK and Färjestads BK. He finished his career in England with the London Lions in 1973–74. On 27 January 1965, he became the first European-trained player to play in the National Hockey League (NHL).

Sterner made his hockey debut at 15 when he was accepted onto a second division club where he made a name for himself with his speed and scoring ability. On 12 November 1959, he made his international debut with Tre Kronor in a friendly match against Czechoslovakia's team. He scored his first goal in that game, which Tre Kronor won 11–3. He was the team's youngest player of all time. Through the late 1950s and early 1960s, he was one of Sweden's most popular players. He is also credited with inventing the "stick to skate to stick" manoeuvre. At the 1962 World Ice Hockey Championships, Sterner scored what he described as his most memorable goal when he scored the 3–0 goal against Team Canada. His team won the game 5–3 and took the gold medal. At the 1963 World Championship, he scored a hat trick against Canada in a 4–1 win. After the game, he and teammate Sven "Tumba" Johansson met King Gustaf VI Adolf and received a royal congratulations.

His first Olympics came in 1960 in Squaw Valley. The team did not earn a medal, but from that point on he was a dominating centre in international play. By 1963, the New York Rangers had taken interest, and in October, Sterner made the trip for training camp. The parties signed a five-game try-out agreement, but Sterner declined to play that season in order to conserve his amateur status for the 1964 Winter Olympics. The Swedish Olympic hockey team won a silver medal, and Sterner then attended the NY Rangers training camp in 1964 where he displayed excellent skills. However, the NHL, unlike the International Ice Hockey Federation (IIHF), permitted hitting and physical play on any point of the ice; international players were not allowed to hit in the offensive zone. Allowing him time to adjust to the North American game, the Rangers offered him a start with the St. Paul Rangers of the Central League, which he accepted. After two months, he had adapted to the different style of play and was promoted to the Baltimore Clippers of the American Hockey League. Finally, on 27 January 1965, he joined the Rangers in a game against the Boston Bruins, becoming the first European to play in the NHL.

Ultimately, Sterner played only four games in the NHL, and he did not register a point although Rangers coach Red Sullivan praised Sterner for his puck handling skills. But he had been reluctant to play physically or to instigate physical play. He was sent back down to the AHL, and it soon became clear that he was not willing to return to the NHL for the 1965-66 season although he had signed a two year contract. As much as his skills carried him through games in the AHL, he simply did not have the training to play 60-minute games with full contact. In 1969, the IIHF adopted the same body-checking rules as the NHL, and four years later, Börje Salming joined the Toronto Maple Leafs, ending up playing 17 years in the NHL.[4] Eight years after leaving the Rangers, Sterner and the Swedish national team finally faced the best Canadian NHL players in two exhibition games in Stockholm that were part of Team Canada's preparation for the Summit Series against the USSR. On September 16 1972, Sterner scored against Canada as the Swedes only narrowly lost the game. He was offered a contract by the Chicago Cougars of the rival World Hockey Association but declined the offer.

Sterner, his wife Pia, and their family currently live on a farm near Karlstad, where they keep four horses. He nicknames his horses after former teammates and friends; when one of the horses smashed his nose, he nicknamed it Alexander Ragulin.

Ulf's Stats

TEAM STAFF HISTORY				
S	TEAM	LEAGUE	ROLE ON TEAM	NOTES
1977-78	Vänersborgs HC	Division 2	Player-Coach	
1986-87	SV Bayreuth	Germany2	Head Coach	
1989-90	Hammarö HC	Division 2	Head Coach	
1990-91	Hammarö HC	Division 2	Head Coach	Fired mid-season

S	TEAM	LEAGUE	GP	G	A	TP	PIM	+/-	POST	GP	G	A	TP	PIM	+/-
1954-55	Deje IK	Division 2	-	-	-	-	-	-							
1955-56	Deje IK	Division 2	-	-	-	-	-	-							
1956-57	Forshaga IF	Division 1	7	3	0	3	-	-							
1957-58	Forshaga IF	Division 1	14	2	0	2	-	-							
1958-59	Forshaga IF	Division 1	11	7	8	15	-	-							
	Sweden (all)	International	-	-	-	-	-	-							
1959-60	Forshaga IF	Division 1	14	17	6	23	14	-							
	Sweden	OG	5	0	1	1	0	-							
	Sweden B (all)	International	2	1	-	-	-	-							
	Sweden (all)	International	8	4	-	-	-	-							
1960-61	Forshaga IF	Division 1	13	14	8	22	2	-							
	Sweden	WC	7	5	0	5	2	-							
	Sweden (all)	International	13	6	-	-	-	-							
1961-62	Västra Frölunda IF	Division 1	20	18	13	31	31	-	Playoffs	7	6	4	10	5	-
	Sweden	WC	7	9	7	16	2	-							
1962-63	Västra Frölunda IF	Division 1	21	21	10	31	6	-	Playoffs	7	7	4	11	0	-
	Sweden (all)	International	-	-	-	-	-	-							
	Sweden	WC	7	7	2	9	2	-							
1963-64	Västra Frölunda IF	Division 1	19	11	6	17	16	-	Playoffs	7	1	4	5	10	-
	Sweden	OG	7	6	5	11	0	-							
1964-65	New York Rangers	NHL	4	0	0	0	0	-							
	St. Paul Rangers	CPHL	16	12	9	21	2	-							
	Baltimore Clippers	AHL	52	18	26	44	12	-	Playoffs	5	1	0	1	2	-
1965-66	Rögle BK	Division 2	21	46	14	58	-	-	Qualification	6	11	3	15	-	-
	Sweden (all)	International	-	-	-	-	-	-							
	Sweden	WC	7	4	1	5	0	-							
1966-67	Rögle BK	Division 1	19	4	11	15	11	-							
	Sweden	WC	7	2	3	5	7	-							
1967-68	Färjestad BK	Division 1	21	16	8	24	19	-							
1968-69	Västra Frölunda IF	Division 1	19	19	20	39	10	-	Qualification	7	5	7	12	2	-
	Sweden (all)	International	-	-	-	-	-	-							
	Sweden "C"	WC	10	5	9	14	8	-							
1969-70	Färjestad BK	Division 2	22	17	26	43	-	-	Qualification	5	3	4	7	2	-
	Sweden "C"	WC	10	1	7	8	7	-							
1970-71	Färjestad BK	Division 1	20	14	10	24	27	-15	Playoffs	14	10	3	13	14	-
	Sweden (all)	International	-	-	-	-	-	-							
	Sweden	WC	10	2	2	4	2	-							
1971-72	Färjestad BK	Division 1	28	15	21	36	18	-	Playoffs	14	5	6	11	24	-
1972-73	Färjestad BK	Division 1	28	17	17	34	52	-	Playoffs	14	10	2	12	29	-
	Sweden	WC	9	5	2	7	6	-							
1973-74	London Lions "A"	International	64	27	88	115	71	-							

S	TEAM	LEAGUE	GP	G	A	TP	PIM	+/-
1974-75	🇸🇪 BK Bäcken	Division 2	22	14	31	45	63	-
1975-76	🇸🇪 IFK Bäcken	Division 1	22	17	23	40	31	-
1976-77	🇸🇪 IFK Bäcken	Division 1	24	14	24	38	38	-
1977-78	🇸🇪 Vänersborgs HC	Division 2	15	17	16	33	-	-
1978-79	🇸🇪 Forshaga IF	Division 3	5	-	-	-	-	-
1982-83	🇸🇪 Hammarö HC	Division 3	-	-	-	-	-	-
1983-84	🇸🇪 Skattkärrs HC	Division 4	12	4	15	19	-	-
1984-85	🇸🇪 Skåre BK	Division 4	-	-	-	-	-	-
1988-89	🇸🇪 Hammarö HC	Division 2	-	-	-	-	-	-
1989-90	🇸🇪 Hammarö HC	Division 2	1	0	0	0	0	-

S	TEAM	LEAGUE	GP	G	A	TP	PIM	+/-	POST	GP	G	A	TP	PIM	+/-
1961-62	🇸🇪 Västra Frölunda IF	Ahearne Cup	-	-	-	-	-	-							
1962-63	🇸🇪 Västra Frölunda IF	Ahearne Cup	-	-	-	-	-	-							

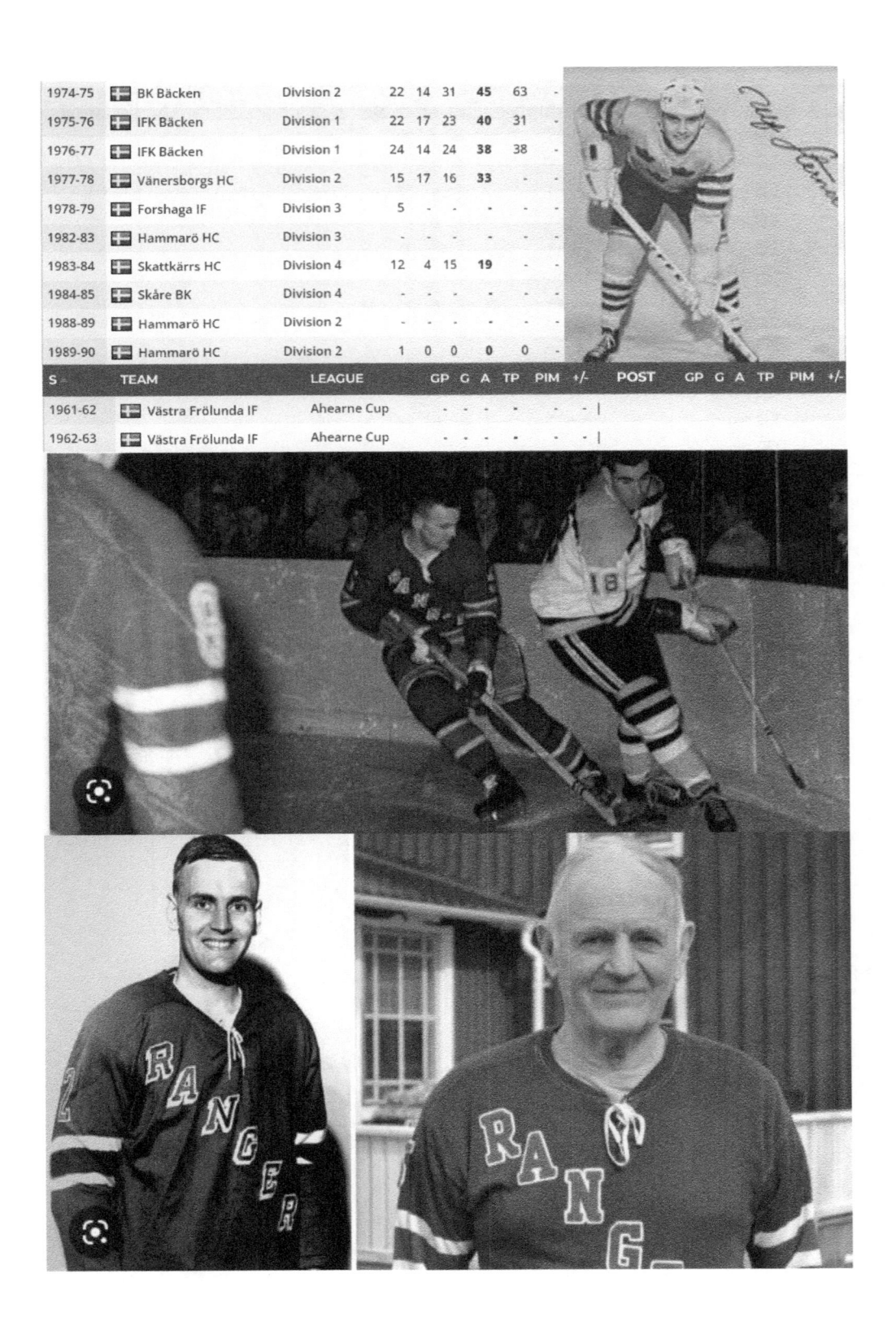

The NHL in the UK

Mike Korney

Michael Wayne Korney was born on September 15, 1953 and is a Canadian retired professional ice hockey player. He played in 77 games in the National Hockey League with the Detroit Red Wings and New York Rangers between 1973 and 1978..

Mike played 2 years for his hometown Dauphin Kings, winning Manitoba in his final year (1971–72), before moving up to the Western Canada Hockey League with the Winnipeg Jets. HE was selecte by the Detroit Red Wings in 4th round (59th overall) in the 1973 NHL Amateur Draft.

Mike's Stats

S	TEAM	LEAGUE	GP	G	A	TP	PIM	+/-	POST	GP	G	A	TP	PIM	+/-
1970-71	Dauphin Kings	MJHL	45	15	31	46	38	-							
1971-72	Dauphin Kings	MJHL	41	16	33	49	64	-							
1972-73	Winnipeg Jets	WCHL	68	20	29	49	92	-							
1973-74	Detroit Red Wings	NHL	2	0	0	0	0	-3							
	Virginia Wings	AHL	19	1	1	2	15	-							
	Port Huron Wings	IHL	7	1	0	1	9	-							
	London Lions	International	31	15	10	25	33	-							
1974-75	Detroit Red Wings	NHL	30	8	2	10	18	-9							
	Virginia Wings	AHL	2	0	0	0	0	-							
	Providence Reds	AHL	3	1	0	1	0	-							
	Springfield Indians	AHL	1	0	0	0	0	-							
	Hampton Gulls	SHL-Sr.	13	0	1	1	35	-							
1975-76	Detroit Red Wings	NHL	27	1	7	8	23	-8							
	New Haven Nighthawks	AHL	21	8	9	17	31	-							
	Oklahoma City Blazers	CHL	18	8	6	14	20	-	Playoffs	4	0	0	0	2	-
1976-77	Kansas City Blues	CHL	74	17	24	41	82	-	Playoffs	10	1	6	7	13	-
1977-78	Maine Mariners	AHL	15	2	4	6	20	-							
	Milwaukee Admirals	IHL	3	0	0	0	2	-							
	Salt Lake Golden Eagles	CHL	54	12	8	20	75	-	Playoffs	6	2	4	6	6	-

S	TEAM	LEAGUE	GP	G	A	TP	PIM	+/-	POST	GP	G	A	TP	PIM	+/-
1978-79	New York Rangers	NHL	18	0	1	1	18	4							
	New Haven Nighthawks	AHL	5	1	3	4	0	-							
	Tulsa Oilers	CHL	11	0	9	9	36	-							
1979-80	Syracuse Firebirds	AHL	73	11	16	27	87	-	Playoffs	4	1	2	3	18	-
1980-81	Cranbrook Royals	WIHL	-	-	-	-	-	-							
	Trail Smoke Eaters	WIHL	15	1	10	11	24	-							
1981-82	Cranbrook Royals	WIHL	-	-	-	-	-	-							

S	TEAM	LEAGUE	GP	G	A	TP	PIM	+/-	POST	GP	G	A	TP	PIM	+/-
1981-82	Cranbrook Royals	Allan Cup	5	1	6	7	2	-							

Rick McCann

Richard Leo McCann was born on May 27, 1944 and died on September 3, 2013, he was a Canadian ice hockey player who played 43 games in the National Hockey League with the Detroit Red Wings between 1967 and 1974. Internationally he played for the Canadian national team at the 1966 World Championships.

S	TEAM	LEAGUE	GP	G	A	TP	PIM	+/-	POST	GP	G	A	TP	PIM	+/-
1964-65	Michigan Tech	NCAA	-	-	-	-	-	-							
1965-66	Team Canada	International	-	-	-	-	-	-							
	Canada	WC	2	0	0	0	2	-							
1966-67	Memphis Wings	CPHL	61	15	26	41	23	-	Playoffs	1	0	0	0	0	-
1967-68	Detroit Red Wings	NHL	3	0	0	0	0	0							
	Fort Worth Wings	CPHL	68	20	51	71	98	-	Playoffs	13	5	11	16	13	-
1968-69	Detroit Red Wings	NHL	3	0	0	0	0	-1							
	Fort Worth Wings	CHL	67	22	49	71	63	-							
1969-70	Detroit Red Wings	NHL	18	0	1	1	4	-2							
	Fort Worth Wings	CHL	47	15	24	39	29	-	Playoffs	7	2	4	6	4	-
1970-71	Detroit Red Wings	NHL	5	0	0	0	0	-2							
	Baltimore Clippers	AHL	62	18	20	38	21	-							
1971-72	Detroit Red Wings	NHL	1	0	0	0	0	0							
	Tidewater Red Wings	AHL	69	13	38	51	39	-							
1972-73	Virginia Wings	AHL	66	12	44	56	75	-	Playoffs	11	1	9	10	4	-
1973-74	London Lions "C"	International	70	25	55	80	28	-							
1974-75	Detroit Red Wings	NHL	13	1	3	4	2	-4							
	Virginia Wings	AHL	65	19	48	67	60	-	Playoffs	5	1	4	5	0	-
1975-76	New Haven Nighthawks	AHL	73	15	42	57	47	-	Playoffs	3	0	0	0	0	-

Bill McKenzie

In an era when the chances of a collegiate hockey player making it to the NHL were slim to none – let alone a goaltender – Saint Thomas, Ontario's own Bill McKenzie was the exception to the rule. An undrafted netminder, McKenzie would go on to play 91 games in the NHL across six seasons.

Electing to go the US collegiate route, he played three seasons for Ohio State University beginning with the 1969-70 season. As the starting goaltender for the Buckeyes, the team assembled a combined record of 63-21-1 during McKenzie's tenure, including a 24-5 record in 1972. He backstopped the Buckeyes to their first Central Collegiate Hockey Association championship in 1972. McKenzie was named the 1972 CCHA Tournament MVP and named to the 1972 All-Tournament Team.

Bill McKenzie played for three different teams across six season in the NHL – one of which was the Kansas City Scouts (Photo Credit: Kansas City Scouts team issued press photo).

Having graduated from OSU following the 1972 championship, McKenzie still ranks within the top-3 in program history for season shutouts (four in both 1970 and 1972) and career shutouts (10). He was the school's career wins leader until 2004 with 54 victories to his credit. McKenzie also still holds top-10 marks in the program for single-season goals against average of 2.25 in 1972, and for a career (2.74).

Though not selected in the draft, it is clear to see why McKenzie would garner interest from NHL clubs. A school record achieving goalie with solid numbers and a championship to boot? Taking a stab at the netminding scholar simply made sense.

Debuting in Detroit

On Oct. 4, 1972, McKenzie was signed as a free agent by the Detroit Red Wings. Though an "Original Six" team and ultimately the winners of 11 Stanley Cup championships, the Red Wings of the 1970s were rather abysmal. The club failed to make the playoffs for seven straight seasons from 1970-71 through 1976-77, and only made the postseason once during the entire decade.

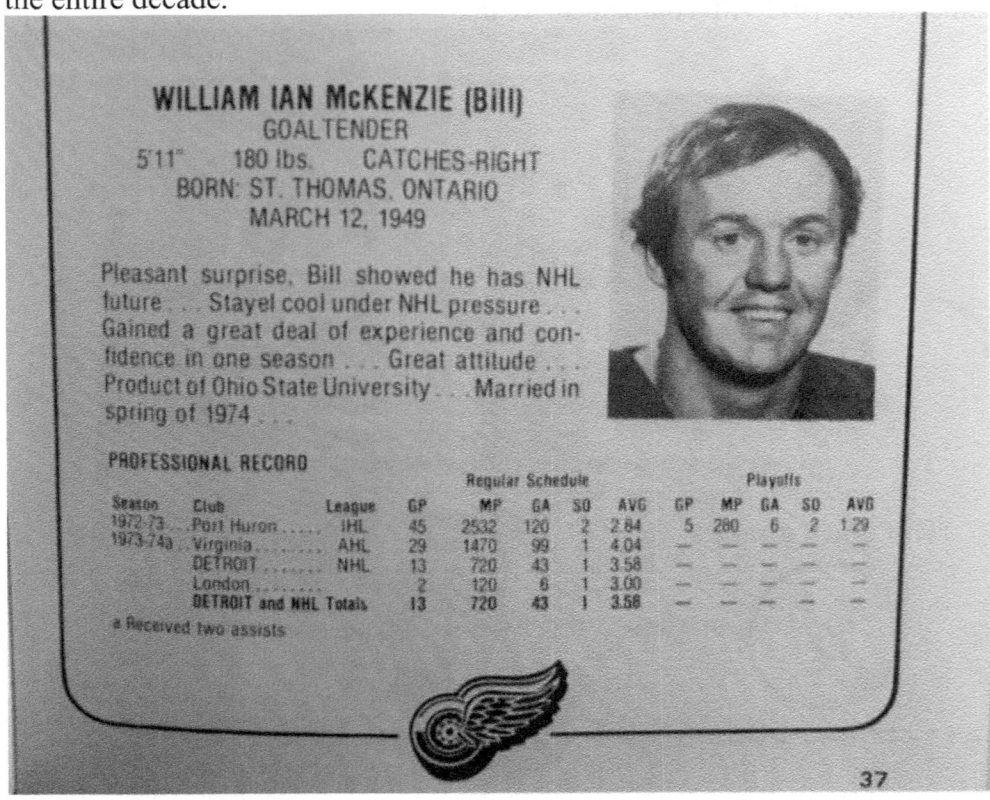

Goaltender Bill McKenzie began his NHL career with the Detroit Red Wings in 1973-74 (Photo Credit: Detroit Red Wings 1974-75 Media Guide).

McKenzie certainly at least had the potential to be a diamond in the rough. The Red Wings assigned him to their IHL affiliate for the 1972-73 season, the Port Huron Flags. McKenzie assumed the starting goaltending duties on a primarily veteran club. He backstopped the team to a winning record of 41-31-1 and a berth in the Turner Cup Final. Unfortunately, McKenzie and the

Flags would lose to the Fort Wayne Komets in four straight games. McKenzie in turn was named the IHL's Rookie of the Year.

Proving his worth within the organization, McKenzie would see his first NHL action during the 1973-74 season. He would split the season between two other clubs – the AHL's Virginia Red Wings and the independent London Lions – but earned himself a call-up to the parent club in December of 1973.

McKenzie made his NHL debut on Dec. 18 and earned the Red Wings a tie against the visiting Los Angeles Kings. He remained with the team for the rest of the month, all of January and into February. McKenzie earned a record of 4-4-4, and pitched his first NHL shutout on Jan. 12, 1973 in 6-0 win over the Kings.

When the 1974-75 season came around, veteran goaltender Jimmy Rutherford handled the bulk of the Detroit netminding duties while the team utilized three young prospects – McKenzie, Doug Grant, and Terry Richardson – as revolving backups. McKenzie would begin the season in Virginia, but would be called up in the back half of the season as Grant and Richardson were sent down.

McKenzie went 1-9-2 in 13 games for Detroit from January 1975 into April. He would play his final game in a Red Wings uniform on Apr. 5, 1975 on the road against the Pittsburgh Penguins.

Traded to Kansas City
Bill McKenzie is one of just five goalies to ever play for the Kansas City Scouts (Photo Credit: Kansas City Scouts 1975-76 Media Guide).

On Aug. 22, 1975, McKenzie and veteran defender Gary Bergman were traded from the Red Wings to an equally struggling club – the Kansas City Scouts – in exchange for goaltender Peter McDuffe and centerman Glen Burdon.

In terms of finding a successful hockey club, joining the Scouts likely put McKenzie in a worse situation. But going with the notion that every cloud has its silver lining, the Kansas City/Colorado franchise afforded McKenzie his fullest NHL action and his longest tenure with an NHL organization.

In what would be their final season in Kansas City, McKenzie assumed the full-time backup duties for the Scouts in behind starting netminder Denis Herron. McKenzie would see his fullest amount of NHL action to that point by playing 22 games in 1975-76.

Unfortunately, amid a woeful Scouts line-ups, he assembled a rough record of 1-16-1. The only victory McKenzie earned for Kansas City was an Oct. 22, 1975 4-2 victory over the Washington Capitals.

Never truly catching on in Missouri, the Scouts would relocate to Colorado in July of 1976 and became known as the Rockies.

The Minors and the Rockies
During the club's first season in Colorado, McKenzie's appearances were few and far in between. The main goaltending duties for the Rockies fell to veterans Doug Favell and Michel Plasse during 1976-77, while McKenzie made just five appearances for a record of 0-2-1. He made one appearance in October, two in November, and one each in December and February.

This would signal the beginning of a continuous bouncing around for McKenzie. From 1976-77 through 1979-80, he played for eight different teams across three different leagues. He would suit up specifically for the Rockies in 1977-78 and 1979-80.

But there were three particularly positive things that happened to McKenzie during this range of seasons.

First, during the 1976-77 season he suited up for four different teams – the last of which was the Kansas City Blues of the Central Hockey League. McKenzie manned the Blues' net for all 10 of their playoff games, and backstopped them to the Adams Cup championship. McKenzie was additionally awarded as the CHL's Playoff MVP for his heroics.

Secondly, McKenzie did his part to help the Rockies make the playoffs for the 1977-78 season – the *only* time ever that either the Scouts or Rockies version of the franchise made it to the postseason. McKenzie played 12 games that season and went 3-6-2. For a Rockies team (19-40-21) that sneaked into the playoffs by a mere two points, McKenzie's three wins and two ties were imperative to ensure the club's playoff appearance.

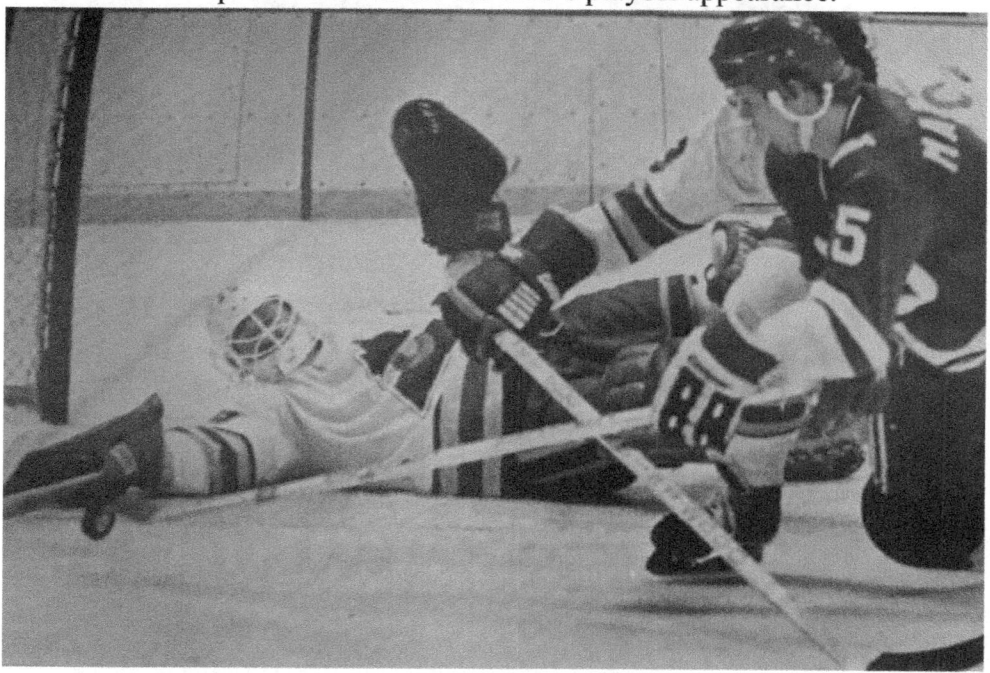

Colorado Rockies goalie Bill McKenzie makes a save against the Hartford Whalers' Mark Howe (Photo Credit: Colorado Rockies 1979-80 Media Guide).

Lastly, in what would be his final professional season, McKenzie played his fullest amount of NHL action in 1979-80. Led by head coach Don Cherry and firepower from the likes of Lanny McDonald and Rene Robert, the Rockies went 19-48-13.

A less than impressive record, but McKenzie was one of their few bright spots. He set career highs in games played (26), wins (9), and saves (528). McKenzie was also the only Rockies goalie that season (of which there were four) to record a shutout when he whitewashed the Pittsburgh Penguins on Mar. 28, 1980 by a score of 5-0.

Post Playing Career

Following his retirement after the 1979-80 season, McKenzie returned to his alma mater. For 18 seasons he served as an assistant coach at Ohio State for both their men's and women's hockey programs. In 2001 McKenzie became only the second hockey player inducted into OSU's Hall of Fame.

Bill McKenzie set career highs for games played, wins and saves during the 1979-80 season while with the Colorado Rockies (1977-78 Colorado Rockies Media Guide).

Bill's Stats

TEAM STAFF HISTORY				
S	TEAM	LEAGUE	ROLE ON TEAM	NOTES
2006-07	Ohio State Univ.	NCAA (W)	Goaltending Coach	Volunteer
2007-08	Ohio State Univ.	NCAA (W)	Goaltending Coach	Volunteer
2008-09	Ohio State Univ.	NCAA (W)	Goaltending Coach	Volunteer
2009-10	Ohio State Univ.	NCAA (W)	Goaltending Coach	Volunteer

S	TEAM	LEAGUE	GP	GAA	SV%	SO	WLT	POST	GP	GAA	SV%	SO	WLT
1969-70	Ohio State Univ.	NCAA	25	3.12	.907	4	-						
1970-71	Ohio State Univ.	NCAA	24	2.74	-	-	-						
1971-72	Ohio State Univ.	NCAA	21	2.26	-	-	-						
1972-73	Port Huron Wings	IHL	45	2.84	-	-	-	Playoffs	5	1.29	-	-	-
1973-74	Detroit Red Wings	NHL	13	3.59	.885	1	4-4-4						
	Virginia Wings	AHL	29	4.04	-	-	-						
	London Lions	International	2	3.00	-	-	-						
1974-75	Detroit Red Wings	NHL	13	4.71	.862	0	1-9-2						
	Virginia Wings	AHL	14	2.82	-	-	-						
1975-76	Kansas City Scouts	NHL	22	5.20	.845	0	1-16-1						
1976-77	Rhode Island Reds	AHL	2	4.80	-	-	-						
	Colorado Rockies	NHL	5	2.41	.921	0	0-2-1						
	Oklahoma City Blazers	CHL	6	4.02	-	-	-						
	Kansas City Blues	CHL	10	2.92	-	-	-	Playoffs	10	2.18	-	-	-
1977-78	Colorado Rockies	NHL	12	3.87	.879	0	3-6-2						
	Hampton Gulls	AHL	12	3.53	-	-	-						
	Philadelphia Firebirds	AHL	5	4.33	-	-	-						
1978-79	Tulsa Oilers	CHL	35	5.09	-	-	-						
1979-80	Colorado Rockies	NHL	26	3.49	.871	1	9-12-3						
	Fort Worth Texans	CHL	9	3.34	-	-	-						

Thomas Mellor

Thomas Robert Mellor was born on January 27, 1950 and is an American former professional ice hockey defenseman. He played 26 games in the National Hockey League with the Detroit Red Wings during the 1973–74 and 1974–75 seasons. Internationally Mellor played for the American national team at the 1972 Winter Olympics, winning a silver medal.

Before being drafted by the Detroit Red Wings, Mellor played hockey for Boston College. In the 1968–69 season, he scored nine goals and 19 points in his 17-game rookie season. In his sophomore season, he scored 21 goals and 44 points in 26 games. He scored a hat trick for Boston College in a 13–6 win over Rensselaer Polytechnic Institute. In his junior year in the NCAA he had 40 points in 25 games for the Boston Eagles. During his years at Boston College, he led Boston College in assists on two occasions (1971: 30; 1973: 45) and was ranked third for most assists in a season at Boston College. He was also a two-time recipient (1971, 1973) of Boston College's Norman F. Dailey Memorial Award as the team's Most Valuable Player. He was inducted into the Boston College Varsity Club Athletic Hall of Fame in 1980.

Mellor was drafted 68th overall by the Detroit Red Wings in 1970 NHL Amateur Draft and played 26 regular season games in the National Hockey League for Detroit between 1973 and 1975. Mellor also played in the American Hockey League for the Virginia Wings; in the International Hockey League for the Toledo Goaldiggers; and in the Swedish Elitserien with Västra Frölunda. As a player in the IHL, he was named to the First-Team All-Star Team, he won the James Gatschene Memorial Trophy and the Governor's Trophy in 1977, his last season as a professional player before retiring.

As an amateur, Mellor represented the United States national team at the 1972 Winter Olympics in Sapporo, winning a silver medal.[4] Mellor also played in the 1971, 1972 and 1973 Ice Hockey World Championship tournaments.

Mellor was formally inducted into the Rhode Island Hockey Hall of Fame in 2022. At the same enshrinement ceremony, his 101-year-old father, Don

Mellor, a pioneer youth hockey organizer, was honoured by the Hall with the Malcolm Greene Chace Memorial Trophy for "Lifetime Achievement of a Rhode Islander to the game of hockey."

Tom's Stats

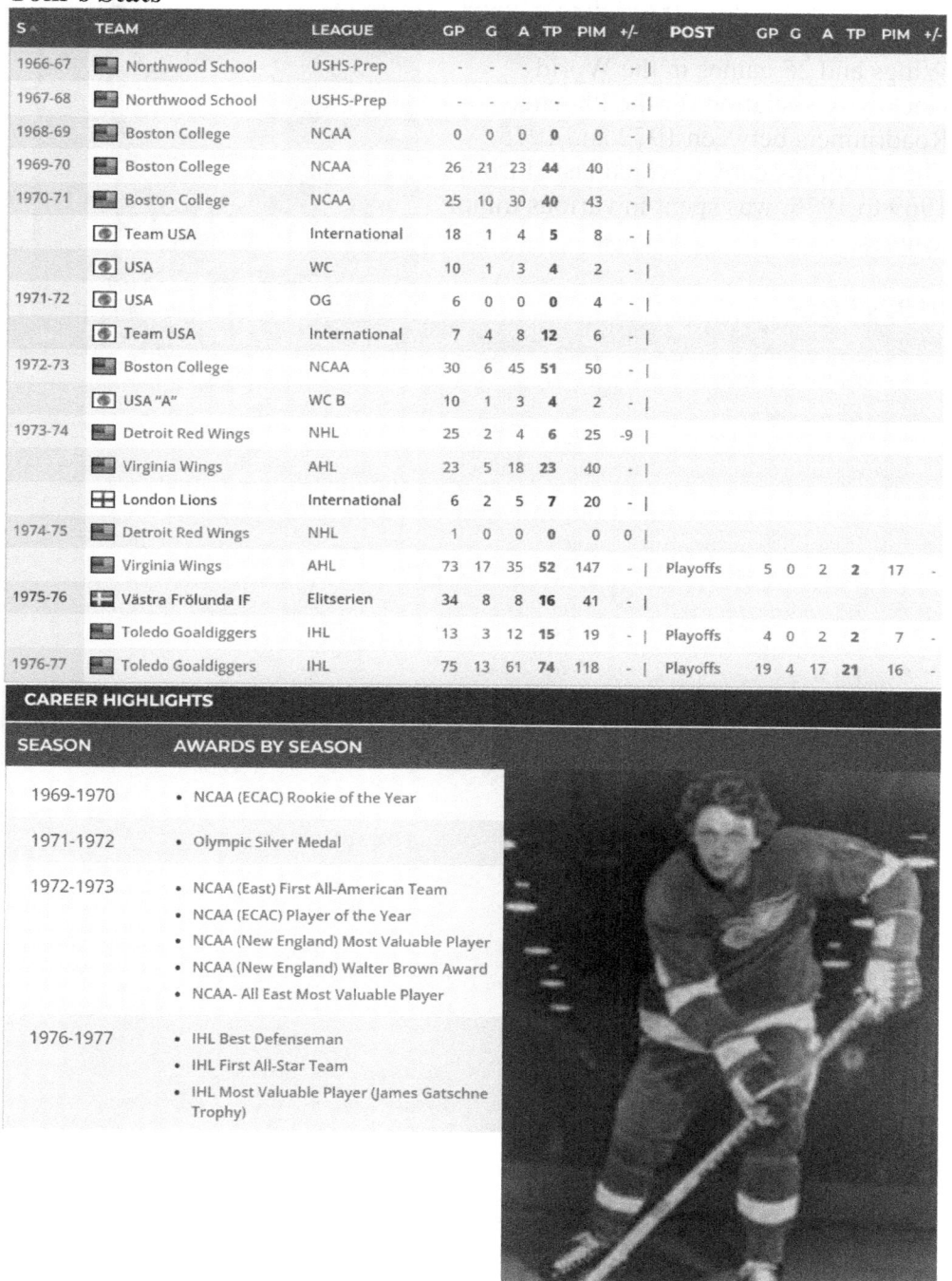

S	TEAM	LEAGUE	GP	G	A	TP	PIM	+/-	POST	GP	G	A	TP	PIM	+/-
1966-67	Northwood School	USHS-Prep	-	-	-	-	-	-							
1967-68	Northwood School	USHS-Prep	-	-	-	-	-	-							
1968-69	Boston College	NCAA	0	0	0	0	0	-							
1969-70	Boston College	NCAA	26	21	23	44	40	-							
1970-71	Boston College	NCAA	25	10	30	40	43	-							
	Team USA	International	18	1	4	5	8	-							
	USA	WC	10	1	3	4	2	-							
1971-72	USA	OG	6	0	0	0	4	-							
	Team USA	International	7	4	8	12	6	-							
1972-73	Boston College	NCAA	30	6	45	51	50	-							
	USA "A"	WC B	10	1	3	4	2	-							
1973-74	Detroit Red Wings	NHL	25	2	4	6	25	-9							
	Virginia Wings	AHL	23	5	18	23	40	-							
	London Lions	International	6	2	5	7	20	-							
1974-75	Detroit Red Wings	NHL	1	0	0	0	0	0							
	Virginia Wings	AHL	73	17	35	52	147	-	Playoffs	5	0	2	2	17	-
1975-76	Västra Frölunda IF	Elitserien	34	8	8	16	41	-							
	Toledo Goaldiggers	IHL	13	3	12	15	19	-	Playoffs	4	0	2	2	7	-
1976-77	Toledo Goaldiggers	IHL	75	13	61	74	118	-	Playoffs	19	4	17	21	16	-

CAREER HIGHLIGHTS

SEASON	AWARDS BY SEASON
1969-1970	• NCAA (ECAC) Rookie of the Year
1971-1972	• Olympic Silver Medal
1972-1973	• NCAA (East) First All-American Team • NCAA (ECAC) Player of the Year • NCAA (New England) Most Valuable Player • NCAA (New England) Walter Brown Award • NCAA- All East Most Valuable Player
1976-1977	• IHL Best Defenseman • IHL First All-Star Team • IHL Most Valuable Player (James Gatschne Trophy)

Rick Newell

Gordon Richard Newell was born on February 18, 1948 and is a Canadian retired professional ice hockey player who played seven games in the National Hockey League for the Detroit Red Wings and 25 games in the World Hockey Association for the Phoenix Roadrunners between 1972 and 1975. The rest of his career, which lasted from 1969 to 1978, was spent in various minor leagues.

Rick's Stats

S	TEAM	LEAGUE	GP	G	A	TP	PIM	+/-	POST	GP	G	A	TP	PIM	+/-
1964-65	Winnipeg Rangers	MJHL	35	5	13	18	74	-	Playoffs	5	1	8	9	15	-
1965-66	Winnipeg Rangers	MJHL	3	0	2	2	6	-							
1966-67	Univ. of Minnesota-Duluth	NCAA	22	6	13	19	68	-							
1967-68	Univ. of Minnesota-Duluth "A"	NCAA	18	1	7	8	52	-							
1968-69	Univ. of Minnesota-Duluth "C"	NCAA	18	1	6	7	16	-							
1969-70	Univ. of Minnesota-Duluth	NCAA	17	3	4	7	28	-							
	Omaha Knights	CHL	6	0	0	0	4	-							
1970-71	Omaha Knights	CHL	69	6	17	23	110	-	Playoffs	11	1	4	5	4	-
	Providence Reds	AHL	19	1	6	7	15	-							
1971-72	Omaha Knights	CHL	53	8	21	29	76	-							
	Phoenix Roadrunners	WHL-Sr.	1	0	0	0	0	-							
	Providence Reds	AHL	19	1	6	7	15	-							
1972-73	Virginia Wings	AHL	68	24	23	47	125	-	Playoffs	9	2	3	5	6	-
	Detroit Red Wings	NHL	3	0	0	0	0	-1							
1973-74	Virginia Wings	AHL	50	9	22	31	44	-							
	Detroit Red Wings	NHL	3	0	0	0	0	-1							
	London Lions	International	17	12	11	23	63	-							
1974-75	Tulsa Oilers	CHL	22	5	9	14	24	-							
	Phoenix Roadrunners	WHA	25	0	4	4	39	-	Playoffs	5	0	1	1	2	-
1975-76	Tucson Mavericks	CHL	57	9	23	32	104	-							
	Syracuse Blazers	NAHL-Sr.	6	1	3	4	0	-							
1976-77	Did not play														
1977-78	Phoenix Roadrunners	PHL-Sr.	35	10	32	42	28	-							

Nelson Pyatt

Frederick Nelson Pyatt was born on September 9, 1953 and is a Canadian former professional ice hockey player. Pyatt was born in Port Arthur, Ontario. Drafted in 1973 by both the Detroit Red Wings of the National Hockey League and the Minnesota Fighting Saints of the World Hockey Association, Pyatt also played for the Washington Capitals and Colorado Rockies.

He is the father of Jesse and former NHL players Tom and Taylor Pyatt.

Nelson's Stats

S	TEAM	LEAGUE	GP	G	A	TP	PIM	+/-	POST	GP	G	A	TP	PIM	+/-
1970-71	Thunder Bay Marrs	TBJHL	-	-	-	-	-	-							
1971-72	Oshawa Generals	OHA-Jr.	54	17	29	46	27	-	Playoffs	12	3	3	6	10	-
1972-73	Oshawa Generals "C"	OHA-Jr.	26	13	19	32	7	-							
1973-74	Detroit Red Wings	NHL	5	0	0	0	0	-2							
	London Lions	International	61	35	28	62	4	-							
1974-75	Detroit Red Wings	NHL	9	0	0	0	2	-2							
	Virginia Wings	AHL	14	3	4	7	12	-							
	Washington Capitals	NHL	16	6	4	10	21	-14							
1975-76	Washington Capitals	NHL	77	26	23	49	14	-56							
1976-77	Colorado Rockies	NHL	77	23	22	45	20	-17							
1977-78	Colorado Rockies	NHL	71	9	12	21	8	-23							
1978-79	Colorado Rockies	NHL	28	2	2	4	2	-17							
	Philadelphia Firebirds	AHL	7	3	1	4	0	-							
1979-80	Colorado Rockies	NHL	13	5	0	5	2	-5							
	Fort Worth Texans	CHL	45	20	17	37	11	-	Playoffs	15	5	1	6	2	-
1980-81	VER Selb 1953	Germany2	22	37	26	63	4	-							
1981-82	VER Selb 1953	Germany2	46	80	30	110	32	-							
1982-83	Wiener EV	Austria	24	28	24	52	25	-							

S	TEAM	LEAGUE	GP	G	A	TP	PIM	+/-	POST	GP	G	A	TP	PIM	+/-
1970-71	Thunder Bay Marrs	Centennial Cup	5	3	4	7	7	-							

Terry Richardson

Terrance Paul Richardson was born on May 7, 1953 and is a Canadian retired ice hockey goaltender. He played 20 games in the National Hockey League with the Detroit Red Wings and St. Louis Blues between 1973 and 1979. The rest of his career, which lasted from 1973 to 1981, was spent in the minor leagues. Richardson was selected 11th overall by Detroit in the 1973 NHL Amateur Draft.

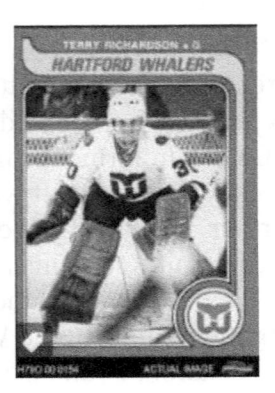

Richard began his career with the New Westminster Bruins during the 1971–72 season. He recorded three shutouts that year with a 3.06 goals against average (GAA). He had a record of 31–22–5 in 1972–73.

In 1973, Richardson was selected in the first round by the Red Wings. Richardson played in nine games that year finishing with one win and four losses and a dismal 5.33 goals against average. He was sent down to the Virginia Wings of the American Hockey League for conditioning and even was sent to the United Kingdom for a short time to play for the London Lions. The following year he returned to the Wings, but his skill did not. Richardson played only four games for the club and ended with a 6.83 GAA and one win before being sent back down to Virginia. The following season was no better, as the one NHL game that Richarson started ended in a loss with the score of 7–0 going to the Boston Bruins. He spent the rest of that year playing of both the Springfield Indians and the New Haven Nighthawks of the AHL.

The Red Wings decided to give Richardson one last shot with their club as he would start five games in the 1976–77 season, but again would disappoint, ending with one win and three losses. Richardson spent the rest of that year with the Kalamazoo Wings of the International Hockey League, leading them into the playoffs. However Kalamazoo would get knocked out in the second round. In 1977–78, Richardson played for the Kansas City Red Wings of the Central Hockey League, where he played a full season but finished with a 27–32–2 record.

On July 26, 1978, Richardson was signed as free agent by the St. Louis Blues, and found himself playing for their farm team, the Salt Lake Golden Eagles. Here he would have his best season to date, finishing with a 30–7–3 record in 40 games and leading the Eagles to the top of the CHL. He would even get called up for a single game with the Blues, but again watched as puck after puck got by in a 9–1 loss at the hands of the Minnesota North Stars.

In the summer of 1979, Richardson was involved in two trades. One from the Blues to the New York Islanders (along with Barry Gibbs) for future considerations on June 9 and from the Islanders to the Hartford Whalers for Ralph Klassen on June 14. He finished his career within the Whalers organization as he posted a 15–22–7 record in 46 games while playing again for the Springfield Indians in the 1979–80 season.

Terry's Stats

S	TEAM	LEAGUE	GP	GAA	SV%	SO	WLT	POST	GP	GAA	SV%	SO	WLT
1970-71	New Westminster Royals	BCJHL	-	-	-	-	-						
1971-72	New Westminster Bruins	WCHL	49	3.07	-	-	-	Playoffs	5	3.80	-	-	-
1972-73	New Westminster Bruins	WCHL	68	3.77	-	-	-	Playoffs	5	6.40	-	-	-
1973-74	Detroit Red Wings	NHL	9	5.35	.828	0	1-4-0						
	Virginia Wings	AHL	14	3.54	-	-	-						
	London Lions	International	14	3.12	-	-	-						
1974-75	Detroit Red Wings	NHL	4	6.86	.758	0	1-2-0						
	Virginia Wings	AHL	30	3.57	.882	-	-	Playoffs	2	3.52	-	-	-
1975-76	Detroit Red Wings	NHL	1	7.00	.806	0	0-1-0						
	Springfield Indians	AHL	20	4.28	-	-	-						
	New Haven Nighthawks	AHL	4	3.46	.500	-	-	Playoffs	2	2.86	-	-	-
1976-77	Detroit Red Wings	NHL	5	4.02	.869	0	1-3-0						
	Kalamazoo Wings	IHL	65	3.62	-	-	-	Playoffs	10	3.08	-	-	-
1977-78	Kansas City Red Wings	CHL	63	3.17	.888	-	-						
1978-79	St. Louis Blues	NHL	1	9.00	.750	0	0-1-0						
	Salt Lake Golden Eagles	CHL	40	2.53	.896	-	-	Playoffs	7	3.17	-	-	-
1979-80	Hartford Whalers	NHL	0	-	-	-	-						
	Springfield Indians	AHL	46	3.67	.880	-	-						
1980-81	Delta Hurry Kings	BCSHL	-	-	-	-	-						

TEAM STAFF HISTORY

S	TEAM	LEAGUE	ROLE ON TEAM	NOTES
2009-10	Washington Capitals	NHL	Scout	Amateur Scout
2010-11	Washington Capitals	NHL	Scout	Amateur Scout
2011-12	Washington Capitals	NHL	Scout	Amateur Scout
2012-13	Washington Capitals	NHL	Scout	Amateur Scout
2013-14	Washington Capitals	NHL	Scout	Amateur Scout
2014-15	Washington Capitals	NHL	Scout	Amateur Scout
2015-16	Washington Capitals	NHL	Scout	Amateur Scout
2016-17	Washington Capitals	NHL	Scout	Amateur Scout
2017-18	Washington Capitals	NHL	Scout	
2018-19	Washington Capitals	NHL	Scout	

Murray Wing

Murray Alan Wing was born on October 14, 1950 and is a Canadian retired professional ice hockey defenceman who played in one game in the National Hockey League with the Detroit Red Wings during the 1973–74 season, on April 7, 1974 against the Chicago Black Hawks. The rest of his career, which lasted from 1971 to 1977, was spent in the minor leagues.

Murray's Stats

S	TEAM	LEAGUE	GP	G	A	TP	PIM	+/-	POST	GP	G	A	TP	PIM	+/-
1967-68	Westfort Hurricanes	TBJHL	18	4	6	10	25	-							
1968-69	Westfort Hurricanes	TBJHL	36	22	25	47	58	-							
1969-70	Univ. of North Dakota	NCAA	0	-	-	-	-	-							
1970-71	Univ. of North Dakota	NCAA	29	3	10	13	18	-							
1971-72	Oklahoma City Blazers	CHL	71	12	15	27	79	-	Playoffs	6	0	0	0	14	-
1972-73	Boston Braves	AHL	57	2	10	12	37	-	Playoffs	10	2	6	8	2	-
	San Diego Gulls	WHL-Sr.	6	0	0	0	2	-							
1973-74	Detroit Red Wings	NHL	1	0	1	1	0	-2							
	London Lions	International	71	21	21	42	24	-							
1974-75	Thunder Bay Twins "A"	USHL Sr.	44	16	35	51	23	-							
1975-76	Thunder Bay Twins	OHA Sr.	22	3	15	18	8	-							
1976-77	Thunder Bay Twins	OHA Sr.	12	2	11	13	2	-							

S	TEAM	LEAGUE	GP	G	A	TP	PIM	+/-	POST	GP	G	A	TP	PIM	+/-
1967-68	Westfort Hurricanes	M-Cup	11	2	2	4	11	-							
1968-69	Fort William Canadiens	M-Cup	6	1	3	4	9	-							

The Resurgence of the Sport in the UK

The 1980's and 1990's

Ron Plumb played 26 games in the NHL for the Hartford Whalers during the 1979/80 season and had also notched up over 1000 games at minor pro level in a 16 year career in North America before he arrived at Fife Flyers as player coach for the 1984/85 season.

In terms of playing, defenceman Plumb notched up 54 goals and 135 assists with 206 PIM in 94 games over 2 seasons.

As a coach, he led the Flyers to 2nd place in the Heineken League Premier Division table - just 2 points behind champions Durham Wasps, after having finished 7th the season before. They went on to win the British Championship for the first time since 1978 at the Heineken Play Offs at Wembley, the last time that they would win a national title.

In his second season at Kirkcaldy, the Flyers finished 5th in the league but still qualified for the Wembley Play Offs, losing out to Murrayfield Racers in the semi final.

Long term Fife Flyers player and former GB international Chic Cottrell said of Plumb:

"Ron arrived with Danny Brown and Dave Stoyanovich and immediately blended in with the local lads. The arrival of three professional players of such a high calibre – especially with Ronnie being ex-NHL - was a huge boost to the team."

"Ronnie very quickly adapted to the fact that the rest of the team were locals who had full time jobs and families, and that hockey was a sport not a job. The training sessions were fun and Ronnie created a trophy called the "Jock Strap Cup" that we played for on a regular basis. These games were very intense but kept things fun and meaningful."

"On the ice, Ronnie was a "lead by example" coach who was always 100% committed in every game. Never a coach to badmouth any of the players and always encouraged you even during difficult times."

"As a player you always wanted to play your best for Ronnie we all felt part of a team with a strong bond. His legacy is Wembley where we won the play off final in 1985 and added to Flyers history."

Ron Plumb

Ronald William Plumb was born on July 17, 1950 and is a Canadian former professional ice hockey defenceman. Ron is the brother of Robert Plumb.

Plumb was born in Kingston, Ontario. A Peterborough Petes junior player who won the Max Kaminsky Trophy as the league's best defenceman in 1970, Plumb was drafted ninth overall by the Boston Bruins in the 1970 NHL Amateur Draft. After two seasons with their Central Hockey League farm club Oklahoma City Blazers, the Bruins protected him in the June, 1972 expansion draft. But with little chance to play with the veteran-laden NHL team, he jumped to the unproven World Hockey Association Philadelphia Blazers only weeks later.

He remained with the Blazers as they moved to Vancouver in the following season. Plumb then played for the San Diego Mariners in 1975, the Cincinnati Stingers for the following three seasons, and the New England Whalers. He then played one season in the National Hockey League with the Hartford Whalers, remaining in the organization for two more years, but playing in the AHL with the Springfield Indians.

In the WHA, Plumb won the Dennis A. Murphy Trophy as the WHA's best defenceman in 1977, and was also selected a First or Second Team All-Star for much of the league's history. His total of 549 career games in the WHA is the second most overall, trailing only the 551 games played by André Lacroix. Lacroix was his teammate in Philadelphia, San Diego and New England.

Plumb followed his North American pro career with three seasons in Europe, 1983 with ERC Freiburg in the 2.Bundesliga, then 1984–1986 with the Fife Flyers in the British Hockey League.

Plumb was inducted into the Kingston and District Sports Hall of Fame on May 2, 2008.

In 2010, he was elected as an inaugural inductee into the World Hockey Association Hall of Fame.

Ron's Stats

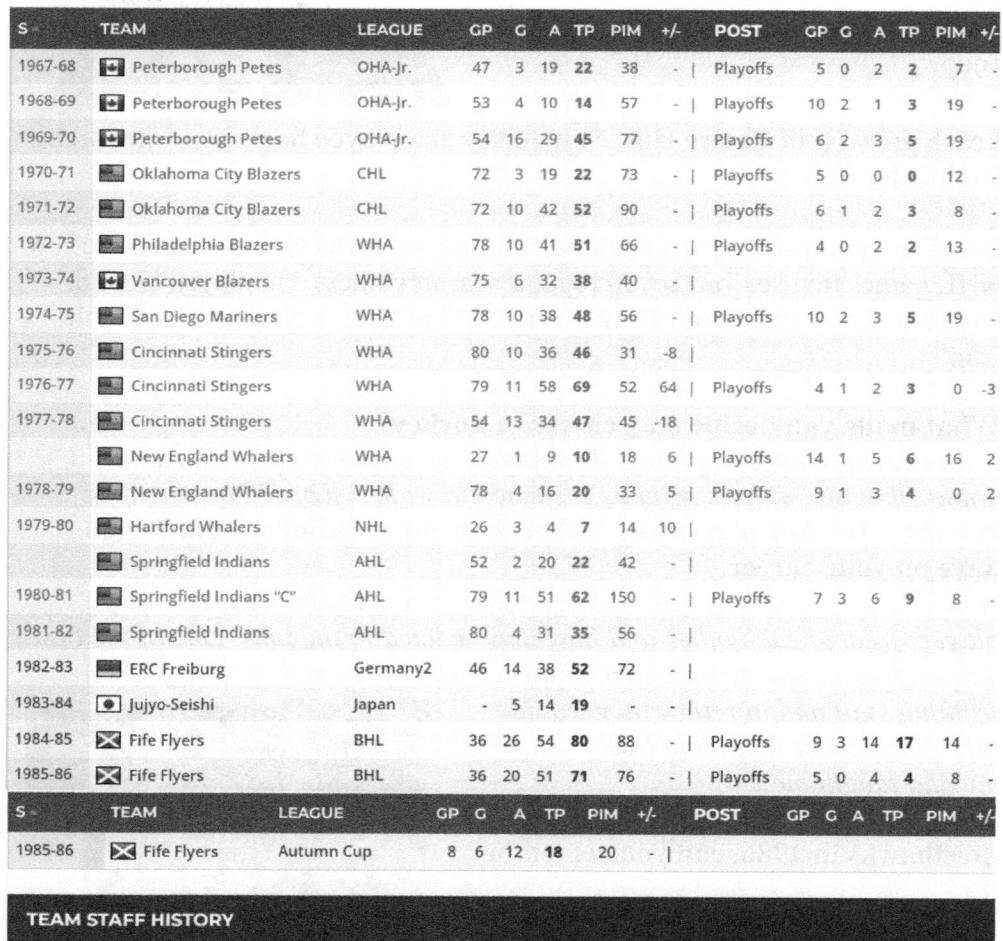

S	TEAM	LEAGUE	GP	G	A	TP	PIM	+/-	POST	GP	G	A	TP	PIM	+/-
1967-68	Peterborough Petes	OHA-Jr.	47	3	19	22	38	-	Playoffs	5	0	2	2	7	-
1968-69	Peterborough Petes	OHA-Jr.	53	4	10	14	57	-	Playoffs	10	2	1	3	19	-
1969-70	Peterborough Petes	OHA-Jr.	54	16	29	45	77	-	Playoffs	6	2	3	5	19	-
1970-71	Oklahoma City Blazers	CHL	72	3	19	22	73	-	Playoffs	5	0	0	0	12	-
1971-72	Oklahoma City Blazers	CHL	72	10	42	52	90	-	Playoffs	6	1	2	3	8	-
1972-73	Philadelphia Blazers	WHA	78	10	41	51	66	-	Playoffs	4	0	2	2	13	-
1973-74	Vancouver Blazers	WHA	75	6	32	38	40	-							
1974-75	San Diego Mariners	WHA	78	10	38	48	56	-	Playoffs	10	2	3	5	19	-
1975-76	Cincinnati Stingers	WHA	80	10	36	46	31	-8							
1976-77	Cincinnati Stingers	WHA	79	11	58	69	52	64	Playoffs	4	1	2	3	0	-3
1977-78	Cincinnati Stingers	WHA	54	13	34	47	45	-18							
	New England Whalers	WHA	27	1	9	10	18	6	Playoffs	14	1	5	6	16	2
1978-79	New England Whalers	WHA	78	4	16	20	33	5	Playoffs	9	1	3	4	0	2
1979-80	Hartford Whalers	NHL	26	3	4	7	14	10							
	Springfield Indians	AHL	52	2	20	22	42	-							
1980-81	Springfield Indians "C"	AHL	79	11	51	62	150	-	Playoffs	7	3	6	9	8	-
1981-82	Springfield Indians	AHL	80	4	31	35	56	-							
1982-83	ERC Freiburg	Germany2	46	14	38	52	72	-							
1983-84	Jujyo-Seishi	Japan	-	5	14	19	-	-							
1984-85	Fife Flyers	BHL	36	26	54	80	88	-	Playoffs	9	3	14	17	14	-
1985-86	Fife Flyers	BHL	36	20	51	71	76	-	Playoffs	5	0	4	4	8	-

S	TEAM	LEAGUE	GP	G	A	TP	PIM	+/-	POST	GP	G	A	TP	PIM	+/-
1985-86	Fife Flyers	Autumn Cup	8	6	12	18	20	-							

TEAM STAFF HISTORY

S	TEAM	LEAGUE	ROLE ON TEAM	NOTES
1984-85	Fife Flyers	BHL	Player-Coach	
1985-86	Fife Flyers	BHL	Player-Coach	
1995-96	Fife Flyers	BHL	General Manager	

Jamie Leach

William "Jamie" Leach was born on August 25, 1969 and is a Canadian-born American former National Hockey League right wing. He is the son of former NHLer Reggie Leach. He was included on both Stanley Cup winning pictures with Pittsburgh in 1991 and 1992.

Leach grew up in Cherry Hill, New Jersey and played hockey at Cherry Hill High School East.

Leach did not qualify for a Cup inscription in 1991 as he had played too few NHL games that season (seven regular season games). He played enough games with the Pittsburgh Penguins in 1992 to get his name on the Stanley Cup.

What made you decide on a career in hockey?
It was because my dad played. I wanted to go with him. I was a rink rat, doing what dad did. As soon as I learned to walk, I learned to skate.

Having a Hockey player as a father, how much influence did Reggie have on your career.
He was a huge influence and being amongst the players I learned how players treated each other and how they reacted to the fans. One of the best lessons was in how to take care of the training staff and in return they would take care of you. Valuable lessons that my dad taught me.

Your first senior goal was for Hamilton Steelhawks in 1986, can you remember it?
I played in the Western League the year before and scored in that league, but I cant remember either goal.

You were drafted by Pittsburgh in 1987 in round 3, how did you feel on finding this out?
To make it you really had to be in the top 3 rounds. I went to the draft in Detroit with a team mate. I went to support my buddy, but my coach told me to wear a

suit "Just in case". The draft selectors took a time out, then announced my name which took me by complete surprise. I was a surprise draft by the penguins. I ran downstairs and shook everyone's hand. It was a great day that I will never forget.

You made your NHL debut for the Penguins in 1989, do you remember your debut?

Yes it was against the Rangers. It was a blur leading up to it. The Penguins flew in my mum and dad so it was a special occasion. After all the hard work that I had put in, it had finally happened. I had played in exhibition games, but it was great to get a chance to play in Pittsburgh

You got an assist in your 1st season in the NHL can you remember it?

It was in my debut game, it was great to look up at the scoreboard and see my name on it.

Your 1st NHL goal came in 1990-91 Season can you remember it?

As to my first NHL goal, its something I always wanted to score and that is clear as day in my mind. The excitement and relief that it had finally happened. I followed the puck to the blueline, then went to the net, the puck went towards the goal and rebounded off Patrick Roy, I missed the puck but it dribbled in.

In 1993 you moved from Pittsburgh to the Hartford Whalers, what was the reason for the move?

After many years of having a contract, I found myself not playing much. I had a meeting with the Penguins and said I would rather go to the minors- so I could play. They agreed to put me on their waivers list and Hartford picked me up.

Later that year you moved to your 3rd NHL side in the Florida Panthers, what was the reason behind this move?

Florida signed me as a free agent. Hartford didn't offer me a contract. I felt part of history as I was signed by Florida in their first ever season in the NHL. They had the best boot camps that I had ever played in. I did however, play most of the season with the Cyclones in Cincinnati.

How did it feel to become a full international when you iced for Canada?

I played for the Canadian junior team first where I scored my first two goals with the national programme. I was into my 2nd year of my contract with Florida

and grabbed the opportunity and learned a lot with them. The Spengler Cup was a great experience and something I didn't really get a chance to do.

What was the deciding factor behind your move from the USA to sign for the Sheffield Steelers?

After returning from my Team Canada experience, I was to sign a 1 year contract with the Sabres, but it didn't happen. I went to the Rochester Americans and won the Calder Cup with them instead. Being aged 26/27 years old I was getting older, so when Ken Priestly contacted me in the Summer I listened. He asked me to consider the UK. I spent time on the phone discussing things with Kenny. I had the chance to go to the Phillie Flyers camp, but Ken persuaded me to accept a contract offer from Sheffield.

After a season in Sheffield what influenced you to sign for Nottingham Panthers?

Shannon Hope slashed me in the face and broke my cheek bone, it was not a good situation to be in, nothing happened as a result of the incident. Even the Super League didn't take any action. At the end of the season, Mike Blaisdell, who knew my dad called me and asked me to come to Nottingham. As a Steeler, I loved playing in Nottingham but not the netting. I did love the atmosphere, they had a decent team and bunch of fans. It was a no brainer to go.

You had 4 seasons in Nottingham, controversial question for you, who had the better team, Sheffield Steelers or the Nottingham Panthers?

Both are really good hockey clubs. Every year both clubs are competitive. In my 3rd year at Nottingham, we played every game possible including the finals. Nottingham were the best, but I have great respect for Sheffield as they had a great rivalry between the clubs.

Did you enjoy your time in the UK?

I did. I didn't stay in the USA and pursue a contract there because I was enjoying the game in the UK. In my 1st year we attended a training camp in Edinburgh, it was twice a day on the ice held in a party atmosphere. I had a conversation with my mum who advised me to just play and enjoy it, which I did. I loved playing in the UK as well as living here. It was the highlight of my career and I enjoyed playing every game.

What do you remember most about it?

The pubs! Nobody can emulate pubs like they do here. Meeting the guys for a pint or two in North America is completely different, no sports chants etc. the UK has great atmosphere with singing

and interacting with the fans. Most arenas had bars and it was nice talking to people who enjoy the game, Both myself and Steve Carpenter managed to change attitudes of people in Nottingham where we converted football fans into hockey fans. It was an awesome feeling. I enjoyed Nottingham for its city. It was quaint and small and I enjoyed hanging out there.

You won honours at both Sheffield and Nottingham, what was the best honour that you have won on the ice?

The Stanley Cup. I wasn't involved very much in winning it, but it was nice to be around and involved. No one understands just how hard it is to win it. Its 2 or 3 levels up from the standard season. The play off weekend is for the fans in the UK but its not as good as in North America. I did also win the Calder Cup whilst with the Rochester Americans.

When did you decide to retire from playing, was it after Nottingham released you, or before?

I told Nottingham just before Christmas that I would not be returning. I had a chance to comeback and do some coaching and that was something that I had always wanted to do and something I should have done whilst still with the Panthers. It was a big regret that I said no to doing it.

What was the best rink that you have played in and why?

The Philadelphia Spectrum not just because of watching my dad play there. It was a cool experience walking in, not as Reggie's son, but as an NHL player and it was neat to see the security guards who knew me growing up. I finally got to play there and as I stepped onto the ice a Philly fan tried to wreck my day with abuse. I scored there as well for Hartford and that was special, especially as only 20 fans were cheering for me.

What was the worst rink that you have played in and why?

Peterborough, it had a stupid hump in the neutral zone and I got my helmet stuck in the netting. It definitely was the worst professional rink that I have played in.

Which team had the best fans in all the clubs that you have played for and why?

Davos in Switzerland definitely. I played there in the Spengler Cup. The stadium has a high roof with great acoustics and you can hear the fans cheering from the changing room. I really was awesome. I enjoy watching the Spengler Cup on TV to this day because of the experiences I had there. It was cool! As to the ~UK Nottingham had great fans!

Who was the best player that you have played with?
That has to be Mario Lemieux, he had speed and a great skillset. His hands, passing, stick handling were amazing and I was lucky to be on the ice with him.

Who was the best player that you have played against and why?
That's a tough one. Ive played against lots of good players. Id probably choose Brendan Shanahan. He was really good, a big fast man who was mean and tough who had a great NHL career.

Who was the toughest player that you have played against and why?
Link Gaetz when he played for Kalamazoo Wings. It seemed like we played then every 2nd week. He was very tough, he would hurt you and not even blink twice! He was not a good skater so I could escape from him.

What was your best memory of being on the ice?
My 1st NHL goal is one. I don't have many memories but I do fondly remember both my dad and I playing against each other in an Alumni game. I was lucky to be asked by the penguins to play against dad's team mates and it was treated like a regular NHL game. We had a packed stand of 16,000 just to watch the game. It was memorable for so many things but most definitely because it was the last game Bobby Clark played in and I lined up against my dad!

What was your most memorable game and why?
The Alumni match plus the Stanley Cup winning game.

Who has influenced you the most in your career and why?
My dad. He got me started and his team mates who helped me whilst I hung out at the rink. I got an opportunity that no one else got. Me skating at the rink was special, I always enjoyed doing it!

You are currently running your own Ice Hockey Coaching school in Canada, are you enjoying it?
Ive always enjoyed doing it. I wasn't allowed back into the UK to coach when I finished at Nottingham because I didn't have a certificate. Ive been doing this job since 2006 and visited over 100 communities. I would love to come to the UK and do an Ice Hockey School or help at Nottingham, where it would be the best of both worlds!

Jamie's Stats

S	TEAM	LEAGUE	GP	G	A	TP	PIM	+/-	POST	GP	G	A	TP	PIM	+/-
1983-84	Cherry Hill High	USHS-NJ	60	48	51	99	68	-							
1984-85	Philadelphia Jr. Flyers	NEJHL	70	35	35	70	24	-							
1985-86	New Westminster Bruins	WHL	58	8	7	15	20	-							
1986-87	Hamilton Steelhawks	OHL	64	12	19	31	67	-	Playoffs	9	1	1	2	4	-
1987-88	Hamilton Steelhawks	OHL	64	24	19	43	79	-	Playoffs	14	6	7	13	12	-
1988-89	Niagara Falls Thunder	OHL	58	45	62	107	47	-	Playoffs	17	9	11	20	25	-
	Canada U20	WJC-20	7	1	4	5	2	-							
1989-90	Pittsburgh Penguins	NHL	10	0	3	3	0	3							
	Muskegon Lumberjacks	IHL	72	22	36	58	39	-	Playoffs	15	9	4	13	14	-
1990-91	Pittsburgh Penguins	NHL	7	2	0	2	0	-1							
	Muskegon Lumberjacks	IHL	43	33	22	55	26	-							
1991-92	Pittsburgh Penguins	NHL	38	5	4	9	8	-2							
	Muskegon Lumberjacks	IHL	3	1	1	2	2	-							
1992-93	Pittsburgh Penguins	NHL	5	0	0	0	2	-2							
	Hartford Whalers	NHL	19	3	2	5	2	-5							
	Cleveland Lumberjacks	IHL	9	5	3	8	2	-6	Playoffs	4	1	2	3	0	-1
	Springfield Indians	AHL	29	13	15	28	33	3							
1993-94	Florida Panthers	NHL	2	1	0	1	0	-2							
	Cincinnati Cyclones	IHL	74	15	19	34	64	-5	Playoffs	11	1	0	1	4	-2
1994-95	Cincinnati Cyclones	IHL	11	0	2	2	9	-5							
	San Diego Gulls	IHL	0	0	0	0	0	0	Playoffs	4	0	0	0	0	0
	Team Canada	International	41	12	26	38	26	-							
1995-96	Rochester Americans	AHL	47	12	14	26	52	-3	Playoffs	2	0	0	0	0	-1
	South Carolina Stingrays	ECHL	5	6	1	7	4	3							
1996-97	Sheffield Steelers	BISL	36	17	20	37	26	-	Playoffs	8	4	5	9	12	-
1997-98	Nottingham Panthers	BISL	39	20	25	45	36	-	Playoffs	5	1	1	2	2	-
1998-99	Nottingham Panthers "C"	BISL	32	16	13	29	14	-	Playoffs	8	4	5	9	0	-
1999-00	Nottingham Panthers "C"	BISL	42	17	29	46	18	-	Playoffs	6	2	3	5	12	-
2000-01	Nottingham Panthers "C"	BISL	46	16	10	26	16	-	Playoffs	6	1	3	4	2	-

S	TEAM	LEAGUE	GP	G	A	TP	PIM	+/-	POST	GP	G	A	TP	PIM	+/-
1994-95	Team Canada	Spengler Cup	-	-	-	-	-	-							
1996-97	Sheffield Steelers	Autumn Cup	10	13	4	17	4	-							
1997-98	Nottingham Panthers	Autumn Cup	11	6	7	13	2	-							
1998-99	Nottingham Panthers	Autumn Cup	12	8	9	17	10	-							
1999-00	Nottingham Panthers	Autumn Cup	9	2	5	7	4	-							
2000-01	Nottingham Panthers	Autumn Cup	10	2	3	5	6	-							
2002-03	Île-des-Chênes North Stars	Allan Cup	4	2	2	4	2	-							

JAMIE LEACH
PROFESSIONAL HOCKEY COACH

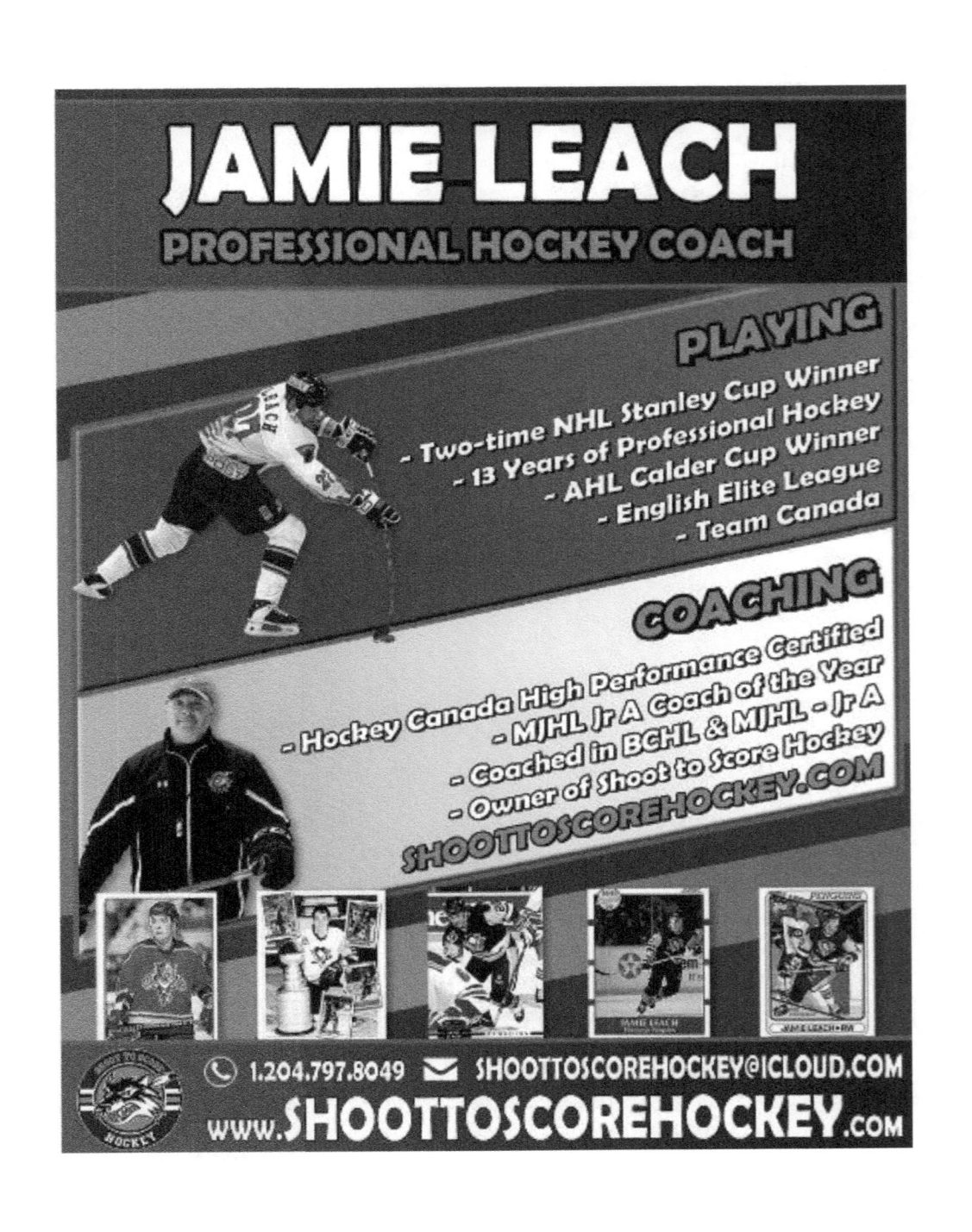

PLAYING
- Two-time NHL Stanley Cup Winner
- 13 Years of Professional Hockey
- AHL Calder Cup Winner
- English Elite League
- Team Canada

COACHING
- Hockey Canada High Performance Certified
- MJHL Jr A Coach of the Year
- Coached in BCHL & MJHL - Jr A
- Owner of Shoot to Score Hockey

SHOOTTOSCOREHOCKEY.COM

1.204.797.8049 SHOOTTOSCOREHOCKEY@ICLOUD.COM
www.SHOOTTOSCOREHOCKEY.com

Fred Perlini

Fred has written a few lines especially for this book:

1. What made you start to play ice hockey?

I started to play hockey because my father introduced me to the game and growing up in cold Sault ste Marie Ontario Canada, the winters were long and everyone practically had a back yard rink to skate or an outdoor school rink to play on with family and friends. It was our culture growing up in a cold steel mill town, as it was across Canada. My dad played pro and was an exceptionally good athlete and great hockey player. When I was young, I would hear legendary stories of him and his greatness of skill on the pond. I had seen it first-hand and wanted to play like him. Obviously watching hockey night in Canada every Saturday on tv 📺 was a way to watch your heroes play every Saturday night, and it started my dream between 5-10 years old to be a professional player one day. When we were not in school, I was basically on the outdoor rink practicing my skills. It was all fun playing in -10 degrees and colder temperatures to hone your skills. In those days I played once a week @ indoor facilities with my Team. But no doubt in those early days it was all about learning the game and it was simple because we grew up in a cold climate.

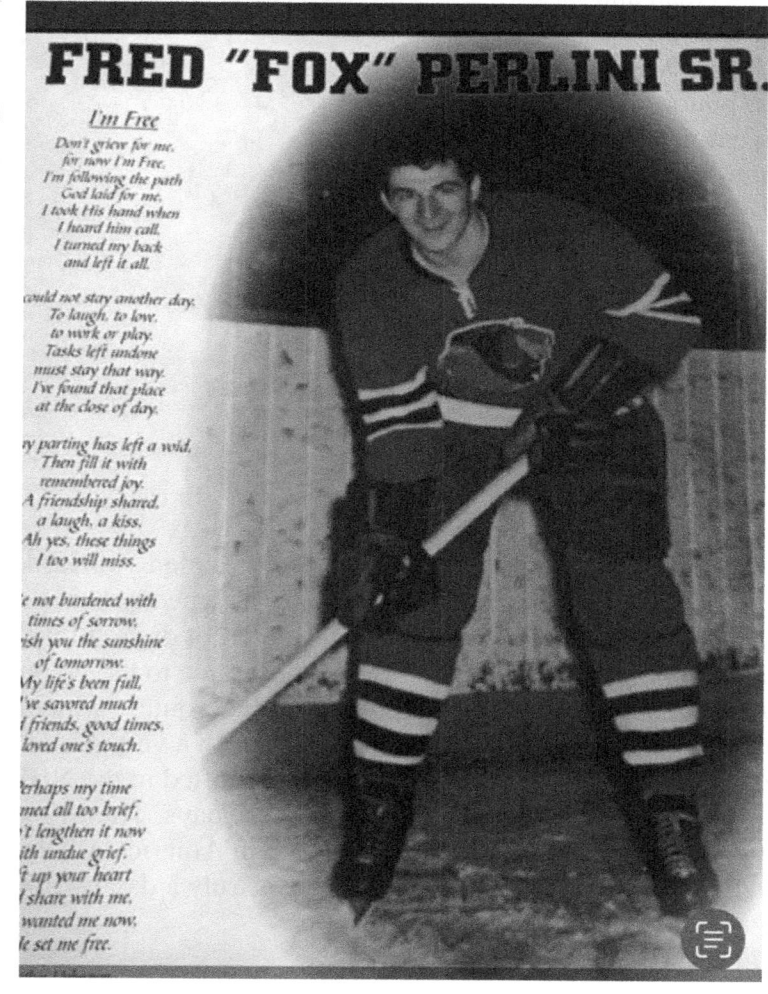

2. How did it feel when Toronto drafted you in 1980?

Drafted by the Toronto Maple Leafs in 1980 was an honour. Anyone who grows up in Canada, especially the province of Ontario is lying to you if they say they don't want to put that jersey on in the NHL. There was only 16 NHL teams than and playing for the Toronto Marlies , the junior club was an easy transition into the organization. Guys like Darryl Sittler , Borje Salming and many others whom I had watched on tv 5 years earlier I was soon to skating beside. The tradition of the leaf's, an original 6 hockey club is historical. Also, Maple Leaf Gardens where I played all my junior games was soon to become my home rink as a pro. It was my 2nd home in those days. The day I got drafted I was working in construction as a 17 year old . Somebody came to the working site to congratulate me as it was on the local radio around 12 lunch time. I finished my shift at 4 , went home and celebrated with a very proud family. Things gave sure changed as both my sons were drafted in the NHL and it was live on TV. It's celebrated like a wedding these days. The whole family is in attendance @ the draft itself with all North America watching and Europe as well. Boy have times changed, but it was truly a day I will never forget.

3. How did it feel when the Maple Leafs gave you your debut in 1981-82 season?

I was fortunate to get called up into the big leagues as a 19 year old which was rare in those days. I made my debut vs St. Louis blues @ Maple Leaf Gardens. I had an assist and after the game we flew out to Detroit vs the wings and I had a goal and assist as well as second star. I must admit I felt very comfortable out there like I belonged.

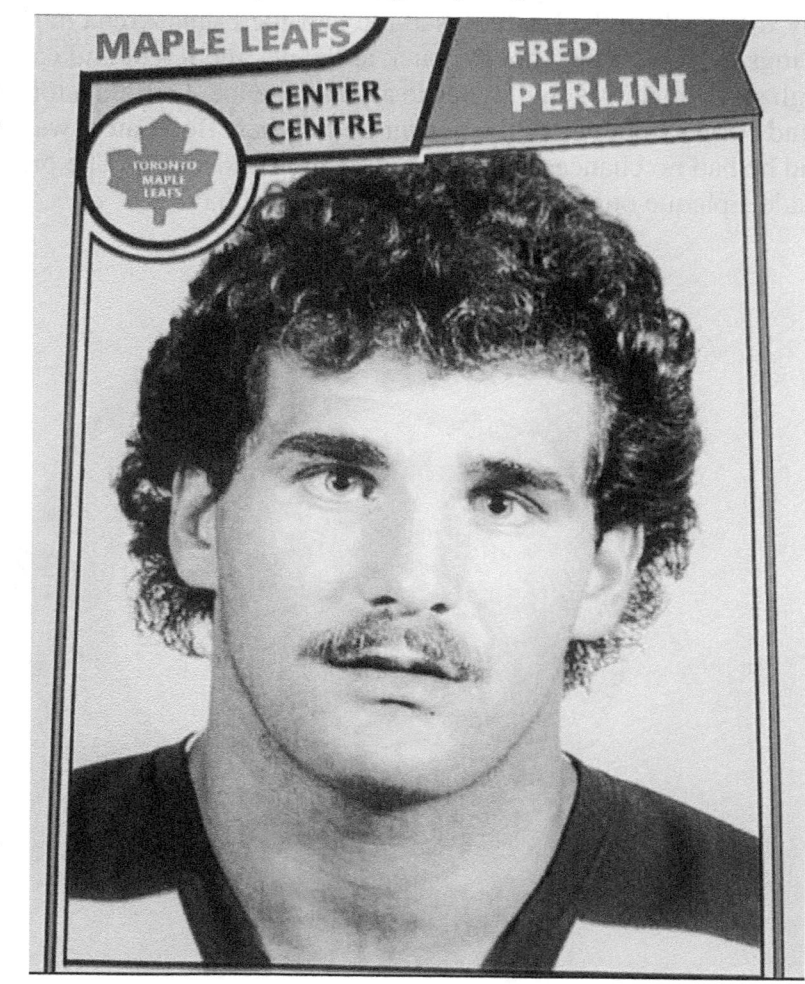

I was still a junior and I ended my junior career with the Marlies that season so although I played 7 games and had 5 points at the end of that NHL season, I still had a responsibility to end my junior season out in the playoffs before heading pro. This was a great way of breaking into NHL games and feeling like I belonged. That season was my last year in the juniors, and I had 111 points in 60 games and 14 points on 10 playoff games. It was a great year to play both junior and pro in the same year. It's still a record to score a hattrick in the juniors during a game in the afternoon vs Niagara of the OHL and scoring an NHL goal that night vs the Blackhawk s wearing the Leaf jersey!

4. Do you remember your first goal for the Leafs? Who was it against?
My first goal for the Leafs was at the Old Joe Louis Arena in Detroit vs the Wings. Darryl Sittler shot the puck at the net and a rebound came out to the high slot which was my favourite area on the ice. I riffled a top shelfer left hand corner right where the peanut butter goes, Bob Sauve was in the nets and he had no chance. It was a good feeling and still is. The organization made a plaque out of that puck in which I still have.

Fred Perlini's 1st. NHL Goal
December 31, 1981
Toronto 5 at Detroit 2

5. What made you leave the Baltimore Skipjacks in 1986 and sign for the Nottingham Panthers?
The reason I left the AHL Baltimore Skipjacks is I simply thought there was a lot of politics within organizations on what players were called up to the bigs and what players stayed in the minors. So, I figured I should go abroad and play and enjoy the game once more. I was originally going to Italy to play on a good contract, but my Italian passport fell through, so I received a call from Alex Dampier who was head coach of GB & the Panthers and I thought I'd go over and play until a bigger contract came up over in Switzerland or Germany, but low and behold I loved it in the UK and played in the country for another 10 seasons and coached for 10.

6. You remained in the UK playing for 10 clubs which was your favourite club to play for overall? And what was your favourite in the UK?
My son Brendan was born in Guildford in the UK and played there until he was 12 and was also an NHL first round pick, I don't think people understand how hard that is to achieve!

Plus Brett also played there in and developed there, I got a full ride at Michigan state, 200 thousand dollar scholarship, that's pretty special. Then drafted to Anaheim, and obviously won MVP at whole rod championships for GB, my point is they both were developed in UK at Guildford

Yes, I played for 10 teams. Each organization added something a little different which when I look back on had a great deal to do with helping me develop as a person, husband and father. I guess playing my first year in Nottingham was special simply because of the old stadium and it was my first experience in the UK playing hockey and having fun again, coming out of the grind of North America pro hockey. That first year in Notts helped me love the game again. Also playing my last 3 years in Guildford and raising my family there was pretty special, helping to build the hockey club up on and off the ice and giving back the junior part of the organization was special.

Above: Brendan as a under 10 with his coach

7. What was your favourite memory playing ice hockey?
Favourite memories of playing hockey are playing at my school outdoor rink with all our neighbourhood family and friends Up in Sault Ste. Marie. My dad would make the local rink at St Mary's elementary school for the whole neighbourhood. At night my favourite time when it was cold the majority of the kids would be indoors. So, my dad would flood the rink with a fireman hose. We'd let the rink freeze, watch a period of hockey night in Canada and after the game on a Saturday night we'd be back at it on the ice imitating our favourite players we had just watched. My dads' older friends would be out there and they all could skate like the wind. Marcel Fortier and my dad were the best two skaters I have ever seen so I'd try to keep up with them. It was ecstasy just skating on a sheet of glass ice , cold blowing off your face and the rink lit up with street lights. Those memories were the best times for me.

Having fun and developing your skill, it was all backyard hockey. My dad also built a rink in my own backyard and I spent hours out in the cold with my dad , brothers and friends just playing the sport we loved.

8. What was your favourite rink to play in and why?
My favourite rink to play in was Maple Leaf Gardens. The Mecca of hockey revolved around Toronto back in the day , and I was fortunate to play 3 years for the Marlies in that rink. As well as play pro with the leaf's there.

9. Who was the best player you played against and why?
The best player I played against was Wayne Gretzky. I watched him play in my home town the Soo when he was 16. I have seen all of his magic as a kid . He was so far advanced, always a step ahead of everyone. Again, I saw it first hand when we played the Oilers. There is a reason why he holds all the records, he anticipated well because he was smarter than anyone else.

As a kid I loved how Geordie Howe played the game , tough as nails , could score and play a two way game, also I loved Bobby Hull, just watching him skate and shoot rockets he transformed the game with his curved stick.

Above with Bobby Hull

10. Who was the best player you played with and why?

Darryl Sittler was the best player I played with. First of all he was very underrated. I watched him in the 70s play for the leaf's when he scored a record 10pts in an NHL game . In the 80s I was fortunate to become a teammate and friend. He played the game the right way, was strong on face offs, played a 200ft game , was good in both ends of the ice . Could score, make plays and was tough to play against. He could also drop the mitts if needed. He was the captain and a great leader and always went out of his way to help me with my game. He also was a big time player for Canada when called upon.

11. What expectations did you have on playing in the UK and were they met?
Expectations on playing in the UK when I first arrived were to score goals , that's what the teams wanted me to do as an established scorer throughout my career. As time moved on, I felt an obligation to give back so when I ran the Guildford junior programme for close to 10 years I felt like I had helped develop the game and grow it throughout the southwest. I feel I developed a lot of local talent as well as kids and juniors through the country to love the game, a lot of them have gone on to play pro.

12. Did you prefer playing in North America or in the UK?
Playing hockey in North America at the pro level is the ultimate. When you can play in the national league vs anything outside of it nothing compares. But I will say there is always other ways to prolong your career as I did when things were not going in the right direction. There are great teams in countries across Europe/ UK that put hockey on a good universal platform to grow the game

13. Which team in your opinion had the best fans and why?
The best fans that I played in front of were the Nottingham Panther's in the old stadium, my reasons for this were they were close to the ice so you can hear them , cheer , sing and clap loud. Plus, they would clap for the opposing team if they or a top player from that team made a nice play. The atmosphere across Europe in general is great with the singing and all its parallel's with football chanter. In North America it's Toronto and Montreal. Very educated hockey fans because they live and breath it as football is in Great Britain

14. Which team was the best to play for and why?
In the UK it's hard to judge I had good seasons with all of them. In Notts it was fun but a lot relied on the imports to produce because the team was young and up and coming. In Fife it was easier to be a goal scorer because Steve Moria was my Centre man and it was a veteran team, Altrincham was a lot of fun dropping down and learning to become a player coach with a good bunch of players and guys. Same thing in Deeside I brought two good imports with me so there was a lot more responsibility. And of course came Guildford at the end , where everything came full circle from a scorer to a coach and teacher to retired player with his number in the rafters.

15. What is your favourite memory from ice hockey on or off the ice?
My favourite memories on or off the ice was when I scored a goal and an assist in Detroit and was named 2nd star & The Great Darryl Sittler quoted "hey Freddy nothing to this league, you look great out there and you belong." I guess that's the ultimate complaint u can get from one of the best players to play the game.

16. In your opinion do you feel the standard of play in the uk is improving?
The standard in the UK is definitely improving. I watched all the games that my son Brett has played in Nottingham and the fan base and league has gone from strength to strength. Also, because Brett is a part of the GB team I look at the levels they have progressed through in the last 4-5 years to get to the world championship pool and put hockey on the map.

17. How do you feel watching you son Brett play hockey?
Watching Brett play in the UK and in Europe brings back so many memories of me playing overseas, the pressure imported players are under to produce is always going to be there when you're a paid professional, but to see him handle it all on and off the ice has made his mom Vicki & I proud

18. Being a cousin of Kevin Conway why didn't you stay and play more games for the Telford Tigers other than the 5 games played in 1990-91 season?
I played a few games in Telford and Basingstoke just to fill in and play along side Kevin who has had a tremendous career over there . Other thing's were transpiring at that time in the direction of becoming a player coach, that's the direction I wanted to go . I felt I had more to give to the game than just scoring goals

19. Having played BD2, BD1, BHL, and EPHL in the UK which league did you enjoy playing in the mist?
Having played in all levels across the board as a player for me scoring goal's was always fun . Playing in the highest level in the country was awesome. Going down to a lower standard in the country was to get experience at playing and coaching. It all worked out and I enjoyed the whole process

20. You coached the Deeside Dragons for a season why didn't you remain in coaching?
Being a player coach in Deeside and Altringham was a process to start the player coaching role. It all transpired into getting experience. It came full circle to Guildford when I ran the junior programs and was in charge of 7-8 teams , the coaches , the kids , the prospects going to our pro team . All this experience has led me to my own business where we run clinics across the USA and Canada. I work with pros as well on all their skill sets. I also have a job in the states where I run a prep school hockey program. It's enough to keep me busy at my age of 60.

PLAYER BIOGRAPHY AND TRIVIA

Drafted 1979, 5 #55 overall by Toronto Marlboros in the OHL Priority Selection

Number 11 retired by Guildford Flames

Cult/Star player for Guildford Flames

Cult/Star player for Streatham IHC

Drafted by the Toronto Maple Leafs in 1980 in round 8, 158th overall.

Fred's Stats

S	TEAM	LEAGUE	GP	G	A	TP	PIM	+/-	POST	GP	G	A	TP	PIM	+/-
1978-79	Sault Ste. Marie Legion Midget AA	NOHA	27	57	50	107									
1979-80	Toronto Marlboros	OMJHL	67	13	18	31	12		Playoffs	4	0	1	1	5	
1980-81	Toronto Marlboros	OHL	55	37	29	66	48		Playoffs	5	0	0	0	4	
1981-82	Toronto Marlboros	OHL	68	47	64	111	75		Playoffs	10	4	9	13	8	
	Toronto Maple Leafs	NHL	7	2	3	5	0	-2							
1982-83	St. Catharines Saints	AHL	76	8	22	30	24								
1983-84	Toronto Maple Leafs	NHL	1	0	0	0	0	0							
	St. Catharines Saints	AHL	79	21	31	52	67		Playoffs	7	1	1	2	17	
1984-85	St. Catharines Saints	AHL	77	21	28	49	26								
1985-86	Baltimore Skipjacks	AHL	25	6	4	10	6								
1986-87	Nottingham Panthers	BHL	35	89	82	171	135		Playoffs	4	6	8	14	8	
1987-88	Fife Flyers	BHL	35	103	73	176	34		Playoffs	6	20	14	34	0	
1988-89	Deeside Dragons	BD1	24	103	69	172	42								
1989-90	Trafford Metros	BD1	25	81	59	140	14								
1990-91	Telford Tigers	BD1	5	9	8	17	2								
	Blackburn Blackhawks	BD2	21	83	49	132	48								
1991-92	Streatham Redskins	BD2	23	93	53	146	42		Qualification	6	12	4	16	48	
1992-93	Streatham Redskins	BD2	31	135	91	226	20		Qualification	6	17	9	26	4	
1993-94	Basingstoke Beavers	BHL	1	0	0	0	0								
	Lee Valley Lions	BD1	20	71	47	118	26								
1994-95	Guildford Flames	BD1	44	78	57	135	40								
1995-96	Guildford Flames	BD1	50	90	56	146	51		Qualification	6	3	8	11	0	
1996-97	Guildford Flames	EPIHL	27	32	18	50	14		Playoffs	10	6	6	12	0	

S	TEAM	LEAGUE	GP	G	A	TP	PIM	+/-
1974-75	Sault Ste. Marie Peewee	QC Int PW	-	-	-	-	-	
1986-87	Nottingham Panthers	Autumn Cup	3	4	5	9	6	
1987-88	Fife Flyers	Autumn Cup	5	17	7	24	15	
	Fife Flyers	Scottish Cup	3	5	4	9	-	
1989-90	Trafford Metros	Midlands Cup	6	11	11	22	-	
1991-92	Streatham Redskins	Autumn Trophy	4	16	7	23	4	
1992-93	Streatham Redskins	Autumn Trophy	3	10	3	13	4	
1994-95	Guildford Flames	Autumn Trophy	6	12	16	28	12	
1995-96	Guildford Flames	Autumn Cup	8	11	6	17	33	
1996-97	Guildford Flames	Autumn Cup	2	2	1	3	2	

TEAM STAFF HISTORY

S	TEAM	LEAGUE	ROLE ON TE...
1988-89	Deeside Dragons	BD1	Player-Coach
2011-12	Belle Tire 16U AAA	T1EHL 16U	Asst. Coach

Frank Pietrangelo

(Interview in 2000) VOTED the Superleague, Writers and Supporters player-of-the-year, in addition to the players' player as well as being selected for the Superleague's All Star team and having the best save percentage in the top flight, Frankie Pietrangelo was truly a champion last season. But things change. This time around Storm have seen their crown slip and after overcoming a broken rib and a groin injury Frankie now finds himself at the end of the regular season trying to get over knee surgery in order to be fit for the play-offs.

"It's getting better slowly but surely, it's only been a couple of weeks since the operation and I'm surprised how well it's gone," he said: "although I'm still a little way away from playing. I feel I can do more than what they're letting me do but I don't want to be foolish, if I'm back for the play-offs great, if not I'll prepare for next season." In fact, last season – his first in British ice hockey – was so good he signed up for another two-part way through the title winning campaign.

Although he's found out it's not been all smooth running he's already had one major success, the B&H Cup in which he played a major part, claiming back-to-back shutouts in the semis over tonight's opponents the Cardiff Devils (4-0 and 0-0) before saving all five penalty shots in the shoot-out with London after the Knights had snatched a late equaliser to tie the final 4-4, which even overtime couldn't alter. "Kurt told us how important the B&H would be because you get to carry it all season with you as it's the first championship to be decided. I thought we should have won it last year; I mean we only lost one game (to Nottingham). Then when we beat Cardiff this year in the first leg I knew there was no way we'd not get to the final, and as I like our team in one-off games I'd already planned the party at my house. Penalties aren't a fair way to decide a game, but someone's got to lose – we'd lost some heartbreakers in the EHL that way, so there you go." But then winning has been a way of life for the 36-year-old native of Niagara Falls.

After starting out playing minor and Junior B in his hometown he spent two seasons with Brampton before going to the University of Minnesota. "I was offered scholarships at 23 of the 30 colleges available and I chose Minnesota for a couple of reasons. My main goal was to play hockey, education came second. I wanted to get my education don't get me wrong, but I wanted to get to the NHL and at the time Minnesota was producing NHL players. Plus I would have been the first Canadian to have gone there since 1964 since they tended to take just kids from within the state, so it would have been a big thing and I would get a lot of attention and it worked, I was drafted at the end of my first year by Pittsburgh (4th round, 63rd overall 1983) although I stayed on to complete my degree majoring in business. "After college I spent my first year as a pro with the Muskegon Lumberjacks in the IHL, as the Penguins didn't want to sign me at the time. Rick Lee was coaching Muskegon and he gave me what turned out to be the biggest break of my career and at the end of that season I was signed by Pittsburgh. "The Penguins had a new coach in Bob Johnson at the start of the 1990-91 season and although I was back-up to Tom Barrossa he played me in the game that clinched the divisional championship and then the last regular game of the season in New York, to stay sharp in case they needed me in the play-offs. Barrossa got injured and he brought me in and I played my part in lifting the Stanley Cup. Everyone had written us off and when I was brought in, I just felt I had nothing to lose, if we won, I was a hero if we lost no one would blame me."

But along with the ups come the downs. "The following season Bob Johnson died of a brain tumour and Scotty Bowman came in. We didn't see eye to eye about a number of things, I wasn't playing much, and I was getting frustrated. I'd been with the club six and a half years by this time (1992) and had developed a good relationship with the general manager Craig Patrick. So I asked to be traded. He said he'd find me a place I could be the number one goalie and that's what he did, that's how I ended up at Hartford. The team wasn't very good but I got to play a lot, although it was difficult going from the top to the very bottom and given the choice again I probably wouldn't have done it."

After a couple of seasons with the Whalers I went to the Islanders, but it was the season of the players strike so the owners locked us out and sent me down to the Minnesota Moose, where I played alongside Kris Miller, but I broke my finger and then had double knee surgery and ended up retiring. But for the strike and the injuries I'd probably have played a few more seasons in the NHL. "It wasn't the end of the world, I was only 30-years old, and I was ready to move on I guess, but a friend of mine, Bob Manno, phoned me up and asked me to join him in Bolzano, Italy, which was like a new start or me. My parents come from Italy and I'd got my passport in 1988, because I thought if I don't make it in the NHL maybe I could go play in Europe, in fact it was always my intention to pay in Europe at some stage. Bolzano flew my wife Kim and me out to have a look around and we immediately fell in love with the place, I was also given a clean bill of health and we made the move. My goal changed, it was no longer to make it back to the NHL but to enjoy life hockey and my family and I went out there intending to give it a year and see where it took me. 'We won the Italian championship and so the following year I figured that if I was going to stay in Europe I wanted to play at the highest level, which is the DEL and I moved to Kaufbeurer – for less money. I figured if I bit the bullet for a year the opportunities would arise, but the team went bust after three months and I went back to Italy and joined Asiago.

"To be honest I didn't enjoy the hockey in Germany. There were long bus rides and two-day practices, it was too much like back home in the minors and I wasn't getting the time with my family that I wanted. Also the kids – Paige, Jessica and Dylan – were getting a little confused going from an Italian school to a German school and back again and we decided we had to think more about their education and I contacted my agent Gary Seigo about a move to Britain. I spoke to guys I knew who were already playing here and I'd watched the hockey on satellite TV. So, I thought if I got fixed up in an English-speaking environment my kids would benefit and I could play a few more years. I had offers from other British clubs, but Manchester was the only place to go to. It's central, the arena spoke for itself and it's a big city with lots to see and do. I came here expecting to win and to make a contribution and I've achieved that so far."

But this time out injuries have stalked the club, especially the defensive unit "Last season we stayed healthy right up until the play-offs. This year we started without Dave Morrison and Ruby, then we lost our best defenceman in Neumeier and we've been dropping like flies at the back ever since, including myself". Along with a less than successful showing in the league came the criticism, something Frank is not afraid of addressing. "There's not a lot you can you do about it Sometimes it stings you, sometimes you laugh it off, sometimes it gets to you. I try not to let it affect me because people are going to try and say things about you – good and bad – no matter what. When you're up they want to bring you down, that's just the nature of the business. People don't always know what's really going on behind the scenes, they don't care, they come to the game to see you play well and I suppose they have a right to that because we're professional athletes and we're supposed to perform to the best of our ability every night. But everyone has bad days the problem is when we have bad days everybody's pointing the finger, although they tend to forget what you've achieved up till that point. I'm happy with myself and I try not to bring it home with me, you forgive you just never forget, I guess.

"I've not had the season I had last year but who on the team has? Last year is not this year. Last year we were we were outstanding defensively, this year we're not but it's not fair to compare oranges and apples. Last year was a career year for me, that's how much it meant to me personally and I don't ever see me duplicating those numbers again, that's life. But when I come back next year, I'll still be expecting to win another championship. It's going to be different; it will probably be my last year as a player so I'm not going to put any extra pressure on myself. I always go into games expecting to win and I always go into a season expecting to win a championship.

We'll probably have quite a few changes but hopefully we'll get in some good characters. Dave Morrison and Ruby were huge losses this year. Dave is one of the best leaders I have ever played for. He'd do things that would hurt him personally, which is a true test of a leader. Ruby was a real character; he came to play every night and he's one of the greatest guys I've ever met. On top of losing them we've also lost the likes of Rick and Darren and plenty of others, the turnover's been tremendous, whereas Bracknell have been like we were last year – stable.

Despite an indifferent season by his own high standards Frank still sees himself as a major part of the Storm set-up, someone others look up to. "I can see the way the players react around me when I play, and I try to be as positive a role model as I can. I'd like to think they take notice of my work ethic; this is my 14th year as a pro and you have to work at it. I physically and mentally prepare myself to play every night and I like to think I do the best I can every night. I think the guys feel comfortable around me, not just on the ice, the friendships you get from the game are just as important as winning trophies or the numbers you put up. "Now we've got to focus on the play-offs, we are more than capable of winning them but in this league anybody can beat anybody so who knows who will make the final four, after that it's a one-off and I don't think there are any favourites."

Interview by Peter Collins March 2000

Frank's Player Stats

S	TEAM	LEAGUE	GP	GAA	SV%	SO	WLT	POST	GP	GAA	SV%	SO	WLT
1979-80	Niagara Falls Canucks	GHL	12	5.31	-								
1980-81	Brampton Chevies	OPJHL	28	5.78	-								
1981-82	Niagara Falls Canucks	GHL	-	-	-								
	Brampton Warriors	OJHL	36	3.09	-								
1982-83	Univ. of Minnesota	NCAA	25	3.55	.885								
1983-84	Univ. of Minnesota	NCAA	20	3.47	.887								
1984-85	Univ. of Minnesota	NCAA	17	3.42	.873								
1985-86	Univ. of Minnesota	NCAA	23	3.55	.880								
1986-87	Muskegon Lumberjacks	IHL	35	3.42	-			Playoffs	15	2.99	-		
1987-88	Pittsburgh Penguins	NHL	21	3.99	.867								
	Muskegon Lumberjacks	IHL	15	2.97	-								
1988-89	Pittsburgh Penguins	NHL	15	4.03	.890								
	Muskegon Lumberjacks	IHL	13	3.00	-			Playoffs	9	3.07			
1989-90	Pittsburgh Penguins	NHL	21	4.33	.867								
	Muskegon Lumberjacks	IHL	12	3.30	-								
1990-91	Pittsburgh Penguins	NHL	25	3.94	.880			Playoffs	5	3.13	.899		
1991-92	Pittsburgh Penguins	NHL	5	5.33	.846								
	Hartford Whalers	NHL	5	2.35	.923			Playoffs	7	2.68	.922		

S	TEAM		LEAGUE	GP	GAA	SV%	SO	WLT	POST	GP	GAA	SV%	SO	WLT
1992-93	Hartford Whalers		NHL	30	4.85	.858								
1993-94	Hartford Whalers		NHL	19	3.60	.875								
	Springfield Indians		AHL	23	3.33	.881			Playoffs	6	4.26	.842		
1994-95	Minnesota Moose		IHL	15	4.12	.870								
1995-96	Did not play													
1996-97	HC Bolzano		Italy	39	3.77	.874								
1997-98	Kaufbeurer Adler		DEL	14	4.47	.927								
	Asiago		Italy	32	3.16	.894								
1998-99	Manchester Storm		BISL	38	1.92	.931			Playoffs	6	1.83	.941		
1999-00	Manchester Storm		BISL	19	3.89	.866								
2000-01	Manchester Storm		BISL	9	3.82	.882								

S	TEAM	LEAGUE	GP	GAA	SV%	SO	WLT	POST	GP	GAA	SV%	SO	WLT
1998-99	Manchester Storm	Euro HL	6	3.21	.897								
	Manchester Storm	Autumn Cup	10	2.10	.916								
1999-00	Manchester Storm	Euro HL	5	3.58	.897								
	Manchester Storm	Autumn Cup	9	1.95	.923								
2000-01	Manchester Storm	Autumn Cup	7	4.12	.861								

TEAM STAFF HISTORY

S	TEAM	LEAGUE	ROLE ON TEAM	NOTES
2008-09	The Hill Academy Varsity	CAHS	GM/Head Coach	
2009-10	Mississauga Rebels U16 AAA	GTHL U16	Head Coach	
	The Hill Academy Varsity	CAHS	GM/Head Coach	
2010-11	Mississauga Rebels U16 AAA	GTHL U16	Head Coach	
	The Hill Academy	CAHS	GM/Head Coach	
2011-12	Niagara Falls Canucks	GOJHL	Asst. Coach	
2013-14	Niagara Falls Canucks	GOJHL	Asst. Coach	
2015-16	Niagara Falls Canucks	GOJHL	GM/Head Coach	
	Niagara Falls Canucks	GOJHL	Franchise Owner	
2016-17	Niagara Falls Canucks	GOJHL	Head Coach	
2017-18	Niagara Falls Canucks	GOJHL	Head Coach	
2019-20	Niagara Falls Canucks	GOJHL	Head Coach	

CAREER HIGHLIGHTS

SEASON	AWARDS BY SEASON
1996-1997	• Italy Champion
1998-1999	• BISL Champion • BISL First All-Star Team
1999-2000	• B&H Cup Champion

Kurt Kleinendorst

(Interview from 2000) "I have a lot of good friends here and I was never just going to leave town without saying goodbye, but I'm very comfortable with my decision and as good as I have it here, and as much as I've enjoyed my three years here, I'm 100 per cent sure I'm making the right decision. I made my mind up the last time I went home. I really have enjoyed my time here and I don't regret a minute of it, but it's time to leave."

"Contrary to what most people seem to think I have no job to go back to, I just want to go home. I came up with the 1 May deadline, I told David Davies I would know by then and he would have been as patient with me as I needed him to be, but that would not have been fair to him or anyone else involved with the club. Even though 1 May doesn't work – NHL, AHL, IHL teams don't make decisions until after their play-offs sometime in June, so as you can see I made my decision for personal reasons. Sometimes you have to dare yourself to be daring and after 30 June I don't know what I'll be doing. I'm hopeful something is going to open up for me, if it doesn't, I'm doing what I'm doing for all the right reasons."

"My son Kolin turned 13 this month and I sat there and realised that he's just a few years away from college. So the way I see it is I've got two years or so to spent with him before he moves on, becomes less dependent on me, it was just something I had to do, although there were other reasons."

"Last year we had some situations player-wise that made things really difficult and it wore on me after a while and one of the things I miss a lot is working with younger players. Guys that enjoyed playing for you, that have learned something from you – other than two or three guys that wasn't the case here this year."

"I'll give you a few examples. Barry Nieckar was pretty much done and dusted when I got him down in Raleigh and I wasn't the one that put him in the NHL. BUT I did give him a chance along the way, I got him into Hartford's training camp, and he went on to play parts of four years in the NHL. I miss that and I realised I wanted to go back and be part of nurturing younger players and help them reach their goals like I did with Weaves. I got

Kris Miller when he had no place left to go and got him a place in three different training camps and I love being able to call a player up to tell him I've got them a place in Ottawa's camp, or Hartford's camp or whoever's camp because you can see real progress."

"A worst case scenario for me would be I don't get a hockey job and I take a year off and coach a youth team in Salt Lake City, Utah, where I live, which to be honest isn't such a bad deal. I'd be able to spend quality time with my son, help the youth programme in the area and it would be something I really do enjoy."

"I don't have these visions of me being an NHL coach anytime soon, I'm not even sure I'd want to be an NHL coach at all. But, say, AHL players I think would have the right attitude because they're trying to get into the NHL, they'll listen to what you say, they'll believe in you as a coach and realise you might have an influence on where they might go. But all that is on the periphery, the reason I'm going home is I want to spend more time with my family, that's what it's all about."

"My time in Manchester has taught me many valuable lessons. There have been situations where I've looked back at the way I've handled things and thought I could have done it better, but that's what I've enjoyed, it's been a constant challenge and similar problems will come again and I'll be able to handle them better because of what I've learned in my time here. Another thing that helped me make my decision was the future of Superleague. It's going more towards what the ECHL is like as with the wage cap wages are not all that great anymore. You can no longer identify the players you like, talk to their agents and put offers in front of them. It's not going to be like that anymore. You are going to have to get a list of 50 players and shoot down that list convincing them that it is a good opportunity for them and that although the money is not great it is worth coming over for, and it's something I just don't want to do. I did it in the ECHL for five years and it's not in my heart to do it anymore. The standard is going to drop a little bit and it means the Frankie Pietrangelos and Ed Courtenays are going to be a thing of the past because clubs won't be able to afford them – if we hadn't have signed Frankie on a two year deal he wouldn't have been back because we wouldn't have been able to afford him. Same with Ed Courtenay. Guys like them are at a point in their careers where they're going to say, 'no thank you' and retire."

" Having said that, I think the players that are already contracted to come back will do so, in fact I've been trying to talk to all five of them about that. I think it'll be good for them. Kris Miller has been with me here for three years and it would be real easy for him to get stale in the fourth year, a new coach will freshen things up for him and it should wear well for all of them. Come November it's just going to be like when Woody left, only it'll be Kurt's left – what are we going to do? But like we got on with the job after Woody went the new coach will get on with the job after I've gone. I feel I'm leaving the programme here in better shape than it was in when I arrived, I've made my mark now it's time to move on."

"But all things are relative, every team will have the same budget to work to and I think it will open the door for British players to make it in Superleague. All of a sudden you'll have bottom-end North Americans competing with upper-end British talent, and if I had a Canadian that's the same calibre as a Brit and I could get the Brit for a little less money, I'd take the Brit and I think most coaches would, so if that's one of the things Superleague wanted to accomplish I think it will work."

"Back home we have public buildings that cater for ice and roller hockey as well as private ones put up by businessmen who want to make a little money as well as putting something back into the community. So, if it works back there, Utah, which is still not noted as being a hockey hotbed, I can't understand why it's not happened in Manchester. The kids here don't have enough ice time, they practice once a week and play one game a month which is a real shame because the interest in ice hockey is phenomenal. Most of the venues I know of are used every single minute, which means there's room for somebody else to come in, build a rink and absorb the surplus demand for ice and make money. Maybe nobody's ever really had a proposal put before them that makes sense, but surely there's someone out there that's got a boat load of money and wants to give something back."

"I'm not leaving because I'm not happy, I've leaving because I want to go home, and I don't think anyone can fault me for that. I really didn't feel in my heart I could come back and do the kind of job I've done for the last three years, if I had it would have been a big mistake for everybody. As for who will take over there's two ways to look at it. If David Davies feels he needs somebody quickly it'll be Dave Whistle. He knows the league; he's expressed an interest in the job and David Davies has expressed an interest in him. If he doesn't want a quick fix and he wants to go out and find the very best guy available and use Ottawa like he did with me then it will take longer. Ottawa brings a great networking capacity, if you give up the bond because you've gone on your own then that's the price you pay. But Dave is a good guy and a good coach, he knows the league and the players, and he's showed he can be a success."

(c) Peter Collins 2000

Kurt's Player Stats

S	TEAM	LEAGUE	GP	G	A	TP	PIM	+/-	POST	GP	G	A	TP	PIM	+/-
1976-77	Grand Rapids High	USHS-MN	-	-	-	-	-			-					
1977-78	Grand Rapids High	USHS-MN	-	-	-	-	-			-					
1978-79	Grand Rapids High	USHS-MN	-	-	-	-	-			-					
1979-80	Providence College	NCAA	32	10	17	27	4			-					
1980-81	Providence College	NCAA	32	16	20	36	18			-					
1981-82	Providence College	NCAA	33	30	27	57	14			-					
	USA	WC	-	-	-	-	-			-					
1982-83	Providence College "C"	NCAA	41	33	39	72	30			-					
1983-84	Tulsa Oilers	CHL	24	4	9	13	10		Playoffs	9	2	2	4	7	
	Team USA	International	-	-	-	-	-			-					
1984-85	Salt Lake Golden Eagles	IHL	44	21	21	42	10			-					
	New Haven Nighthawks	AHL	3	0	0	0	0			-					
	Toledo Goaldiggers	IHL	13	4	9	13	21		Playoffs	6	1	3	4	7	
1985-86	Salt Lake Golden Eagles	IHL	24	5	12	17	21			-					
	Indianapolis Checkers	IHL	45	11	22	33	22		Playoffs	1	0	0	0	0	
1986-87	Peliitat	I-divisioona	27	16	7	23	17			-					
	ECD Iserlohn	Germany	0	0	0	0	0		Playoffs	1	1	0	1	0	
1987-88	Utica Devils	AHL	9	0	1	1	0			-					
	Turbana Panda's Rotterdam	Netherlands	42	39	32	71	16			-					
1988-89	ERC Ingolstadt	Germany3	17	29	21	50	43		Relegation	5	3	2	5	14	
1989-90	Salt Lake Golden Eagles	IHL	5	1	1	2	2			-					
	ERC Selb	Germany4	-	-	-	-	-		Relegation	12	15	20	35	4	

TEAM STAFF HISTORY

S	TEAM	LEAGUE	ROLE ON TEAM	NOTES
1991-92	Raleigh IceCaps	ECHL	Head Coach	
1992-93	Raleigh IceCaps	ECHL	Head Coach	
1993-94	Raleigh IceCaps	ECHL	Head Coach	
1994-95	San Diego Gulls	IHL	Asst. GM/Asst. Coach	
1995-96	Raleigh IceCaps	ECHL	Head Coach	
	Raleigh IceCaps	ECHL	Dir. of Hockey Operations	
1996-97	Raleigh IceCaps	ECHL	Head Coach	
	Raleigh IceCaps	ECHL	Dir. of Hockey Operations	

Season	Team	League	Role	Notes
1997-98	Manchester Storm	BISL	GM/Head Coach	
1998-99	Manchester Storm	BISL	GM/Head Coach	
1999-00	Manchester Storm	BISL	GM/Head Coach	
2000-01	New Jersey Devils	NHL	Asst. Coach	
2001-02	New Jersey Devils	NHL	Scout	
	New Jersey Devils	NHL	Asst. Coach	Promoted mid-season
2002-03	New Jersey Devils	NHL	Scout	
2003-04	New Jersey Devils	NHL	Scout	
2004-05	New Jersey Devils	NHL	Scout	
2005-06	New Jersey Devils	NHL	Scout	
2006-07	Lowell Devils	AHL	Head Coach	
2007-08	Lowell Devils	AHL	Head Coach	
	USA	WC	Asst. Coach	
2008-09	Lowell Devils	AHL	Head Coach	
2009-10	USNTDP Juniors	USHL	Head Coach	
	USA U18	WJC-18	Head Coach	Gold Medalist
2010-11	Binghamton Senators	AHL	Head Coach	
2011-12	Binghamton Senators	AHL	Head Coach	
2012-13	Univ. of Alabama-Huntsville	NCAA	Head Coach	
2013-14	Iowa Wild	AHL	Head Coach	
2014-15	Iowa Wild	AHL	Head Coach	Fired mid-season
2015-16	ERC Ingolstadt	DEL	Head Coach	Replaced Emanuel Viveiros mid-season
2016-17	Binghamton Senators	AHL	Head Coach	
2017-18	Belleville Senators	AHL	Head Coach	
2019-20	Nürnberg Ice Tigers	DEL	Head Coach	

CAREER HIGHLIGHTS

SEASON	AWARDS BY SEASON
1980-1981	• NCAA (ECAC) Tournament MVP
1981-1982	• NCAA (ECAC) All-ECAC
1982-1983	• NCAA (All-East) Senior All-Stars • NCAA (East) First All-American Team • NCAA (ECAC) All-ECAC • NCAA (New England) - All New England • NCAA Top Collegiate Player (Hobey Baker Award) Finalist

Trivia

Kurt and his brother Scot were the first brothers to be drafted into the NHL on the same year (1980 round 4 #77 overall by New York Rangers)

Tony Hand

S	TEAM	LEAGUE	GP	G	A	TP	PIM	+/-	POST	GP	G	A	TP	PIM	+/-
1981-82	Murrayfield Racers	SNL	8	2	6	8	12			-					
	Murrayfield Racers	Northern	11	2	1	3	0			-					
	Great Britain U18	EJC-18 C	4	6	4	10	0			-					
1982-83	Murrayfield Racers	BHL	22	18	21	39	23		Playoffs	2	2	1	3	0	
	Great Britain U18	EJC-18 C	3	3	2	5	2			-					
1983-84	Murrayfield Racers	BHL	30	52	43	95	28		Playoffs	6	10	5	15	6	
	Great Britain U18	EJC-18 C	6	9	7	16	4			-					
	Great Britain U20	WJC-20 C	4	6	3	9	16			-					
1984-85	Murrayfield Racers	BHL	36	72	92	164	36		Playoffs	6	13	11	24	4	
	Great Britain U18	EJC-18 C	3	4	0	4	0			-					
1985-86	Murrayfield Racers	BHL	32	79	85	164	49		Playoffs	6	13	13	26	4	
	Great Britain U20	WJC-20 C	5	10	1	11	6			-					
1986-87	Victoria Cougars	WHL	3	4	4	8	0			-					
	Murrayfield Racers	BHL	35	105	111	216	86		Playoffs	6	9	19	28	4	
	Great Britain U20	WJC-20 C	5	8	5	13	16			-					
1987-88	Murrayfield Racers	BHL	36	81	111	192	54		Playoffs	5	17	6	23	16	
1988-89	Murrayfield Racers	BHL	35	86	126	212	57		Playoffs	4	8	10	18	12	
	Great Britain	WC D	4	6	12	17	2			-					
1989-90	Murrayfield Racers	BHL	32	53	91	144	26		Playoffs	6	9	10	19	10	
	Great Britain	WC D	-	-	-	-	-			-					
1990-91	Murrayfield Racers	BHL	34	60	96	156	46		Playoffs	7	8	17	25	8	
	Great Britain	WC C	8	9	12	21	12			-					
1991-92	Murrayfield Racers "A"	BHL	36	60	80	140	46		Playoffs	5	8	12	20	2	
	Great Britain	WC C	5	6	12	18	4			-					
1992-93	Murrayfield Racers "C"	BHL	35	66	119	185	100		Playoffs	7	14	19	33	8	
	Great Britain	WC B	7	6	8	14	2	12		-					
1993-94	Murrayfield Racers "C"	BHL	44	72	150	222	44		Playoffs	6	9	15	24	10	
	Great Britain	WC	6	0	0	0	0	-17		-					
1994-95	Edinburgh Racers "C"	BHL	42	71	136	207	28		Playoffs	8	13	21	34	20	
1995-96	Sheffield Steelers	BHL	35	46	77	123	65		Playoffs	8	6	10	16	4	
1996-97	Sheffield Steelers	BISL	41	13	32	45	26		Playoffs	8	3	6	9	4	
1997-98	Sheffield Steelers	BISL	44	14	44	58	18		Playoffs	9	2	9	11	4	
1998-99	Sheffield Steelers "A"	BISL	36	11	27	38	6		Playoffs	5	1	4	5	0	
	Great Britain	WC Q	4	1	0	1	6			-					
1999-00	Ayr Scottish Eagles "A"	BISL	40	8	35	43	52		Playoffs	7	0	4	4	0	
	Great Britain	WC Q	3	1	0	1	4	0		-					
	Great Britain	WC B	7	2	8	10	2	3		-					
2000-01	Ayr Scottish Eagles "A"	BISL	46	19	36	55	42		Playoffs	7	2	5	7	0	
	Great Britain	WC D1	5	3	13	16	0	11		-					

Season		Team	League	GP	G	A	TP	PIM			GP	G	A	TP	PIM
2001-02		Dundee Stars	BNL	44	25	79	104	18		Playoffs	10	7	17	24	4
		Great Britain "A"	WC D1	5	2	4	6	2	1		-				
2002-03		Dundee Stars	BNL	36	22	58	80	99			-				
2003-04		Edinburgh Capitals	BNL	36	21	63	84	38		Playoffs	11	2	14	16	2
2004-05		Belfast Giants	EIHL	30	10	27	37	48		Playoffs	8	0	6	6	34
2005-06		Edinburgh Capitals	EIHL	43	14	36	50	2		Playoffs	4	2	2	4	0
2006-07		Manchester Phoenix	EIHL	51	17	55	72	60		Playoffs	2	0	0	0	20
		Great Britain	WC D1	5	0	3	3	0	0		-				
2007-08		Manchester Phoenix	EIHL	53	21	51	72	50		Playoffs	2	0	2	2	4
2008-09		Manchester Phoenix	EIHL	52	17	50	67	74			2	1	1	2	0
2009-10		Manchester Phoenix	EPIHL	54	25	95	120	52		Playoffs	3	1	3	4	4
2010-11		Manchester Phoenix	EPIHL	54	25	108	133	65		Playoffs	3	2	3	5	0
2011-12		Manchester Phoenix	EPIHL	21	6	26	32	12		Playoffs	3	0	3	3	4
2012-13		Manchester Phoenix	EPIHL	47	10	67	77	52		Playoffs	4	3	6	9	8
2013-14		Manchester Phoenix	EPIHL	53	18	64	82	104		Playoffs	4	1	7	8	2
2014-15		Manchester Phoenix	EPIHL	44	11	46	57	36		Playoffs	4	0	4	4	0

S		TEAM	LEAGUE	GP	G	A	TP	PIM
1983-84		Murrayfield Racers	Autumn Cup	7	0	2	2	54
1984-85		Murrayfield Racers	Autumn Cup	8	5	2	7	24
1985-86		Murrayfield Racers	Autumn Cup	9	22	23	45	15
		Murrayfield Racers	Scottish Cup	10	27	26	53	12
1986-87		Murrayfield Racers	Autumn Cup	2	7	1	8	4
		Murrayfield Racers	Scottish Cup	10	28	28	56	20
1987-88		Murrayfield Racers	Autumn Cup	6	16	12	28	6
		Murrayfield Racers	Scottish Cup	3	4	9	13	-
1988-89		Murrayfield Racers	Autumn Cup	8	14	22	36	10
1989-90		Murrayfield Racers	Autumn Cup	7	11	16	27	12
		Murrayfield Racers	Scottish Cup	4	7	9	16	30
1990-91		Murrayfield Racers	Autumn Cup	11	17	34	51	30
		Murrayfield Racers	Scottish Cup	5	9	14	23	-
1991-92		Murrayfield Racers	Autumn Cup	2	1	7	8	0
1992-93		Murrayfield Racers	Autumn Cup	6	10	11	21	0
1993-94		Murrayfield Racers	Autumn Cup	11	12	24	36	20
1994-95		Edinburgh Racers	Autumn Cup	12	17	34	51	14
1995-96		Sheffield Steelers	Autumn Cup	12	23	18	41	14
1996-97		Sheffield Steelers	Autumn Cup	10	6	16	22	10
1997-98		Sheffield Steelers	Autumn Cup	12	6	14	20	2
1998-99		Sheffield Steelers	Autumn Cup	10	8	6	14	8
1999-00		Ayr Scottish Eagles	Autumn Cup	8	3	6	9	0
2000-01		Ayr Scottish Eagles	Autumn Cup	8	3	5	8	14
		Ayr Scottish Eagles	BISL Cup	3	1	3	4	0
2001-02		Dundee Stars	Findus Cup	6	7	10	17	6

Season	Team	Competition	GP	G	A	Pts	PIM
2002-03	Dundee Stars	Findus Cup	10	7	15	22	6
2003-04	Edinburgh Capitals	Findus Cup	12	5	13	18	16
2004-05	Belfast Giants	Crossover Cup	14	5	16	21	2
	Belfast Giants	EIHL Cup	6	4	6	10	10
2005-06	Edinburgh Capitals	EIHL Cup	6	1	2	3	0
	Edinburgh Capitals	EIHL KO Cup	2	1	3	4	0
2006-07	Manchester Phoenix	EIHL Cup	4	1	3	4	0
2007-08	Manchester Phoenix	EIHL Cup	4	2	8	10	2
	Manchester Phoenix	EIHL KO Cup	2	1	2	3	4
2008-09	Manchester Phoenix	EIHL Cup	8	2	13	15	0
	Manchester Phoenix	EIHL KO Cup	6	1	5	6	12
2009-10	Manchester Phoenix	EPIHL Cup	2	0	2	2	0
2010-11	Manchester Phoenix	EPIHL Cup	2	2	2	4	0
2012-13	Manchester Phoenix	EPIHL Cup	2	1	4	5	0
2013-14	Manchester Phoenix	EPIHL Cup	2	0	6	6	10

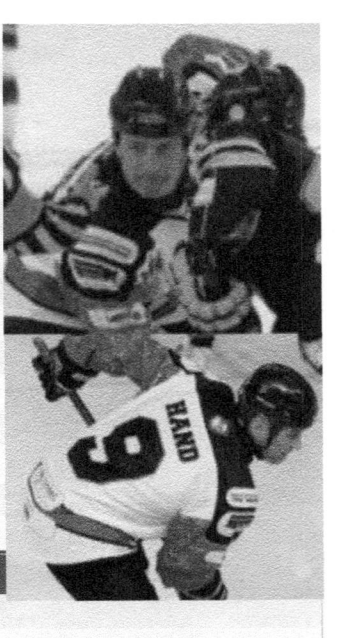

S	TEAM	LEAGUE	ROLE ON TEAM	
2001-02	Dundee Stars	BNL	Player-Coach	
2002-03	Dundee Stars	BNL	Player-Coach	Stepped down midseason
2003-04	Edinburgh Capitals	BNL	Player-Coach	
2004-05	Belfast Giants	EIHL	Player-Coach	
2005-06	Edinburgh Capitals	EIHL	Player-Coach	
2006-07	Manchester Phoenix	EIHL	Player-Coach	
2007-08	Manchester Phoenix	EIHL	Player-Coach	
	Great Britain	WC D1	Asst. Coach	
2008-09	Manchester Phoenix	EIHL	Player-Coach	
	Great Britain	OGQ	Asst. Coach	
2009-10	Manchester Phoenix	EPIHL	Player-Coach	
2010-11	Manchester Phoenix	EPIHL	Player-Coach	
2011-12	Manchester Phoenix	EPIHL	Player-Coach	
	Great Britain	WC D1A	Head Coach	
2012-13	Manchester Phoenix	EPIHL	Player-Coach	
	Great Britain	OGQ	Head Coach	
	Great Britain	WC D1A	Head Coach	
2013-14	Manchester Phoenix	EPIHL	Player-Coach	
2014-15	Manchester Phoenix	EPIHL	Player-Coach	
2015-16	Manchester Phoenix	EPIHL	Head Coach	
2016-17	Manchester Phoenix	EPIHL	Head Coach	
2017-18	Great Britain U18	WJC-18 D2A	Head Coach	
2018-19	Murrayfield Racers	SNL	Director	
	Murrayfield Racers	SNL	Head Coach	
2019-20	Murrayfield Racers	SNL	Director	
	Murrayfield Racers	SNL	Head Coach	
	Great Britain U20	WJC-20 D2A	Team Manager	

Tony was interviewed by the author and provided the following interesting answers to questions that were asked of him:

1. **What attracted you to the sport of ice hockey?**
   I used to play football and rugby but liked skating with my brothers at the Murrayfield rink since I was 9 years old and that is how I become interested in skating which developed into my love for ice hockey.
2. **Who has influenced you the most during your playing career?**
   A lot of people have influenced me during my career from team members to coaches to family members, a vast amount of people, too many to mention.
3. **What was the best rink that you have played in?**
   The Coliseum in Edmonton would probably be the best, with Belfast in the UK coming close. However, for atmosphere nothing can beat the Murrayfield rink when its full!
4. **What was your best memory as a player?**
   Every time we won a trophy or competition and playing at the Wembley Arena. Also, whilst with the Edmonton Oilers training with Mark Messier and Wayne Gretzky and appearing in an exhibition game for the Oilers.

5. **Best memory as a coach?**
   That would have to be with the Manchester Phoenix and the first time we won the league. I had been thrown out of the game at Swindon for drawing blood, but the team still won the game. Also winning the play offs with Manchester.
6. **What was the best goal that you remember scoring?**
   Playing at Wembley against Nottingham, I beat a few players and put the puck into the top shelf of the net. I think the goal is still available on you tube.
7. **Who was the best player that you have played with?**
   Loads of players, the most natural player was Ed Courteney his talent was fantastic. There were lots of great players in the Elite league that I played with including David-Alexandre Beauregard
8. **And against?**
   That would have to be the former Fife Flyer, Greg Kuznik, he played in the American Hockey League and was great on one to ones. Also, Neal Martin was a good player whilst playing for the Coventry Blaze.
9. **What attracted you to the Manchester Phoenix?**
   Neil Morris. I had spoken to him several times over the years and we agreed to meet at a service station on the M6 as it was about halfway for us both. I was impressed by his passion for the Phoenix and he had a good business plan drawn up and they had the opportunity to do well. Neil was fantastic all the time I was at the club!
10. **How did the set up at Phoenix differ from what you had experienced elsewhere in Scotland Sheffield and Belfast?**
    The set up at all clubs are virtually the same, its just experience that separates the teams off the ice. It's a case of what people can bring into a club. Owners also, need to be fair and accommodating. The only real difference is at Belfast with all the constant flying that is involved. But as a club itself it's a case of tweaking what you have to suit the conditions.

11. **Having coached at several age groups and teams including GB what was your biggest challenge?**
I have coached at many levels involving numerous groups. The biggest challenge is not the professionals who know what they are doing and understanding the level of coaching being given. It's the players who do not understand the game as they all require individual managing.
12. **What was the biggest obstacle that you have encountered in Ice Hockey and how did you overcome it?**
I had not encountered many obstacles, but probably one was when we moved out of the Altrincham rink and found ourselves playing out of the Fylde rink and trying to retain our fanbase whilst keeping the team together. The cost factor was partially overcome as we raised money to keep the team going which was near impossible when we had no rink of our own.
13. **How have you been keeping busy during Covid lockdown?**
I am now the owner of the Murrayfield Racers running a fantastic team and in a great rink. COVID has knocked everything back but I am planning and ready to go again once the Government gives the go ahead. But not knowing how long that will be or if the season will start is a problem. Social distancing will be the main problem for fans returning to watch the sport and that is currently very confusing when you can go to a pub and have a drink with your friends but not go to an ice rink. I find this very frustrating!
14. **How easy was it to become a team director with the Racers and how have you adjusted to it?**
The transition was easy. I was fortunate having coached and played for over 20 years. I understood how the ice hockey business was run. Directors have a duty of care both to the business and to the players. I have good backroom staff to help me, we work together as a good

team and we have surpassed all my expectations for the first 2 years. Being a director has not been a problem at all. It has been a team effort and jointly we have succeeded in what we set out to achieve. The ice rink has been good to us and we needed a good relationship with our landlord for us to be successful. Seldom have we had any issues and Richard Stirling and Willie Kerr have been great to work with. We averaged crowds of 800 last season, which was up 300% on our 1st season. We are moving in the right direction and I am happy with the progressed made by the club on and off the ice.

15. **How did this role differ from what you had experienced at Manchester Phoenix?**
They were similar roles, the only exception being that at Manchester I had no control over the finances, that was left to Neil Morris. so it's a close comparison with the exception of my not signing the cheques in Altrincham. At Murrayfield, I am more involved with the business ensuring that we pay our bills. Thankfully we have good sponsors and fans and have had them for many years here in Edinburgh.

16. **Do you see the Racers re-joining the Elite League at some point or are you happy remaining in the Scottish League?**
Never rule anything out. At this stage with COVID I am thankful we are where we are. The business has survived. We have kept going and are building relationships with the clubs around us. No one knows what is around the corner and under the current circumstances the Elite League business model would be hard to achieve as its all about income. Teams with large arenas, money are struggling and even in normal conditions the smaller teams struggle to compete. We wouldn't want to become the team that was beaten week in week out in the Elite League so are concentrating on building a solid business. Once that is in place we would need to adjust and become more competitive before we could even entertain the concept of joining the Elite League, but who knows what is down the road?

17. **What was it like playing alongside your brother? Was there any sibling rivalry?**
Paul and I have been on the ice together many times over the years, sometimes playing on the same side and sometimes against each other. We were both desperate to win so were both very competitive. As to rivalry, everyone wants to win, but there was never any friction!

Tony Hand
March 2021

Garry Unger

I am pleased to be able to contribute to this book and put across a few thoughts on my very happy time in the UK!

So how did I come to sign for Peterborough? Well it's a long story really, but basically, I was living in Edmonton working for a Trade Development Company selling oil products worldwide, whilst also commentating on the Oilers hockey matches. I was often working abroad and when away I tried to visit different rinks and see matches. I was working with Bruce Wilson who ran Wilson International Trade Consultants, they helped get a few contracts for North Americans in Europe playing hockey. We sent faxes to many clubs in many countries, then mid-August I received a call from Tom Stewart who was in Toronto wanting to look at some players. I had some Oiler guys and Juniors available, so we rented some ice time in Alberta and invited Tom to come and watch even though it was at Midnight. Afterwards, back in my office about 4am, he came in to discuss player options, only he wanted to offer me a contract, even though I was the player's agent. He said:
"Garry you are the best player out there!"

I received an offer to go to Dundee, but my kids were about to start school, so after a few family discussions my contract included numerous flight tickets. My wife came to the UK for a visit for a few days, I went back to Canada in December and then the Kids visited at Easter. We also had tickets thrown in for trips to Paris and Greece! At the end of the season I needed a house for the family to come over and stay in, but Dundee couldn't provide one. I returned home to Canada and about 2 months later Steve Rattle called me and asked what would it take to bring me to Peterborough? He had just signed Todd Bittner and Doug McEwen. I asked for a house, a 4 bedroomed place for my family to come and stay. He said "Yes" and I joined the Pirates.

One of my first games for Pirates was at Medway and I was sat on the bench with Todd and Dougie thinking that this was easy, then we went about 7-2 down after the 2nd period and we all said to each other that we needed to improve as more was expected from us. We turned the match round to win either 11-7 or 11-9. We won most of our games and Todd and Dougie were great players. However, the hockey referees were very sketchy to say the least. One example was a match we were playing down in Southampton. Something broke out in front of the net and a big fight ensued. I attempted to break up the fight and the next thing I knew was the referee had kicked me out of the game. Either Todd or Dougie spoke to the referee as I went off the ice. I was then in the shower when someone came into the changing room and told me that I could play again, so I got changed and went back onto the ice again. I thought to myself "how can I get back at the ref?" and decided that at face off I could "accidentally" wack him in the shin with my stick, but I decided I was a better person and didn't do it. After the match we all were sat in the pub together when the referee came over and shook my hand and told me how pleased he was to meet me and we had a great conversation. I was glad I didn't wack him and I learnt a great lesson in life! The ref was a nice guy and I would have destroyed the reputation I had in his mind.

Then we played Telford in a relegation match. We had a good battle and we won the match to gain promotion to the Premier Division. I went to the Peterborough committee and told them that we were great in the 1st Division, but we would do nothing in the Premier Division with the calibre of the players we had. They were young and not ready for the Premier Division! So we signed Paul Heavey; Peter Smith and the Slater brothers, Grant and Mark, and we put together a good team. However, Doug McEwen went to Cardiff Devils, it was probably the biggest mistake Peterborough ever made to lose him to Cardiff!

Teams that were beating us 13-0 2 years previously were now competing with us and we did well. However, we went all the way to the Cup Final where we played Durham over 2 legs. Durham had a powerhouse team and were top of the league. We had to play the first match in Peterborough and the 2nd in Durham. Before the matches we held a conference call with Durham. Both sides had players working so we arranged both matches for an 8pm face off. Durham came to Peterborough and we tied the match 8-8. For the 2nd leg in Durham we were confident. Chris, our netminder was working late and catching a train so we had a guy waiting at the station to bring him to the rink. We got to the rink at 7pm. Durham were already warming up on the ice. Durham insisted that the match was arranged to start at 7pm and not 8pm that had been agreed. We started at 7:30 without a goalie and had to put a kid in goal. We went 6-0 down by the end of the 1st period and lost the match and final as a result of Durham's tactics!

Two of the committee were a great help to the team in Tony Boon and Tony Medlock. Tony Medlock ran his own car dealership and when Paul Heavey and Pete Smith signed, they needed a job to boost their wages so Tony found them a job in his dealership. Whenever Garry was playing and Peterborough were winning well, he would give the British players valuable match experience. Paul and Pete got close to Tony and when Pirates were winning 13-5 or something similar, I started to give the kids some ice time. Paul got mad at not being given the opportunity to play. I tried to explain my reasons, but Paul was not interested. I was sat on the bench with Paul when with 30 seconds left of the game, Paul leapt off the bench and hit someone on the head as he was mad at me and got thrown out of the game and received a suspension. I tried to coach in the style of the NHL but that didn't suit Paul. Paul and Pete kept going back to Tony complaining about my decisions. We had a Scottish weekend away playing at Fife and Dundee. Tony Medlock travelled up with the team for the matches. We tied the match at Fife, then afterwards the Scots lads asked for time off to visit their families whilst in Scotland to which I approved their requests as long as they were back the following evening to prepare for the Dundee match. They came back on time, had a meal with the rest of the team then went to the bar with Tony Medlock. I told the guys that

Garry Unger Plays in

there was a curfew at 11pm to get ready for the game. I went to my room, then walked down to the bar and all of the guys were drinking with Tony and the other committee members who had travelled for the weekend. Tony was paying for the drinks and said that all was ok. With that I went back to bed. We lost the match at Dundee as a result. On our return to Peterborough I attended the regular Thursday night meeting with the committee and Tony told me that I had no control over the team. I reminded him, that it was him buying them drinks, which he denied and my response was that he and the Scots guys were not running the team!

We were playing Solihull in one of the first matches that I coached. Someone called and said that both Tony's wanted to talk to me. They asked if they could sit on the bench for the match. I told them that there was no room, so they told me to remove some of the young Brits so that they could sit on the bench. They wanted complete control. From then things went downhill for me at the club!

I had a great time in Peterborough as did my 3 girls, even Andy French and Ken McKie came to my daughter's 4th birthday party. My wife was a Personal Trainer delivering aerobics classes throughout the UK. We bought bikes and enjoyed cycling around the town. Dr Guttman was great also, not forgetting Tony Hunter, Alan Walker and Tony Oliver. We loved our time in Peterborough so much that my wife didn't want to return to Canada! I wanted to coach but I was better suited to North America than the UK, so I decided not to return to Peterborough. I signed a contract with the Oxford Stars and offered to commute between Peterborough and Oxford, then I received a call from the USA regarding a new team being formed in Phoenix and would I be interested in coaching them? They wanted to hire me! I had committed to Oxford, then a friend called to say he was going back to the UK, but the contract had been cancelled. I then called Oxford and told them what had happened and offered to stay with Oxford as I had signed a contract with them, or I could swap with my friend. Oxford said that my friend was a good player and agreed to let me return to the USA to coach in Phoenix.

I returned to the USA with nothing but positive thoughts for Peterborough where I have made some firm friends. Dr Guttman fixed my nose after I had broken it 11 times and he even visited me in Calgary.

At the end of my first season I remember going to Brussels to play a friendly. I recently saw a video of the events of us all fooling around and it brought back fond memories of my time there. Playing in the NHL was fun, but I consider my time in Peterborough was just as much fun!

I remember when I was awarded Player of the Year in Dundee, the British Player of the Year award was made by Heineken and won by Tony Hand who got a chance to visit the Calgary training camp. I was in Banff sitting round a camp fire with Glen Sather who is now GM President of the NY Rangers, and was with Edmonton at the time and others. Tony Hand was mentioned as coming over to Canada and was a great prospect. At which point Edmonton said that they would draft him to stop him going to the Flames. Tony arrived to complete his paperwork and could not think about any contacts so listed me as his agent. He scored 11 points in the Juniors whilst in Canada and Glen, the Edmonton owner agreed that Tony had prospects and would have gone on to be the first Scot to play in the NHL, but Tony missed his girlfriend and didn't want Junior hockey so returned home to the UK.

I would like to mention also: Peter Gamble Tony Oliver Dr Guttman Ron Brett and Allen who were all great committee members. To end with I would like to mention Gary Brine whom I played against whilst at Peterborough. He now has a son named Lucas, who is 13 years old and who may well be appearing at the Banff Hockey Academy where I now coach!

THE BANFF HOCKEY ACADEMY
GOALS FOR EDUCATION, HOCKEY, LIFE

Elite Prospects Summary
CAREER STATISTICS

SEASON	TEAM	LEAGUE	GP	G	A	TP	PIM	+/-	POST	GP	G	A	TP	PIM	+/-
1966-67	London Nationals	OHA-Jr.	48	38	35	73	60		Playoffs	6	2	14	5	7	27
	Rochester Americans	AHL	1	0	0	0	0		Playoffs	1	0	0	0	0	
	Tulsa Oilers	CHL	2	2	0	2	2								
1967-68	London Nationals	OHA-Jr.	2	4	1	5	2								
	Toronto Maple Leafs	NHL	15	1	1	2	4	-5							
	Tulsa Oilers	CHL	9	3	5	8	6								
	Rochester Americans	AHL	5	1	3	4	6								

Season	Team	League	GP	G	A	Pts	PIM	+/-		Playoffs	GP	G	A	Pts	PIM
	→Detroit Red Wings	→NHL	13	5	10	15	2	4							
1968-69	→Detroit Red Wings	→NHL	76	24	20	44	33	6							
1969-70	→Detroit Red Wings	→NHL	76	42	24	66	67	24		→Playoffs	4	0	1	1	6
1970-71	→Detroit Red Wings	→NHL	51	13	14	27	63	-32							
	→St. Louis Blues	→NHL	28	15	14	29	41	-4		→Playoffs	6	3	2	5	20
1971-72	→St. Louis Blues	→NHL	78	36	34	70	104	-8		→Playoffs	11	4	5	9	35
1972-73	→St. Louis Blues	→NHL	78	41	39	80	119	7		→Playoffs	5	1	2	3	2
1973-74	→St. Louis Blues	→NHL	78	33	35	68	96	-17							
1974-75	→St. Louis Blues	→NHL	80	36	44	80	123	-1		→Playoffs	2	1	3	4	6
1975-76	→St. Louis Blues	→NHL	80	39	44	83	95	1		→Playoffs	3	2	1	3	7
1976-77	→St. Louis Blues "C"	→NHL	80	30	27	57	56	-12		→Playoffs	4	0	1	1	2
1977-78	→St. Louis Blues	→NHL	80	32	20	52	66	-35							
	→Canada	→WC	10	0	0	0	30								
1978-79	→St. Louis Blues	→NHL	80	30	26	56	44	-44							
	→Canada	→WC	7	2	1	3	12								

Season	Team	League	GP	G	A	Pts	PIM	+/-		Playoffs/Notes	GP	G	A	Pts	PIM
1979-80	➡Atlanta Flames	➡NHL	79	17	16	33	39	2		➡Playoffs	4	0	3	3	2
1980-81	➡Los Angeles Kings	➡NHL	58	10	10	20	40	-17							
	➡Edmonton Oilers	➡NHL	13	0	0	0	6	-9		➡Playoffs	8	0	0	0	2
1981-82	➡Edmonton Oilers	➡NHL	46	7	13	20	69	8		➡Playoffs	4	1	0	1	23
1982-83	➡Edmonton Oilers	➡NHL	16	2	0	2	8	1		➡Playoffs	1	0	0	0	0
	➡Moncton Alpines	➡AHL	8	2	3	5	0								
1983-85	Did not play														
1985-86	➡Dundee Rockets	➡BHL	35	86	48	134	64			➡Playoffs	6	7	6	13	44
1986-87	➡Peterborough Pirates	➡BD1	30	95	143	238	58								
1987-88	➡Peterborough Pirates	➡BHL	32	37	44	81	116			➡Relegation	2	3	3	6	2

TEAM STAFF HISTORY

SEASON	TEAM	LEAGUE	ROLE ON TEAM	NOTES
1987-1988	➡Peterborough Pirates	➡BHL	Player-Coach	Replaced Elwyn Dawkins
1989-1990	➡Phoenix Roadrunners	➡IHL	Head Coach	
1990-1991	➡Phoenix Roadrunners	➡IHL	Asst. Coach	

	New Haven Nighthawks	AHL	Head Coach	Interim
1992-1993	Tulsa Oilers	CHL	Head Coach	
1993-1994	Tulsa Oilers	CHL	Head Coach	
1994-1995	Tulsa Oilers	CHL	Head Coach	
1995-1996	Tulsa Oilers	CHL	Head Coach	
1996-1997	Tulsa Oilers	CHL	Head Coach	
1997-1998	New Mexico Scorpions	WPHL	Head Coach	
1998-1999	New Mexico Scorpions	WPHL	Head Coach	
2001-2002	Tulsa Oilers	CHL	Head Coach	
2002-2003	Tulsa Oilers	CHL	Head Coach	
2003-2004	Alabama Slammers	WHA2	Head Coach	
2004-2005	Motor City Mechanics	UHL	Head Coach	Replace by Steve Shannon midseason
2013-2014	Banff Bears	HJHL	Head Coach	

Rob Robinson

1 – What made you choose Ice Hockey as a career?
I just loved playing hockey and wanted to play at the highest level possible

2 - How did it feel when St Louis Blues drafted you in 1987?
It felt great to get drafted by St Louis... I was probably surprised, I had talked to Buffalo a bit and heard that LA Kings might be interested. I was on the back deck with my Mom when St Louis called to talk to me.

3 – Having a father (Doug) play in the NHL with Chicago, New York Rangers and LA Kings, was that an influence on your playing style?
It is awesome that my Dad played, but I do not have any memories of watching him play. It may be hard to believe but I had more penalty minutes than him!... I had a long fuse.

4 – Having played 22 games for St Louis what was your fondest memory of playing in the NHL?
I think my fondest memory is when Brian Sutter told me I had made the team and to give my parents a call

5 – Do you remember your debut in the NHL?
In New Jersey, made a shitty pinch in the offensive zone and Claude Lemieux scored

6 – You only had 1 assist in the NHL can you remember it?
Brett Hull from Jeff Brown and myself... passed from behind our net to Brownie near the right hash marks in our end and he hit Hully with a beautiful pass through the middle near center ice to send Hul in on a breakaway

7 – Having played in North America what made you head to Europe and play in Austria in 1996?
My buddy Domenic Lavoie (played with him in Peoria) had played in Austria and reached out to me and asked if I would be interested.

8 – After a season in Austria then one in Germany what made you head to the UK?
I headed to the UK because KK offered me a 2 year contract...Frankfurt was offering one year to stay but my wife and I had been in 5 different cities in 5 years and wanted some stability

9 - Why choose to sign for the Manchester Storm?
I was only talking to KK and Manchester. KK was very professional and I knew that the Storm were playing in the Champions league , so I wanted to be a part of that.

10 – Did you have any expectations of playing in the UK?
No expectations, had heard about the MEN Arena and was excited to play there

11 – Were those expectations met?
YES, loved our time in Manchester!

12 – What was your favourite rink to play at?
Men Arena..Sparta Prague was awesome, Nottinghams new arena and Belfast. Training camp in Switzerland and Germany..Zug's rink looking out at the mountains was great!

13 – Who had the best fans and why?
We did..Great fans, supported us and travelled well

14 – Who was the best player that you have played with and why?
Adam Oates...super skilled and hard worker, who played at both ends of the ice

15 – Who was the best player that you have played against and why?
In England I thought Greg Hadden was a really good player

16 – Who was the biggest influence on your career?
My parents and wife, so supportive and helpful

17 – What was your favourite memory of playing hockey?
Winning Championships in the IHL with Peoria, in Austria with VEU Feldkirch and in Manchester..a League Championship and a Benson and Hedges Cup

18 – What do you do now for a living?
In between jobs...working at an Ice Rink right now

19 – What did you think of the standard of play in the UK?
I thought the standard of play amongst the top teams was very good

20 – Is the standard improving in the UK?
I have no idea about today's standard of hockey...but I would suggest that playing in a small building will make it tough for the Storm to sustain a strong team.

We loved our time in Manchester. I was disappointed when KK left and unfortunately my last year there was a struggle. Great people, great friends and great memories. I hope to get back for a visit soon!

Rob's Stats

S	TEAM	LEAGUE	GP	G	A	TP	PIM	+/-	POST	GP	G	A	TP	PIM	+/-
1983-84	St. Catharines Legionnaires	Midget	-	-	-	-	-								
1984-85	St. Catharines Falcons	GHL	12	1	3	4	12								
1985-86	St. Catharines Falcons	GHL	40	5	29	34	28								
	Miami Univ. (Ohio)	NCAA	38	1	9	10	24								
1986-87	Miami Univ. (Ohio)	NCAA	33	3	5	8	32								
1987-88	Miami Univ. (Ohio) "A"	NCAA	35	1	3	4	56								
1988-89	Miami Univ. (Ohio)	NCAA	30	3	4	7	42								
	Peoria Rivermen	IHL	11	2	0	2	6								
1989-90	Peoria Rivermen	IHL	60	2	11	13	72		Playoffs	5	0	1	1	10	
1990-91	Peoria Rivermen	IHL	79	2	21	23	42		Playoffs	19	0	6	6	18	
1991-92	Peoria Rivermen	IHL	35	1	10	11	29		Playoffs	10	0	2	2	12	
	St. Louis Blues	NHL	22	0	1	1	8	-4							
1992-93	Peoria Rivermen	IHL	34	0	4	4	38	-6							
1993-94	Kalamazoo Wings	IHL	67	3	12	15	32	20	Playoffs	5	0	0	0	2	-1
1994-95	Houston Aeros	IHL	70	3	12	15	54	-15	Playoffs	4	0	1	1	4	1
1995-96	Syracuse Crunch	AHL	40	2	6	8	12	-11	Playoffs	16	0	2	2	2	9
1996-97	VEU Feldkirch	Austria	55	4	6	10	30								
1997-98	Frankfurt Lions	DEL	44	0	10	10	51		Playoffs	7	0	2	2	29	
1998-99	Manchester Storm	BISL	42	1	11	12	22		Playoffs	7	0	1	1	6	
1999-00	Manchester Storm	BISL	41	1	6	7	36		Playoffs	5	0	1	1	0	
2000-01	Manchester Storm	BISL	44	0	5	5	16		Playoffs	6	1	0	1	8	

S	TEAM	LEAGUE	GP	G	A	TP	PIM	+/-	POST	GP	G	A	TP	PIM	+/-
1998-99	Manchester Storm	Euro HL	6	0	1	1	6								
	Manchester Storm	Autumn Cup	12	0	3	3	6								
1999-00	Manchester Storm	Euro HL	6	1	1	2	2	-3							
	Manchester Storm	Autumn Cup	11	0	1	1	2								
2000-01	Manchester Storm	Autumn Cup	8	0	2	2	6								

TEAM STAFF HISTORY

S	TEAM	LEAGUE	ROLE ON TEAM	NOTES
2020-21	Honeybaked 16U	16U AAA (W)	Head Coach	

Daryl Evans

Daryl Thomas Evans was born on January 12, 1961 and is a Canadian former professional ice hockey player. He is currently the radio colour commentator for the Los Angeles Kings.

As a youth, Evans played in the 1974 Quebec International Pee-Wee Hockey Tournament with a minor ice hockey team from Toronto.

Evans was born in Toronto, Ontario. Drafted in 1980 by the Los Angeles Kings, Evans also played six games for the Washington Capitals and two games for the Toronto Maple Leafs.

He scored the game winning goal in the 'Miracle on Manchester', one of the most significant goals in LA Kings history.

Evans has been the radio colour commentator for the Los Angeles Kings since 1998, alongside play-by-play voice Nick Nickson.

Evans participates in many charity events for the Kings and teaches sponsored adult hockey Clinics at Toyota Center. Evans is known to be an excellent skater, having built up his ability by skating without laces

Evans resides in Redondo Beach, California and has two children.

Daryl's Stats

S	TEAM	LEAGUE	GP	G	A	TP	PIM	+/-	POST	GP	G	A	TP	PIM	+/-
1977-78	Toronto Nationals U18 AAA	U18 AAA	40	25	35	60	50	-							
1978-79	Niagara Falls Flyers	OMJHL	65	38	26	64	110	-	Playoffs	20	5	5	10	32	-
1979-80	Niagara Falls Flyers	OMJHL	63	43	52	95	47	-	Playoffs	10	5	13	18	6	-
1980-81	Niagara Falls Flyers	OHL	5	3	4	7	11	-							
	Brantford Alexanders	OHL	58	58	54	112	50	-	Playoffs	6	4	5	9	6	-
	Saginaw Gears	IHL	3	3	2	5	0	-							
1981-82	Los Angeles Kings	NHL	14	2	6	8	2	2	Playoffs	10	5	8	13	12	-
	New Haven Nighthawks	AHL	41	14	14	28	10	-							
1982-83	Los Angeles Kings	NHL	80	18	22	40	21	-18							
1983-84	Los Angeles Kings	NHL	4	0	1	1	0	1							
	New Haven Nighthawks	AHL	69	51	34	85	14	-							
1984-85	Los Angeles Kings	NHL	7	1	0	1	2	2							
	New Haven Nighthawks	AHL	59	22	24	46	12	-							
1985-86	Washington Capitals	NHL	6	0	1	1	0	-1							
	Binghamton Whalers	AHL	69	40	52	92	50	-	Playoffs	5	6	2	8	0	-
1986-87	Toronto Maple Leafs	NHL	2	1	0	1	0	-2	Playoffs	1	0	0	0	0	-
	Newmarket Saints	AHL	74	27	46	73	17	-							
1987-88	Newmarket Saints	AHL	57	29	36	65	10	-							
1988-89	Newmarket Saints	AHL	64	29	30	59	16	-	Playoffs	5	1	1	2	0	-
1989-90	Gherdëina	Italy2	32	32	65	97	28	-							
1990-91	Whitley Warriors	BHL	6	10	9	19	6	-	Playoffs	8	18	22	40	6	-

S	TEAM	LEAGUE	GP	G	A	TP	PIM	+/-	POST	GP	G	A	TP	PIM	+/-
1973-74	Toronto Young Nationals	QC Int PW	-	-	-	-	-	-							
1990-91	Whitley Warriors	Autumn Cup	8	18	22	40	6	-							

TEAM STAFF HISTORY

S	TEAM	LEAGUE	ROLE ON TEAM	NOTES
1990-91	Whitley Warriors	BHL	Player-Coach	

Paxton Schulte

Paxton James Schulte was born on July 16, 1972 and is a Canadian former professional ice hockey player.

Schulte was drafted 124th overall in the 1992 NHL Entry Draft by the Quebec Nordiques and played one game for the team during the 1993–94 NHL season, spending much of his tenure in the American Hockey League with the Cornwall Aces. He was part of a blockbuster trade to the Calgary Flames for Vesa Viitakoski in 1996 and again played mostly in the AHL with the Saint John Flames. He did manage to play a second NHL game for Calgary in 1996–97.

He moved to the United Kingdom in 1998, signing for the Bracknell Bees, winning the British Ice Hockey Superleague title in 2000. He then moved to the Belfast Giants for the 2000/2001 season and made a huge reputation with the team, winning the Superleague title in 2002 and the Playoff Championship in 2003 and gained a huge following with Giants fans for his toughness on the ice, but more so for his huge heart and presence off the ice. He returned to America in 2005, playing in the Central Hockey League for the Amarillo Gorillas and the Tulsa Oilers.

He retired in 2006 and is currently spending time on his father's Beef and Buffalo farm in Onoway, Alberta, near Edmonton. He has 2 sons and a daughter.

Schulte returned to Belfast to play in a testimonial game for his friend and former Giants teammate, Todd Kelman on March 13, 2007. His number 27 jersey was retired on March 9, 2007 before the Giants' game against Newcastle Vipers.

Paxton's Stats

S	TEAM	LEAGUE	GP	G	A	TP	PIM	+/-	POST	GP	G	A	TP	PIM	+/-
1988-89	St. Albert Raiders U18 AAA	AMHL	28	22	35	57	38	-							
1989-90	Sherwood Park Crusaders	AJHL	56	28	38	66	151	-							
1990-91	Univ. of North Dakota	NCAA	38	2	4	6	32	-							
1991-92	Spokane Chiefs	WHL	70	42	42	84	172	-	Playoffs	10	2	8	10	48	-
1992-93	Spokane Chiefs	WHL	45	38	35	73	142	-	Playoffs	10	5	6	11	12	-
1993-94	Québec Nordiques	NHL	1	0	0	0	2	0							
	Cornwall Aces	AHL	56	15	15	30	102	-5							
1994-95	Cornwall Aces	AHL	74	14	22	36	217	6	Playoffs	14	3	3	6	29	-3
1995-96	Cornwall Aces	AHL	69	25	31	56	171	-11							
	Saint John Flames	AHL	14	4	5	9	25	-6	Playoffs	14	4	7	11	40	5
1996-97	Calgary Flames	NHL	1	0	0	0	2	1							
	Saint John Flames	AHL	71	14	23	37	274	-7	Playoffs	4	2	0	2	35	1
1997-98	Saint John Flames	AHL	59	8	17	25	133	6							
	Las Vegas Thunder	IHL	10	0	1	1	32	-1	Playoffs	4	0	0	0	4	0
1998-99	Bracknell Bees	BISL	36	9	10	19	152	-	Playoffs	3	0	0	0	14	-
1999-00	Bracknell Bees	BISL	39	12	20	32	110	-	Playoffs	6	3	2	5	4	-
2000-01	Belfast Giants "A"	BISL	48	17	16	33	163	-	Playoffs	6	0	1	1	26	-
2001-02	Belfast Giants "C"	BISL	46	20	17	37	133	-	Playoffs	6	1	3	4	42	-
2002-03	Belfast Giants	BISL	26	13	11	24	107	-	Playoffs	18	7	9	16	48	-
2003-04	Belfast Giants "A"	EIHL	54	21	31	52	352	-	Playoffs	4	0	2	2	66	-
2004-05	Stony Plain Eagles	Chinook HL	12	6	17	23	74	-							
2005-06	Amarillo Gorillas	CHL	4	0	3	3	8	-1							
	Tulsa Oilers	CHL	42	6	15	21	113	-6							
2006-07	Stony Plain Eagles	Chinook HL	8	4	3	7	52	-							
2009-10	Onoway Ice Dogs	NCHL-AB	2	0	0	0	21	-							

S	TEAM	LEAGUE	GP	G	A	TP	PIM	+/-	POST
1998-99	Bracknell Bees	Autumn Cup	8	1	4	5	51	-	
1999-00	Bracknell Bees	Autumn Cup	10	4	8	12	43	-	
2000-01	Belfast Giants	BISL Cup	2	0	0	0	14	-	
2003-04	Belfast Giants	EIHL Cup	2	0	2	2	6	-	

TEAM STAFF HISTORY

S	TEAM	LEAGUE	ROLE ON T
2015-16	PAC Predators U15 AA	NAHL U15	Head Coach

The NHL in the UK

1. **You were drafted by Quebec Nordeques, how did it feel to be drafted into the NHL?**
   It was pretty amazing to be sat with my dad and my agent in the Montreal Forum. The whole event was overwhelming and a big achievement that I was proud to be sharing with my dad2
2. **You have an interesting record in the NHL played 2 and 4 penalty minutes. Can you remember the incidents?**
   Yes on my 1st shift I was called for a hooking penalty, then in my 2nd game it was amazing warming up with Mats Sundin and I remember how amazing it felt to be shoulder to shoulder with him and the other guys.
3. **What happened at both NHL clubs that you only got to play a single game at both sides?**
   At Quebec they used the situation to see how I got on and it was a feeler to see how I adapted, but I had limited opportunities as players were coming back from injury. Same situation at the 2nd NHL side. The bottom guys at NHL clubs and the top players in the AHL there is little difference between them. It's a case of being at the right place at the right time. It's a game of numbers and I think it's between 7500 and 7700 guys that have played in the NHL. That's quite an elite bunch of players.
4. **Can you remember your debut match in the NHL?**
   I warmed up with Valeri Kaminski and Matts Sundin, I called my folks to get them to the game, but lots of it is a blur. I remember Chris Joseph who was with Tampa Bay at the time asked what I was doing there. I remember lots of emotion and the adrenalin rush!
5. **Which league did you prefer playing in?**
   NHL obviously was the tops league, I only wish that I had spent more time there. The American League is a good fighting spot to get into the NHL, I made many good friends in that league. The UK was a comfort to me as I knew I was on the team, so I could focus on being in the team and playing and producing the best product I could on the ice without worrying about my contract.

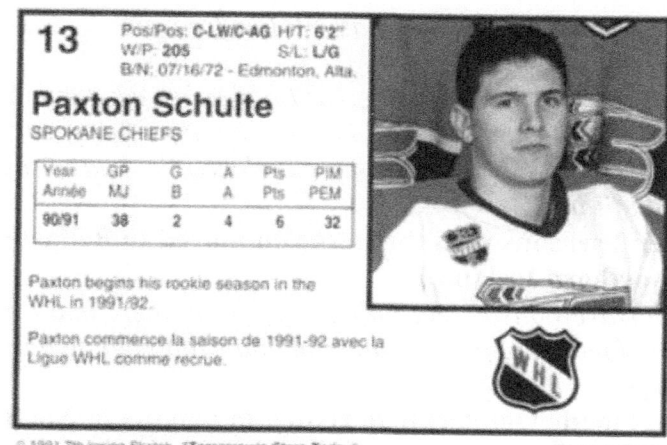

6. **Who was your closet friend on the ice and why?**
   Ladislov Kohn in the AHL as we roomed together, plus in the UK Stewie (Rob Stewart) both on and off the ice at both Bracknell and Belfast.
7. **What made you leave North America to sign for Bracknell**
   It was a good decision as I could be home most nights and be closer to my family and help to make my marriage work. Plus it was a good opportunity to see the world.
8. **What was your favourite memory of playing for the Bracknell Bees?**
   I was trying to help set a record, when Mike Blaisdell and I made contact with each other and we both ended up falling through the Zamboni doors. Also meeting Stewie at the airport. The banter was great, especially between the Canadians in the locker rooms. Kicking around with these guys was often better than the actual playing. We all made friendships that will last forever!
9. **Why sign for Bracknell?**
   It was the only opportunity that I had received. Keith McCambridge knew Dave Whistle and I trusted his opinion and after speaking to Dave I believed in him through his tone of voice and what he had to say and that he thought I would fit in.
10. **After 2 seasons with the Bees you moved to Belfast what made you move to Northern Ireland?**
    Both Dave Whistle and Rob Stewart went there and I had found a coach that trusted me and I got on with him and wanted to be part of his leadership group.
11. **What made you decide to return to playing in North America?**
    Dad had always told me that when hockey stops being fun to get out. It was no longer fun. My son had been born and I went home to spend time with him. My body was tired and I felt rundown and I was not in a good head space for loving the game.
12. **What was your favourite goal scored?**
    Scoring the 1st goal at the Odyssey for the Giants. Whilst I had scored 4 goals in the American Hockey League, scoring the 1st goal in Belfast with the crowd behind me was special. Belfast became an amazing experience for me.
13. **Which team was your favourite to play for?**
    That's tied between the Bees and the Giants because of the players that we had. Great memories at both clubs, no individuals, just a team that played

together as a team. Great guys with great support from the fans, we could all have a beer together after the matches in Bracknell and Belfast. People would also stop you in the street for a chat which was nice.

14. **Who was the best player that you have played with and why?**
    Mats Sundin, Joe Sakic, Marty Murray, Jason Ruff plus off course Stewie both on and off the ice.

15. **Who was the best player that you have played against and why?**
    So many to choose from. Nobody liked me, so all were favourites to play against. Cardiff were always a strong outfit, but I must mention Tony Hand. Very quiet person but has done lots for the sport. I think he holds the record over his career for scoring the most professional points on the ice!

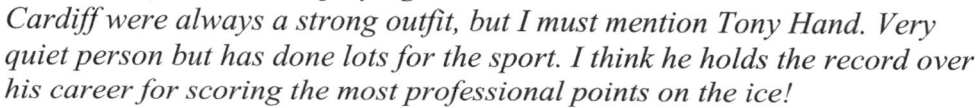

16. **Which rink was your favourite to play in and why?**
    Nottingham's old rink, the fans were always on top of you. Cardiff's old rink was similar. With Bracknell and Belfast you always knew the fans were there.

17. **Out of all the teams that you have played with which team had the best fans and why?**
    Being in the UK the fans were always friendly, intimidating and passionate with their sports and you could sense it be it 200 or 2000 fans in the rinks. Everyone hated me and I always knew when someone had something to say. My heart will always lie with both Bracknell and Belfast. I have a connection with the fans and made friends with a lot of them,

18. **How would you rate the standard of ice hockey in the UK when comparing to North America?**
    When I first arrived I didn't give it the merit it deserved. It's a standard that is improving and producing higher end hockey these days. When I returned to play in a testimonial in 2013 I could see that the levels of interest were rising.

19. **Are you still involved with ice hockey?**
    I work with MCN Sports advising and mentoring kids on the ice. I also get involved with my son, Xander who is now playing hockey.

20. **What was your favourite moment in ice hockey**
    I cant remember a specific- memory, although being called up to the NHL is high on anyone's list. It's what you strive for as a kid. A bittersweet moment was receiving recognition as my jersey was raised in Belfast.

Todd Bidner

Todd Bidner (Photo by Francis Page)

Todd Bidner played 12 games in the NHL for the Washington Capitals in the 1981/82 season as part of a North American pro hockey career that saw him notch up some 470 games from 1978 to 1985 around the various minor leagues.

He joined Fife Flyers in the 1985/86 season and, while a lot of former pro players might be thought of as "one season wonders" looking for an easy payday on these shores, the same could not be said of Bidner.

After a reasonable season with the Flyers where he scored 111 goals and 83 assists in 52 league cup and playoff games, helping the team to a Wembley semi final, he moved to Peterborough where he spent the next four seasons spearheading their promotion back out of HBL Division 1 and bringing Premier Division stability to the Pirates team.

This was all part of an incredible 13 season stint in British ice hockey that saw Bidner play for Telford Tigers, Nottingham Panthers, Bracknell Bees, Humberside Seahawks, Sheffield Steelers, Teeside Bombers, Durham Wasps, Guildford Flames and Blackburn Hawks where he accumulated an impressive total of 497 competitive appearances (which doesn't included pre-season games challenge matches, for which you could easily add another 3 or 4 per season – say 40 or 50 in all...), during which he scored 754 goals and 777 assists with 1508 PIMS.

Bidner also qualified to play for the GB national team and played 4 Olympic qualifying games in the 1993/94 season, scoring 1 goal and 1 assist.

Chic Cottrell played with Bidner on the Fife Flyers team in 1985/6 and against him numerous times after that. He said of the player:

"He was a really strong skater with an eye for goals and was always a difficult guy to play against. For such a tall player he kept a low skating profile that it made it very difficult to knock him off the puck."

"One of his main strengths was an amazing burst of speed from a standing start and he also had good peripheral vision, which allowed him to make smart plays." "I never saw Bids angry and he loved to play. All in all, Todd was a great guy and asset to any team."

Todds Stats

S	TEAM	LEAGUE	GP	G	A	TP	PIM	+/-	POST	GP	G	A	TP	PIM	+/-
1978-79	Toronto Marlboros	OMJHL	64	10	12	22	64	-							
1979-80	Toronto Marlboros	OMJHL	68	22	26	48	69	-							
1980-81	Toronto Marlboros	OHL	67	34	43	77	124	-							
	Hershey Bears	AHL	1	0	0	0	0	-							
1981-82	Washington Capitals	NHL	12	2	1	3	7	-							
	Hershey Bears	AHL	30	6	12	18	28	-							
	Wichita Wind	CHL	15	2	9	11	17	-	Playoffs	7	1	2	3	9	-
1982-83	Moncton Alpines	AHL	59	15	12	27	64	-							
1983-84	Moncton Alpines	AHL	60	17	16	33	75	-							
1984-85	Nova Scotia Oilers	AHL	4	2	2	4	4	-							
	Adirondack Red Wings	AHL	74	22	35	57	61	-							
1985-86	Fife Flyers	BHL	31	71	52	123	116	-	Playoffs	5	7	10	17	10	-
1986-87	Peterborough Pirates	BD1	29	79	112	191	95	-							
1987-88	Peterborough Pirates	BHL	30	50	52	102	86	-	Relegation	2	4	7	11	0	-
1988-89	Peterborough Pirates "A"	BHL	33	76	67	143	70	-							
1989-90	Peterborough Pirates	BHL	13	21	17	38	16	-							
	Telford Tigers	BD1	13	23	42	65	32	-							
1990-91	Telford Tigers	BD1	16	25	24	49	42	-							
	Nottingham Panthers	BHL	20	20	28	48	67	-	Playoffs	6	4	4	8	10	-
1991-92	Bracknell Bees "A"	BHL	19	20	20	40	70	-							
	Humberside Seahawks	BHL	17	21	21	42	50	-	Playoffs	4	4	3	7	12	-
1992-93	Humberside Seahawks	BHL	13	15	18	33	26	-							
	Telford Tigers	BD1	15	22	26	48	92	-							
	Sheffield Steelers	BD1	0	0	0	0	0	-	Qualification	6	7	11	18	10	-
	Teeside Bombers	BHL	36	49	31	80	108	-	Relegation	6	10	7	17	6	-
1993-94	Teeside Bombers	BHL	36	49	31	80	108	-	Relegation	6	10	7	17	6	-
	Great Britain	OGQ	4	1	1	2	-	-							
1994-95	Durham Wasps	BHL	30	30	27	57	141	-	Playoffs	5	3	2	5	4	-
1995-96	Durham Wasps	BHL	21	9	12	21	72	-	Playoffs	1	0	0	0	0	-
	Humberside Hawks	BHL	4	4	4	8	4	-							
1996-97	Guildford Flames	EPIHL	5	2	3	5	2	-							
	Blackburn Hawks	NPIHL	8	14	17	31	6	-	Playoffs	10	9	17	26	22	-
1997-98	Amarillo Rattlers	WPHL	6	1	2	3	7	-2							
1999-00	Peterborough Pirates	BNL	0	0	0	0	0	-	Playoffs	5	2	1	3	39	-
2001-02	Petrolia Squires	OHA Sr.	14	6	5	11	6	-							

S	TEAM	LEAGUE	GP	G	A	TP	PIM	+/-	POST	GP	G	A	TP	PIM	+/-
1985-86	Fife Flyers	Autumn Cup	8	18	10	28	22	-							
	Fife Flyers	Scottish Cup	8	21	11	32	-	-							
1986-87	Peterborough Pirates	Autumn Cup	8	21	18	39	30	-							
1987-88	Peterborough Pirates	Autumn Cup	7	13	16	29	28	-							
1988-89	Peterborough Pirates	Autumn Cup	10	24	29	53	10	-							
1989-90	Peterborough Pirates	Autumn Cup	7	11	8	19	8	-							
1990-91	Telford Tigers	Autumn Cup	8	13	13	26	12	-							
1991-92	Bracknell Bees	Autumn Cup	8	10	10	20	10	-							
1992-93	Humberside Seahawks	Autumn Cup	6	7	6	13	47	-							
1994-95	Teeside Bombers	Autumn Cup	8	7	7	14	57	-							
1995-96	Humberside Hawks	Autumn Cup	10	8	10	18	56	-							
1996-97	Guildford Flames	Autumn Cup	6	0	4	4	20	-							

TEAM STAFF HISTORY

S	TEAM	LEAGUE	ROLE ON TEAM	NOTES
1991-92	Bracknell Bees	BHL	Player-Coach	
2006-07	London Knights	OHL	Asst. Coach	
2010-11	Lambton Shores Predators	GOJHL	Head Coach	
2011-12	Fayetteville FireAntz	SPHL	Head Coach	Replaces Sean Gillam midseason

Al Sims

By the time of his arrival in Scotland to play for the Fife Flyers in 1986, Al Sims had enjoyed an impressive NHL career of over 500 regular season and playoff games over a 10 year period from 1973 to 1983 where had played for Boston Bruins, Hartford Whalers and Los Angeles Kings.

After 2 seasons playing in Germany, the big defenceman spent two seasons at Kirkcaldy, during which he played in 92 league, cup and play off matches, scoring 122 goals and 183 assists with 305 PIM.

After giving up playing – after a season in the IHL with Fort Wayne Comets - Sims moved into coaching and was constantly involved with pro hockey from 1988 to 2016 – including spells in the NHL with the Mighty Ducks of Anaheim as assistant coach and San Jose Sharks, where he was Head Coach for the 1996/97 season.
Chic Cottrell said of Sims:

"Outstanding defence man with a wealth of talent and experience. Deceptively fast for a big guy and exceptional skating talent that allowed him to quickly turn defence in to attack. Al also possessed a wicked accurate slapshot that he could let go really quickly. Many of his shots were one timers and very rarely missed the target. Al was also a master of timing his checks. He had the ability to take away their passing options then dispossess them and change defence into attack All in all a complete player who played hard and added an immense amount of experience to the team I'm sure further into his career he ended up coaching San Jose Sharks

PS You were quite right about Al Sims. He had 3 seasons as asst coach at Anaheim Ducks and then 1 as head coach at San Jose.

Al's Stats

S	TEAM	LEAGUE	GP	G	A	TP	PIM	+/-	POST	GP	G	A	TP	PIM	+/-
1971-72	Cornwall Royals	QMJHL	58	6	24	30	65	-	Playoffs	16	2	9	11	15	-
1972-73	Cornwall Royals "A"	QMJHL	62	13	62	75	54	-	Playoffs	12	2	5	7	8	-
1973-74	Boston Bruins	NHL	76	3	9	12	22	64	Playoffs	16	0	0	0	12	-
1974-75	Boston Bruins	NHL	75	4	8	12	73	29							
1975-76	Boston Bruins	NHL	48	4	3	7	43	6	Playoffs	1	0	0	0	0	-
	Rochester Americans	AHL	21	4	5	9	12	-	Playoffs	7	1	4	5	11	-
1976-77	Boston Bruins	NHL	1	0	0	0	0	1	Playoffs	2	0	0	0	0	-
	Rochester Americans	AHL	80	10	32	42	42	-	Playoffs	12	2	9	11	12	-
1977-78	Boston Bruins	NHL	43	2	8	10	6	11	Playoffs	8	0	0	0	0	-
	Rochester Americans	AHL	31	6	13	19	12	-							
1978-79	Boston Bruins	NHL	67	9	20	29	28	22	Playoffs	11	0	2	2	0	-
	Rochester Americans	AHL	3	0	1	1	4	-							
1979-80	Hartford Whalers	NHL	76	10	31	41	30	9	Playoffs	3	0	0	0	2	-
1980-81	Hartford Whalers	NHL	80	16	36	52	68	-20							
1981-82	Los Angeles Kings	NHL	8	1	1	2	16	-3							
	New Haven Nighthawks	AHL	51	4	27	31	53	-							
1982-83	Los Angeles Kings	NHL	1	0	0	0	0	0							
	New Haven Nighthawks	AHL	76	18	50	68	46	-	Playoffs	12	3	3	6	10	-
1984-85	Genève-Servette HC	NLB	-	-	-	-	-	-							
	EV Landshut	Germany	16	8	12	20	28	-	Playoffs	4	0	4	4	10	-
	New Haven Nighthawks	AHL	13	3	6	9	2	-							
1985-86	Berliner SC Preussen	Germany2	45	27	47	74	106	-							
1986-87	Fife Flyers	BHL	36	52	86	138	95	-	Playoffs	5	6	11	17	0	-
1987-88	Fife Flyers	BHL	30	33	42	75	51	-	Playoffs	6	5	11	16	2	-
1988-89	Fort Wayne Komets	IHL	61	7	30	37	32	-	Playoffs	6	2	2	4	2	-

S	TEAM	LEAGUE	GP	G	A	TP	PIM	+/-	POST	GP	G	A	TP	PIM	+/-
1971-72	Cornwall Royals	M-Cup	3	0	0	0	2	-							
1986-87	Fife Flyers	Autumn Cup	9	16	24	40	34	-							
1987-88	Fife Flyers	Autumn Cup	6	10	9	19	14	-							

TEAM STAFF HISTORY

S	TEAM	LEAGUE	ROLE ON TEAM	NOTES
1988-89	Fort Wayne Komets	IHL	Player-Asst. Coach	
1989-90	Fort Wayne Komets	IHL	GM/Head Coach	
1990-91	Fort Wayne Komets	IHL	GM/Head Coach	
1991-92	Fort Wayne Komets	IHL	GM/Head Coach	
1992-93	Fort Wayne Komets	IHL	GM/Head Coach	
1993-94	Mighty Ducks of Anaheim	NHL	Asst. Coach	
1994-95	Mighty Ducks of Anaheim	NHL	Asst. Coach	
1995-96	Mighty Ducks of Anaheim	NHL	Asst. Coach	
1996-97	San Jose Sharks	NHL	Head Coach	

Mark Pavelich

Mark Pavelich is worthy of note as he was the first player to come and play in the UK direct from having played in the NHL.

Mark Thomas Pavelich was born on February 28, 1958 and died on March 4, 2021. He was an American professional ice hockey forward who played 355 regular season games in the National Hockey League (NHL) for the New York Rangers, Minnesota North Stars, and San Jose Sharks between 1981 and 1991. Pavelich was a member of the 1980 U.S. Olympic hockey team that won the gold medal in what has been called the "Miracle on Ice".

The son of Croatian immigrants, Pavelich grew up in rural Eveleth, Minnesota. He was a star performer on his high school hockey team, Eveleth High School. He attended the University of Minnesota Duluth as an amateur player for three seasons from 1977–1979. Pavelich is best known for being a member of the 1980 U.S. Olympic hockey team that won the gold medal in Lake Placid. In the game against the Soviet Union, Pavelich was credited with two assists, including one on Mike Eruzione's game-winning goal.

He had been a member of the US national side that had won the Olympic gold medal in the famous 1980 "Miracle On Ice" at Lake Placid and went on to play 363 league and play off games for the New York Rangers in the NHL between 1981 and 1986.

Apparently he had fallen out with the new Rangers coach and, with him insisting that he did not want to play in the NHK for the 1986/87 season, Dundee supremo Tim Stewart persuaded the player to sign for the Rockets in the Heineken League Premier Division.

He played 2 games in the Autumn Cup for Dundee – a 6-4 defeat away at Ayr on 14th September in which he scored two assists and then a 1-9 win away to Glasgow Eagles on 20th September 1986, where he scored 4 goals, with Stewart describing him as "the finest skater I have ever seen."

Unfortunately, the New York Rangers claimed they had an option clause on Pavelich under his pro contract and that he was not allowed to play for anybody else without their permission. They complained to the NHL who complained to the IIHF and the international governing body slapped a worldwide ban on Pavelich playing anywhere until the issue was resolved.

The player returned to New York to try and negotiate a release from his contract so that he could play for Dundee but that happy outcome never materialised. What did happen was that the Rockets' win away at Glasgow was overturned for their use of an "ineligible player" and was awarded 5-0 to the Eagles, with Pavelich's 4 goals being wiped from the records.

Mark Pavelich never did get to play for Dundee again – and he never played again for the New York Rangers either. Apparently, after he didn't get his way, he went AWOL for a while, hunting in the wilds of Minnesota. He ended up playing 12 games in the NHL for the Minnesota North Stars later in the 86/87 season and then played for two years in Italy.

Peterborough Pirates' trio of ex NHLers for the 1987/88 season - Todd Bidner, Jim McTaggart and Garry Unger. (Photo by Francis Page / facebook.com/Peterborough Pirates Archive)

Jim McTaggart may only have been a "one season wonder" in terms of his involvement with UK ice hockey, but his arrival at Peterborough part way through the

1987/88 season to play alongside fellow imports Todd Bidner and Garry Unger meant that the Pirates were the first British League outfit to have three former NHL players on their team at the same time.

McTaggart had played 71 games for the Washington Capitals in the NHL between 1980 and 1982 and had been on the same "Caps" team as Todd Bidner in the 1981/82 season.

In fact, Bidner, Unger and McTaggart had all played together for the Moncton Alpines in the AHL for the 1982/83 season, so it is not hard to see how the karate black belt defenceman came to be enticed out of retirement – where he was running a restaurant – to come and play for the Pirates in the Heineken League.

McTaggart's arrival at the East of England Ice Rink brought a level of consistency to the Pirates team that had been lacking since the club's controversial decision to dispense with the services of Doug McEwen after the previous season's promotion from HBL Division 1, and which had led to the proverbial "revolving door" of unsuitable import replacements.

Despite having three ex NHLers on the team, the Pirates finished bottom of the league that season and had to take on Telford Tigers in the two-legged relegation play off. They won by the skin of their collective teeth with Garry Unger scoring the decisive goal with just 72 seconds left to play in what was to be his – and McTaggart's his last ever pro game.

Pavelich married Sue Koski on September 11, 1985. The couple had one daughter, Tarja, in 1987 and divorced in 1989. He married Kara Burmachuk in 1994, and they had no children.

When Pavelich was 18, he accidentally killed his 15-year-old friend Ricky Holgers in a hunting accident. His second wife Kara died at age 44 in an accidental fall from a second-story balcony at their Lutsen, Minnesota home on September 6, 2012.

In April 2014, Pavelich put his Olympic medal up for auction, with bidding beginning at $62,500. The medal sold in May 2014 for $262,900 through Dallas-based auction house Heritage Auctions.

The NHL in the UK

Health and legal issues

Pavelich was arrested on August 15, 2019 for assaulting a neighbour with whom he had earlier been fishing, after he believed the neighbour had put something into his beer. He was charged with four felony counts: second and third-degree assault, possession of a short-barrelled shotgun, and possession of a firearm with a missing or altered serial number. Pavelich was ruled incompetent to stand trial and was ordered committed to a secure treatment facility. In August 2020, Pavelich was granted court approval for transfer to a lower-security setting for treatment. Pavelich's sister, Jean Gevik, stated that she believed he was suffering from chronic traumatic encephalopathy (CTE), and had noticed behavioural changes in the years leading up to the incident which led to his arrest.

Pavelich died on March 3, 2021 at a residential treatment centre in Sauk Centre, Minnesota. His death was ruled a suicide by asphyxiation.

Mark's Stats

S	TEAM	LEAGUE	GP	G	A	TP	PIM	+/-	POST	GP	G	A	TP	PIM	+/-
1974-75	Eveleth-Gilbert High	USHS-MN	-	-	-	-	-	-							
1975-76	Eveleth-Gilbert High	USHS-MN	-	-	-	-	-	-							
1976-77	Univ. of Minnesota-Duluth	NCAA	37	12	7	19	8	-							
1977-78	Univ. of Minnesota-Duluth	NCAA	36	14	30	44	44	-							
1978-79	Univ. of Minnesota-Duluth	NCAA	37	31	48	79	52	-							
1979-80	Team USA	International	53	15	30	45	12	-							
	USA	OG	7	1	6	7	2	-							
1980-81	HC Lugano	NLB	28	24	25	49	-	-							
	USA	WC	8	2	3	5	4	-							
1981-82	New York Rangers	NHL	79	33	43	76	67	21	Playoffs	6	1	5	6	0	-
1982-83	New York Rangers	NHL	78	37	38	75	52	20	Playoffs	9	4	5	9	12	-
1983-84	New York Rangers	NHL	77	29	53	82	96	11	Playoffs	5	2	4	6	0	-
1984-85	New York Rangers	NHL	48	14	31	45	29	1	Playoffs	3	0	3	3	2	-
1985-86	New York Rangers	NHL	59	20	20	40	82	-3							
1986-87	Minnesota North Stars	NHL	12	4	6	10	10	7							
1987-88	HC Bolzano	Italy	36	31	42	73	19	-							
	Zürcher SC	NLB	2	1	2	3	2	-	Playoffs	3	3	0	3	10	-
1988-89	HC Bolzano	Italy	44	23	34	57	42	-							
1989-90	Did not play														
1990-91	Did not play														
1991-92	San Jose Sharks	NHL	2	0	1	1	4	-2							
S	TEAM	LEAGUE	GP	G	A	TP	PIM	+/-	POST	GP	G	A	TP	PIM	+/-
1980-81	HC Davos Loan	Spengler Cup	-	-	-	-	-	-							
1986-87	Dundee Rockets	Autumn Cup	1	0	2	2	0	-							

Jere Gillis

Jere Alan Gillis was born on January 18, 1957 and is an American-born Canadian former professional ice hockey player, actor and stuntman.

Gillis was born in Bend, Oregon and raised in Montreal, the son of skier Gene Gillis (a member of the American alpine skiing team for the 1948 Winter Olympics), and Rhona Wurtele, a Canadian Olympic skier who competed at the 1948 Winter Olympics. His sister Margie Gillis is a dancer and choreographer, and member of the Order of Canada. His older brother Christopher Gillis was also an important dancer and choreographer, and a member of the Paul Taylor Dance Company.

As a youth, Gillis played in the 1970 Quebec International Pee-Wee Hockey Tournament with a minor ice hockey team from Mount Royal, Quebec. Drafted fourth overall in the 1977 NHL amateur draft by the Vancouver Canucks, Gillis played in the National Hockey League (NHL) from 1977 to 1987 for the Canucks, New York Rangers, Quebec Nordiques, Buffalo Sabres and Philadelphia Flyers. From 1988 to 1991, he played in the United Kingdom for Solihull Barons and Peterborough Pirates, finally playing five games in the Quebec Senior Provincial Hockey League in 1996–97.

Jere Gillis NHL collectors card (Dimanche / Derniere Heure, 1977/78)

Jere Gillis had played 405 NHL games for Vancouver Canucks (6 seasons), New York Rangers, Quebec Nordiques, Buffalo Sabres, and Philadelphia Flyers over a 10 year period between 1977 and 1987 and was also a veteran of over 500 minor league games in the QMJHL and AHL by the time he was tempted out of retirement midway the 1988/89 season to resolve the unsettled import merry go round at Solihull Barons in 1988.

He scored an incredible 46 goals and 47 assists in just 18 league games with the Barons but his arrival was too late to salvage the season and Solihull finished in 8th place in the Premier Division table, outside the play off places.

Gillis returned to Solihull for the 89/90 season and with a bit of stability, the team fared much better. He scored 60 goals and 60 assists in 42 league, autumn cup and play off matches and was the Barons' top scorer by some distance - and he even managed to take two weeks off to be a stuntman in James Bond film.

The team finished 4th in the league and made the play offs – although they didn't manage to get to the Wembley finals weekend - but it was certainly a much better season all round.

Gillis took a coaching job at Telford Tigers in Division 1 the following year and played 4 games for them in the Autumn Cup while they resolved import issues player ahead of the regular season. But he was back in Premier Division action shortly after that when Rocky Saganiuk brought him in for 6 games at Peterborough Pirates to cover for the injured Trent Kaese. He scored 13 + 4 and actually finished as the seventh-highest scorer for Peterborough despite having played considerably fewer games than everyone else had.

The game still called to him, though, as Gillis remained in Britain to take a coaching job with the BHL's Telford Tigers in the top division. He had a great run in Telford that season, coaching the team to 4th place in HBL1.

Upon retiring from ice hockey he became a stuntman in movies as well as a Scientologist.

Jere Gillis (in white) in action for Solihull Barons in the 1988/89 Heineken League season. (Photo by Francis Page / facebook.com/Peterborough Pirates Archive)

Jere's Stats

S	TEAM	LEAGUE	GP	G	A	TP	PIM	+/-	POST	GP	G	A	TP	PIM	+/-
1973-74	Sherbrooke Castors	QMJHL	69	20	19	39	96	-	Playoffs	5	1	2	3	0	-
1974-75	Sherbrooke Castors	QMJHL	54	38	57	95	91	-	Playoffs	9	5	3	8	2	-
1975-76	Sherbrooke Castors	QMJHL	60	47	55	102	40	-	Playoffs	17	8	14	22	27	-
	Canada U20	WJC-20	4	1	2	3	2	-							
1976-77	Sherbrooke Castors "C"	QMJHL	72	55	85	140	80	-	Playoffs	18	11	12	23	40	-
1977-78	Vancouver Canucks	NHL	79	23	18	41	35	-24							
1978-79	Vancouver Canucks	NHL	78	13	12	25	33	-31	Playoffs	1	0	1	1	0	-
1979-80	Vancouver Canucks	NHL	67	13	17	30	108	0							
1980-81	Vancouver Canucks	NHL	11	0	4	4	4	0							
	New York Rangers	NHL	35	10	10	20	4	6	Playoffs	14	2	5	7	9	-
1981-82	New York Rangers	NHL	26	3	9	12	16	-2							
	Québec Nordiques	NHL	12	2	1	3	0	2							
	Fredericton Express	AHL	28	2	17	19	10	-							
1982-83	Buffalo Sabres	NHL	3	0	0	0	0	-6							
	Rochester Americans	AHL	53	18	24	42	69	-	Playoffs	16	1	7	8	11	-
1983-84	Vancouver Canucks	NHL	37	9	13	22	7	2	Playoffs	4	2	1	3	0	-
	Fredericton Express	AHL	36	22	28	50	35	-							

S	TEAM	LEAGUE	GP	G	A	TP	PIM	+/-	POST	GP	G	A	TP	PIM	+/-
1984-85	Vancouver Canucks	NHL	37	5	11	16	23	-7							
	Fredericton Express	AHL	7	2	1	3	2	-							
1985-86	Fredericton Express	AHL	29	4	14	18	21	-							
1986-87	Philadelphia Flyers	NHL	1	0	0	0	0	0							
	Hershey Bears	AHL	47	13	22	35	32	-	Playoffs	5	0	0	0	9	
	HC Sierre	NLA	3	2	3	5	0	-							
1987-88	Bruneck/Brunico	Italy	24	20	16	36	10	-							
1988-89	Solihull Barons	BHL	18	46	47	93	12	-							
1989-90	Solihull Barons "C"	BHL	30	50	35	85	16	-	Playoffs	4	2	4	6	6	
1990-91	Peterborough Pirates	BHL	6	13	4	17	22	-							
1996-97	Acton Vale Nova	QSPHL	5	0	3	3	2	-							

S	TEAM	LEAGUE	GP	G	A	TP	PIM	+/-	POST	GP	G	A	TP	PIM	+/-
1969-70	Mont-Royal Peewee	QC Int PW	-	-	-	-	-	-							
1976-77	QMJHL All-Stars	CHL Challenge	6	3	3	6	2	-							
	Sherbrooke Castors	M-Cup	4	4	1	5	0	-							
1989-90	Solihull Barons	Autumn Cup	8	8	21	29	12	-							
1990-91	Telford Tigers	Autumn Cup	4	3	1	4	0	-							

TEAM STAFF HISTORY

S	TEAM	LEAGUE	ROLE ON TEAM	NOTES
1990-91	Telford Tigers	BD1	Head Coach	
1991-92	Telford Tigers	BD1	Head Coach	

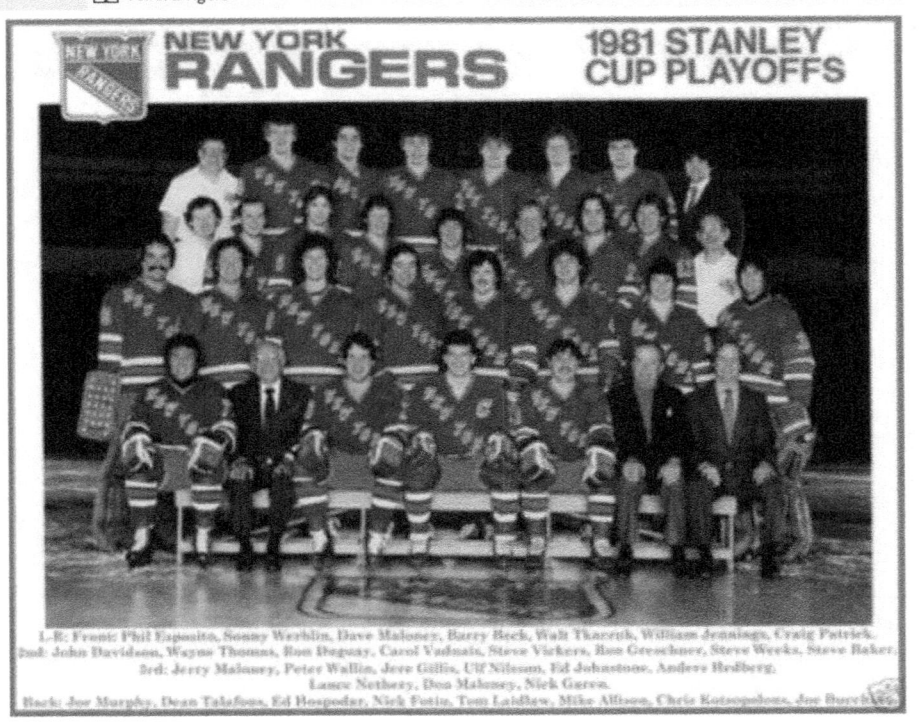

Doug Smail

Douglas Dean Smail was born on 2 September 1957 and is a Canadian former professional ice hockey left winger who played in the National Hockey League (NHL) for 13 seasons from 1980 through 1993.

Smail starred at the University of North Dakota for three seasons from 1977 to 1980, scoring 87 points in 40 games in his final season in the WCHA. His performance was enough to warrant notice from the Winnipeg Jets, and the next season he was a full-time NHL player.

Smail played eleven seasons with Winnipeg, being a top two-way player for them, as he had twelve consecutive seasons in which he scored at least one shorthanded goal, with a total of 28 shorthanded goals in his career.

Perhaps Smail's greatest claim to fame was when he tied the NHL record for fastest goal after the opening faceoff by scoring a goal five seconds after the game started on 20 December 1981. Smail finished his career with the Minnesota North Stars, Quebec Nordiques and Ottawa Senators, but never achieved the success he had in Winnipeg.

After Smail's NHL career was over, he played three seasons in Britain for the Fife Flyers and Cardiff Devils before retiring. He was the first player ever to sign for a British team directly from an NHL team when he signed with Fife from the Senators.

Following on from the Mark Pavelich debacle a few years earlier, Doug Smail became the first player to come to British ice hockey straight from an NHL club when he joined Fife Flyers for the 1993/94 season

Smail had played 887 NHL games in regular season and play offs over a 13 years career with, mainly, Winnipeg Jets (10 seasons) and then a season each at Minnesota North Stars, Quebec Nordiques and Ottawa Senators between 1980 and 1993.

The Fife team had former New York Ranger Mark Morrison as player coach and it turned out to be their best season for years, with the Flyers finishing second in the Heineken League Premier Division – a rather distant 22 points behind champions Cardiff Devils, – and reaching the Wembley playoff semi-finals where they crashed out to Cardiff as well.

Smail scored 74 goals and 95 assists with 114 PIM in 53 league, cup and playoff games for Fife in his only full season there. He had planned to retire at the end the season but was lured back by Cardiff who needed to strengthen their roster for their European Cup semi-final series in Belarus.

He played 3 HBL league games as a warm up for the Devils and then went back to Canada after the European games.

However, Doug was lured out of retirement again by the Flyers and he played 15 league games for them, helping them to 6th place in the final table and a place in the play offs, although they failed to qualify for the Wembley weekend.

Another stint at Cardiff followed after he was called up in January to give the struggling team a bit of extra oomph. He played 15 games for the Devils that season helping them to an unlikely runners up spot in the league table, although they failed to qualify for the Wembley play off weekend and Smail's pro hockey career really did end at that point.

He now resides in Colorado with his wife and three children. Smail was the assistant coach of the U-16 Team Rocky Mountain AAA Hockey program, where he coached alongside former NHL player Rick Berry, and is now the head coach of the Rocky Mountain Roughriders U-18 AAA squad.

Doug's Stats

S	TEAM	LEAGUE	GP	G	A	TP	PIM	+/-	POST	GP	G	A	TP	PIM	+/-
1975-76	Moose Jaw Canucks	SJHL	54	50	44	94	87	-							
1976-77	Moose Jaw Canucks	SJHL	57	60	56	116	-	-							
1977-78	Univ. of North Dakota	NCAA	38	22	28	50	52	-							
1978-79	Univ. of North Dakota	NCAA	35	24	34	58	46	-							
1979-80	Univ. of North Dakota	NCAA	40	43	44	87	70	-							
1980-81	Winnipeg Jets	NHL	30	10	8	18	45	-7							
1981-82	Winnipeg Jets	NHL	72	17	18	35	55	-22	Playoffs	4	0	0	0	0	-
1982-83	Winnipeg Jets	NHL	80	15	29	44	32	0	Playoffs	3	0	0	0	6	-
1983-84	Winnipeg Jets	NHL	66	20	17	37	62	-5	Playoffs	3	0	1	1	7	-
1984-85	Winnipeg Jets	NHL	80	31	35	66	45	12	Playoffs	8	2	1	3	4	-
1985-86	Winnipeg Jets	NHL	73	16	26	42	32	-10	Playoffs	3	1	0	1	0	-
1986-87	Winnipeg Jets	NHL	78	25	18	43	36	18	Playoffs	10	4	0	4	10	-
1987-88	Winnipeg Jets	NHL	71	15	16	31	34	5	Playoffs	5	1	0	1	22	-1
1988-89	Winnipeg Jets	NHL	47	14	15	29	52	12							
1989-90	Winnipeg Jets	NHL	79	25	24	49	63	15	Playoffs	5	1	0	1	0	0
1990-91	Winnipeg Jets	NHL	15	1	2	3	10	-6							
	Minnesota North Stars	NHL	57	7	13	20	38	-2	Playoffs	1	0	0	0	0	-1
1991-92	Québec Nordiques	NHL	46	10	18	28	47	-11							
1992-93	Ottawa Senators	NHL	51	4	10	14	51	-34							
	San Diego Gulls	IHL	9	2	1	3	20	1	Playoffs	9	3	2	5	20	-2
1993-94	Fife Flyers	BHL	41	62	80	142	66	-	Playoffs	7	9	9	18	8	-
1994-95	Fife Flyers	BHL	15	20	9	29	26	-	Playoffs	6	5	9	14	12	-
	Cardiff Devils	BHL	3	2	5	7	2	-							
1995-96	Cardiff Devils	BHL	16	12	14	26	14	-	Playoffs	6	3	5	8	10	-

S	TEAM	LEAGUE	GP	G	A	TP	PIM	+/-	POST	GP	G	A	TP	PIM	+/-
1993-94	Fife Flyers	Autumn Cup	5	3	6	9	40	-							

TEAM STAFF HISTORY

S	TEAM	LEAGUE	ROLE ON TEAM	NOTES
2018-19	Rocky Mountain Roughriders 18U	NAPHL 18U	Head Coach	
2019-20	Rocky Mountain Roughriders 18U	18U AAA	Head Coach	
2020-21	Rocky Mountain Roughriders 18U	18U AAA	Head Coach	
	Hyland Hills Jaguars 16U AA	CCYHL 16U	Asst. Coach	
2021-22	Rocky Mountain Roughriders 18U	T1EHL 18U	Head Coach	
2022-23	Rocky Mountain Roughriders 18U	18U AAA	Head Coach	

Mike Ware

Michael Ware (born March 22, 1967 in York, Ontario) is a Canadian former professional ice hockey player who played for the Edmonton Oilers, as well as in Europe, where he was primarily an enforcer.

Ware began his major junior career with the Hamilton Steelhawks of the OHL in 1984, having been drafted 26th overall in the 1984 OHL priority selection. At the end of his rookie season with the Steelhawks, he was selected by the Edmonton Oilers, 62nd overall in the 1985 NHL Entry Draft. He played a second season in Hamilton, before moving to the Cornwall Royals. Following his season in Eastern Ontario he turned professional.

Ware signed with the Oilers AHL affiliate Nova Scotia Oilers where he registered 253 PIM and 8 points as a rookie during the 1987-88 season. The farm team would relocate within the province, and become the Cape Breton Oilers. Ware remained the with team, but also played two games in the NHL, making his debut in January 1989 in a game against the Los Angeles Kings, where early in his first (and only) shift of the night, he fought Jay Miller. In his next game against the Vancouver Canucks, Ware would register what would be his only point in the NHL, an assist on a Miroslav Fryčer goal. Whilst playing for the affiliate team, his production increased, tallying 12 points and 317 PIM whilst in Cape Breton. The 1989-90 season would again see Ware primarily play in Cape Breton, whilst also playing 3 games in NHL. Ware would return to Nova Scotia for the 1990-91 season, registering 12 points and 176 PIM in 43 games. During his time in Cape Breton, Ware received a 20 game suspension for breaking his stick over the glass, and subsequently throwing it at a referee.

For the 1991-92 season, Ware moved to the U.K. in order to play for the Murrayfield Racers of the British Hockey League. In Edinburgh he would have a stellar season, scoring 60 points in 33 games, whilst also accruing 218 PIM. The team would finish 2nd in the league, before being beaten 9-0 in the playoff semi-finals to eventual champions the Cardiff Devils. Ware would return to the Racers for the following season, again increasing his scoring output, with 71 points in 43 games; the team would finish mid-table and wouldn't make it out the group stages during the playoffs. The team would change its name to the Edinburgh Racers for the 1994-95 season, which would see Ware have a career year, with 79 points in 40 games, and would also see the Racers make it to the playoff final, ultimately losing to the Sheffield Steelers. The following season, Ware would remain in the BHL, but would move to the Cardiff Devils, beginning his association with the club. The Devils would have a strong season, finishing 2nd in the league, however, would crash out in the group stages of the playoffs.

Following the culmination of the 1995-96 season, the BHL would fold, and the BISL would take its place as the top-tier of hockey in the U.K, of which Cardiff were a founding member. Ware remained with the team and was named captain. In the maiden BISL season, The Devils were named league champions, however they lost in the play semi-finals to eventual winners Sheffield Steelers. Ware would subsequently join the Steelers in the off-season, however, the team would struggle, thanks in no small part to the Ayr Scottish Eagles completing the British Grand Slam. For the 1998-99 season, Ware would move to Germany, to play for DEL side Hannover Scorpions. There, Ware managed only 6 points in 44 games, whilst registering 103 PIM. Ware returned the U.K. the following season, signing for the London Knights. With the Knights, Ware totalled 8 points and 90 PIM in 26 games, as the Knights would be crowned British champions after beating the Newcastle Riverkings 7-3 in the playoff final.

Ware returned to the Devils for the 2000-01 season, where he registered 10 points and 155 PIM in 40 games. The team would perform well, finishing 2nd in the league, however, they wouldn't make it passed the group stages in the playoffs. However, at the end of the season the Cardiff Devils went into voluntary liquidation, and as a result were stripped of their BISL franchise. The team would eventually reform and participate in the British National League, which was at the time the second tier of Ice Hockey in the UK. As a result, Ware moved back to the London Knights for the following season, linking up with former Devils teammates Ian MacIntyre, Kim Ahlroos, Steve Thornton and Vezio Sacratini. The team would struggle, finishing 6th out of 7 teams, with Ware producing only 6 points and 33 PIM in 35 games.

The Terminator, as he was known to fans, returned to the Welsh capital for the third time and was named team captain for the 2002-03 season. The Devils made it to the BNL finals, ultimately losing to the Coventry Blaze. Ware had a good season, tallying 32 points and 96 PIM in 30 games.

Following the culmination of the 2002-03 season, the London Knights, as well as the Manchester Storm and Ayr Scottish Eagles all folded, whilst the Bracknell Bees dropped down the BNL. This resulted in the demise of the BISL. Cardiff would be a founding member of the EIHL, which became the new top-tier of hockey in the U.K., and as such Ware remained with the team for the inaugural EIHL season where he remained as team captain. During the season, the Devils awarded Ware a testimonial game as a result of his service with the team, and popularity with the fans. The team would make it to the playoff semi-finals, before losing to the Sheffield Steelers, following which Ware retired from hockey.

Mike's Stats

S	TEAM	LEAGUE	GP	G	A	TP	PIM	+/-	POST	GP	G	A	TP	PIM	+/-
1983-84	Mississauga Reps U18 AAA	GTHL U18	30	14	20	34	50	-							
1984-85	Hamilton Steelhawks	OHL	57	4	14	18	225	-	Playoffs	12	0	1	1	29	-
1985-86	Hamilton Steelhawks	OHL	44	8	11	19	155	-							
1986-87	Cornwall Royals	OHL	50	5	19	24	173	-	Playoffs	5	0	1	1	10	-
1987-88	Nova Scotia Oilers	AHL	52	0	8	8	253	-	Playoffs	3	0	0	0	16	-
1988-89	Edmonton Oilers	NHL	2	0	1	1	11	1							
	Cape Breton Oilers	AHL	48	1	11	12	317	-							
1989-90	Edmonton Oilers	NHL	3	0	0	0	4	-1							
	Cape Breton Oilers	AHL	54	6	13	19	191	-	Playoffs	6	0	3	3	29	-
1990-91	Cape Breton Oilers	AHL	43	4	8	12	176	-	Playoffs	3	0	0	0	4	-
1992-93	Murrayfield Racers	BHL	33	26	34	60	218	-	Playoffs	7	10	7	17	24	-
1993-94	Murrayfield Racers	BHL	43	30	41	71	162	-	Playoffs	6	5	5	10	16	-
1994-95	Edinburgh Racers	BHL	40	38	41	79	218	-	Playoffs	6	8	6	14	6	-
1995-96	Cardiff Devils	BHL	32	16	30	46	169	-	Playoffs	6	0	1	1	37	-
1996-97	Cardiff Devils "C"	BISL	38	6	12	18	79	-	Playoffs	5	0	1	1	29	-
1997-98	Sheffield Steelers	BISL	43	6	8	14	96	-	Playoffs	9	2	0	2	4	-
1998-99	Hannover Scorpions	DEL	44	4	2	6	103	-6							
1999-00	London Knights	BISL	26	6	2	8	90	-	Playoffs	8	0	1	1	8	-
2000-01	Cardiff Devils	BISL	40	2	8	10	155	-	Playoffs	6	1	3	4	8	-
2001-02	London Knights	BISL	35	2	4	6	33	-							
2002-03	Cardiff Devils "C"	BNL	30	12	20	32	96	-	Playoffs	10	3	5	8	43	-
2003-04	Cardiff Devils "C"	EIHL	47	8	14	22	167	-	Playoffs	4	3	1	4	4	-

S	TEAM	LEAGUE	GP	G	A	TP	PIM	+/-
1993-94	Murrayfield Racers	Autumn Cup	11	7	4	11	50	-
1994-95	Edinburgh Racers	Autumn Cup	8	9	5	14	76	-
1995-96	Cardiff Devils	Autumn Cup	9	4	5	9	58	-
1996-97	Cardiff Devils	Autumn Cup	8	1	3	4	49	-
1997-98	Sheffield Steelers	Autumn Cup	11	0	3	3	10	-
1999-00	London Knights	Autumn Cup	9	1	1	2	64	-
2000-01	Cardiff Devils	Autumn Cup	6	0	1	1	40	-
2003-04	Cardiff Devils	EIHL Cup	2	0	0	0	8	-

Darren Banks

Darren Alexander Banks was born on March 18, 1966 and is a Canadian former professional ice hockey player. He played in 20 NHL games with the Boston Bruins between 1992 and 1994, as well as extensively in the minor leagues and briefly in Europe during a career that lasted from 1989 to 2005. During his career he played predominantly as an enforcer.

Banks began his collegiate career in 1986 with the Brock Badgers having previously played for the Leamington Flyers. Banks played for the Badgers for three seasons, with his most productive season coming in his final year, registering 33 points in 26 games, along with 88 PIM. During his time at Brock University, he majored in sociology.

Upon leaving university, Banks turned professional and signed with the Knoxville Cherokees of the ECHL for the 1989–90. In his first season as a pro, Banks would have his most productive season, registering 47 points in 52 games, whilst also accruing 258 minutes in the penalty box. His success in Tennessee would catch the attention of the NHL's Calgary Flames, who signed him to a contract at the end of the ECHL season. The Flames immediately sent him to their IHL affiliate team, the Salt Lake Golden Eagles, for whom he played 6 games. During the season, Banks also played 2 games for the Fort Wayne Komets, also of the IHL.

He returned to the Eagles for the 1990–91 season, playing exclusively for the team. He registered 16 points in 56 games, along with 286 PIM. The following season would again see Banks play exclusively for Salt Lake City, playing 55 games, tallying 10 points and 303 PIM. The off-season would see Banks sign as a free agent for the Boston Bruins in time for the 1992–93 season. Though he played primarily with Boston's farm team in Providence, Banks made his NHL debut on October 8, 1992 against the Hartford

Whalers. He made an impression on his debut; receiving a game misconduct penalty as a result of a fight with Scott Daniels in the 2nd period. Over the course of the season, Banks went on to play an additional 15 games with Boston, and dressed 46 times for Providence. Banks remained in the Bruins system the following season, playing for Boston 4 times, and Providence 41 times. During the season Banks suffered a separated shoulder, and upon returning from injury he played 2 games for Providence before separating his other shoulder; a situation which caused friction with Providence coach Mike O'Connell and culminated with Banks shooting a puck at O'Connell during practice. In the off-season O'Connell was promoted to Assistant General Manager of the Boston Bruins, resulting in Banks being released from the team.

Banks scored exactly two NHL goals. Both came in the same game, an 8-2 Boston road victory over the San Jose sharks on October 15, 1992.

The 1994–95 season would be a nomadic one for Banks, playing 32 games in the AHL for both the Adirondack Red Wings and Portland Pirates, as well as 2 games for IHL side Las Vegas Thunder under coach Chris McSorley, before finishing the season with the Detroit Falcons of the CoHL after joining the team in February 1995. Both Adirondack and the Falcons were farm teams of the Detroit Red Wings. The following season, Banks predominantly played for the Falcons, playing 38 games registering 28 points and 290 PIM. In addition, he played 6 games for the Utica Blizzard, also of the CoHL, before returning to the Las Vegas Thunder towards the end of the season. The 1996–97 season saw Banks play exclusively for the IHL's Detroit Vipers, where he scored 23 points in 64 games and also accrued a career-high 306 PIM. The Vipers had a strong season, finishing on top during the regular season, before being crowned Turner Cup champions by beating the Long Beach Ice Dogs in the playoff final.

Banks began the 1997–98 season with the Québec Rafales also of the IHL, after being traded along with Jeff Parrott by the Vipers in exchange for Stan

Drulia. He played 4 games in Quebec, before moving to the San Antonio Dragons. His stay in Texas was also short, playing 7 games, before returning to the Detroit Vipers with whom he finished the season. The Vipers had another extended playoff run, reaching the final which they ultimately lost to the Chicago Wolves. He returned to the Vipers for the 1998-99 season playing 58 games and scoring 18 points whilst registering 296 PIM.

He would travel overseas for the first time in his career to play for the London Knights of the BISL for the 1999–00 season, reuniting with McSorley. He played 23 games in the capital before courting controversy. In January 2000, following the completion of a game against the Ayr Scottish Eagles, Banks fought Eagles player Cam Bristow and assaulted a match official. As a result of his actions, Banks was suspended for 12 games and faced a £500 fine. However, prior to the resultant suspension and fine being announced, Banks had left the UK and signed for the Port Huron Border Cats of the UHL. In Michigan he played 17 games, registering 8 points and 12 PIM. The following year, Banks signed with the Knoxville Speed, also of the UHL. After 20 games with the Speed, he was traded back to Port Huron, for whom he played 4 games. In addition with his time in the UHL, Banks also played 8 games with WCHL side, Phoenix Mustangs.

Between 2001 and 2003 Banks did not play hockey, however, during the 2003-04 season he signed with the Jacksonville Barracudas of the WHA2, playing 7 games, scoring 3 points and registering 25 PIM. The following year, he played 2 games, with the Kansas City Outlaws of the UHL. Subsequently, Banks retired from professional hockey.

Roller hockey
In addition to his ice hockey career, Banks also played professional roller hockey, which took place in the ice hockey off-season. In the summer of 1995, Banks played for the Anaheim Bullfrogs of the Roller Hockey International league, and, despite initially being unable to stop in roller blades, scored 21 points in 17 games, along with 86 PIM. Banks returned to the Bullfrogs the following season, playing 9 games with the team, before

being traded to the Long Island Jawz in exchange for a sixth-round draft pick and future considerations in July 1996.

Darren's Stats

S	TEAM	LEAGUE	GP	G	A	TP	PIM	+/-	POST	GP	G	A	TP	PIM	+/-
1983-84	Leamington Flyers	GLJHL	5	1	3	4	18	-							
	Windsor Royals	WOHL	-	-	-	-	-	-							
1984-85	Windsor Royals	WOHL	-	-	-	-	-	-							
1986-87	Brock Univ.	CIAU	24	5	3	8	82	-							
1987-88	Brock Univ.	CIAU	26	10	11	21	110	-							
1988-89	Brock Univ.	CIAU	26	19	14	33	88	-							
1989-90	Salt Lake Golden Eagles	IHL	6	0	0	0	11	-							
	Fort Wayne Komets	IHL	2	0	1	1	0	-	Playoffs	1	0	0	0	10	-
	Knoxville Cherokees	ECHL	52	25	22	47	258	-							
1990-91	Salt Lake Golden Eagles	IHL	56	9	7	16	286	-	Playoffs	3	0	1	1	6	-
1991-92	Salt Lake Golden Eagles	IHL	55	5	5	10	303	-							
1992-93	Boston Bruins	NHL	16	2	1	3	64	5							
	Providence Bruins	AHL	43	9	5	14	199	-8	Playoffs	1	0	0	0	0	-
1993-94	Boston Bruins	NHL	4	0	1	1	9	0							
	Providence Bruins	AHL	41	6	3	9	189	-11							
1994-95	Adirondack Red Wings	AHL	20	3	2	5	65	-2							
	Portland Pirates	AHL	12	1	2	3	38	4							
	Las Vegas Thunder	IHL	2	0	0	0	19	-1							
	Detroit Falcons	CoHL	22	9	10	19	51	6	Playoffs	12	3	5	8	59	-3
1995-96	Detroit Falcons	CoHL	38	11	17	28	290	-11							
	Utica Blizzard	CoHL	6	1	2	3	22	0							
	Las Vegas Thunder	IHL	5	0	2	2	10	2	Playoffs	10	0	0	0	54	-1
1996-97	Detroit Vipers	IHL	64	10	13	23	306	16	Playoffs	20	4	5	9	40	4
1997-98	Québec Rafales	IHL	4	0	1	1	9	-2							
	San Antonio Dragons	IHL	7	0	0	0	6	-5							
	Detroit Vipers	IHL	59	16	14	30	175	6	Playoffs	21	2	3	5	97	-3
1998-99	Detroit Vipers	IHL	58	6	12	18	296	10	Playoffs	3	0	0	0	35	-1
1999-00	London Knights	BISL	23	8	2	10	101	-							
	Port Huron Border Cats	UHL	17	3	5	8	12	0							
2000-01	Knoxville Speed	UHL	20	4	7	11	50	-2							
	Port Huron Border Cats	UHL	4	0	0	0	4	1							
	Phoenix Mustangs	WCHL	8	0	1	1	36	-6							
2001-03	Did not play														
2003-04	Jacksonville Barracudas	WHA2	7	1	2	3	25	0							
2004-05	Kansas City Outlaws	UHL	2	0	0	0	2	-1							
S	TEAM	LEAGUE	GP	G	A	TP	PIM	+/-	POST	GP	G	A	TP	PIM	+/-
1999-00	London Knights	Autumn Cup	3	0	2	2	16	-							

Mike Blaisdell

Former NHL winger Mike Blaisdell was the most successful club coach of the 1990s and 2000s, winning 12 trophies at the top level with three different teams, and another three as a player on a fourth. The dozen include Sheffield Steelers' memorable Grand Slam of four titles in 2000-01.

A hard-nosed six-footer from the Canadian prairies, 'Blaiser' plugged his way through over 300 NHL games with Detroit Red Wings, New York Rangers, Pittsburgh Penguins and Toronto Maple Leafs, and toured Europe with Team Canada before coming to England in the middle of the 1990-91 season to join Durham Wasps.

During his two calendar years on the Paul Smith-coached side, he struck up a productive partnership with his fellow countryman Rick Brebant and the Wasps won the Heineken British League and Championships twice, and a Norwich Union Cup. "He has excellent vision," said Smith. "He settled straight into the first line and knew jut where he should be." But when Durham had a slow start to the 1992-93 campaign, club owner Tom Smith – father of the coach – was quick to fire him.

Nottingham Panthers gave him his first job as non-playing coach in 1993-94, a season so marred by financial crises that the Panthers were relieved when their new man got them through to the semi-finals of the British Championships. After recruiting Brebant and retaining the high scoring Paul Adey, Blaisdell guided Panthers to the Benson and Hedges Cup the following term and won his first Coach of the Year trophy.

Taking his full turn on the ice again during the 1995-96 season, he scored his age in goals, 35, and the Panthers went all the way to the Wembley final – only to succumb sickeningly after a penalty shootout against their deadly rivals Steelers, despite 'Blaiser' netting Nottingham's only successful shot.

The tumultuous Superleague era was his finest. The Panthers won two more B&H Cups and reached another Play-off final before Mike tired of the club's money woes and quit early in the 1999-2000 campaign. His four years at neighbouring Sheffield were a huge success as he signed the exciting young

Brit David Longstaff in 2000 and the team won eight trophies, overcoming some unsettling ownership changes.

He won his second Coach of the Year award for Steelers' Grand Slam and a third two years later for their league and cup double. In 2003-04 Sheffield won the first Elite League and the Play-offs, and took the arch enemy Panthers to overtime before bowing out of the Challenge Cup final. This was more than enough to earn the master motivator and shrewd judge of talent his fourth Coach of the Year title.

Michael Walter Blaisdell was born on 18 January 1960 in Moose Jaw, Saskatchewan, Canada. He was inducted into the Hall of Fame in 2004.

Mike's Stats

S	TEAM	LEAGUE	GP	G	A	TP	PIM	+/-	POST	GP	G	A	TP	PIM	+/-
1977-78	Regina Pat Blues	SJHL	60	70	46	116	43	-							
	Regina Pats	WCHL	6	5	5	10	2	-	Playoffs	13	4	7	11	0	-
1978-79	Univ. of Wisconsin	NCAA	23	7	2	9	19	-							
1979-80	Univ. of Wisconsin	NCAA	1	0	0	0	2	-							
	Regina Pats	WHL	63	71	38	109	62	-	Playoffs	18	16	9	25	26	-
1980-81	Detroit Red Wings	NHL	32	3	6	9	10	-							
	Adirondack Red Wings	AHL	41	10	4	14	8	-	Playoffs	12	2	2	4	5	-
1981-82	Detroit Red Wings	NHL	80	23	32	55	48	-							
1982-83	Detroit Red Wings	NHL	80	18	23	41	22	-							
1983-84	New York Rangers	NHL	36	5	6	11	31	0							
	Tulsa Oilers	CHL	32	10	8	18	23	-	Playoffs	9	6	6	12	6	-
1984-85	New York Rangers	NHL	12	1	0	1	11	-4							
	New Haven Nighthawks	AHL	64	21	23	44	41	-							
1985-86	Pittsburgh Penguins	NHL	66	15	14	29	36	-							
1986-87	Pittsburgh Penguins	NHL	10	1	1	2	2	-							
	Baltimore Skipjacks	AHL	43	12	12	24	47	-							
1987-88	Toronto Maple Leafs	NHL	18	3	2	5	2	-5	Playoffs	6	1	2	3	10	-
	Newmarket Saints	AHL	57	28	28	56	30	-							
1988-89	Toronto Maple Leafs	NHL	9	1	0	1	4	-5							
	Newmarket Saints	AHL	40	16	7	23	48	-							
1989-90	Schwenninger ERC	Germany	3	1	0	1	0	-							
	Team Canada	International	50	12	18	30	40	-							

S	TEAM	LEAGUE	GP	G	A	TP	PIM	+/-	POST	GP	G	A	TP	PIM	+/-
1990-91	Albany Choppers	IHL	6	2	0	2	0	-							
	Durham Wasps	BHL	18	36	35	71	114	-	Playoffs	8	24	14	38	18	-
	HC Sierre	NLA	5	4	0	4	6	-							
1991-92	Durham Wasps	BHL	36	74	52	126	86	-	Playoffs	8	11	13	24	22	-
1992-93	Durham Wasps	BHL	13	23	18	41	46	-							
1993-94	Did not play														
1994-95	Nottingham Panthers	BHL	11	7	10	17	60	-							
1995-96	Nottingham Panthers	BHL	33	26	33	59	77	-	Playoffs	8	1	6	7	4	-
1996-97	Nottingham Panthers	BISL	7	2	2	4	6	-							
1997-98	Did not play														
1998-99	Nottingham Panthers	BISL	3	0	1	1	2	-							
1999-00	Did not play														
2000-01	Sheffield Steelers	BISL	4	0	1	1	0	-							

S	TEAM	LEAGUE	GP	G	A	TP	PIM	+/-	POST	GP	G	A	TP	PIM	+/-
1979-80	Regina Pats	M-Cup	4	4	5	9	0	-							
1989-90	Team Canada	Spengler Cup	.	.	.	.	.	-							
1991-92	Durham Wasps	Autumn Cup	9	10	20	30	54	-							
1992-93	Durham Wasps	Autumn Cup	9	18	10	28	22	-							
1994-95	Nottingham Panthers	Autumn Cup	3	4	4	8	6	-							
1995-96	Nottingham Panthers	Autumn Cup	11	8	7	15	43	-							
1996-97	Nottingham Panthers	Autumn Cup	8	4	4	8	6	-							

TEAM STAFF HISTORY

S	TEAM	LEAGUE	ROLE ON TEAM	NOTES
1993-94	Nottingham Panthers	BHL	Head Coach	
1994-95	Nottingham Panthers	BHL	Head Coach	
	Great Britain	WC B	Asst. Coach	
1995-96	Nottingham Panthers	BHL	Player-Coach	
	Great Britain	WC B	Asst. Coach	
1996-97	Nottingham Panthers	BISL	Head Coach	
	Great Britain	WC B	Asst. Coach	
1997-98	Nottingham Panthers	BISL	Head Coach	
1998-99	Nottingham Panthers	BISL	Head Coach	
1999-00	Nottingham Panthers	BISL	Head Coach	Replaced by Alex Dampier
	Sheffield Steelers	BISL	Head Coach	Replaced Don McKee
2000-01	Sheffield Steelers	BISL	Head Coach	
2001-02	Sheffield Steelers	BISL	Head Coach	
2002-03	Sheffield Steelers	BISL	Head Coach	
2003-04	Sheffield Steelers	EIHL	Head Coach	
2004-05	Regina Pats	WHL	Asst. Coach	
2005-06	Nottingham Panthers	EIHL	Head Coach	
2015-16	Yale Hockey Academy Elite 15s	CSSHL U16	Head Coach	

The Present Day
2000 to Date
Jared Staal

Jared John Staal was born on August 21, 1990 and is a Canadian former professional ice hockey player and current coach. He is currently an assistant coach for the AHL's Charlotte Checkers.

Staal moved into coaching after retiring from playing in 2017, following a season with the Edinburgh Capitals of the Elite Ice Hockey League (EIHL). Staal was previously a member of the Carolina Hurricanes of the National Hockey League (NHL). He is the younger brother of Eric Staal of the Florida Panthers, Marc Staal of the Florida Panthers, and Jordan Staal of the Carolina Hurricanes. He is also the cousin of Jeff Heerema, formerly of the Nottingham Panthers.

Staal grew up in his hometown of Thunder Bay, Ontario playing 'AAA' hockey for the Thunder Bay Kings. He was drafted in the first round of the 2006 Ontario Hockey League (OHL) Priority Selection Draft by the Sudbury Wolves (11th overall).

Staal played the 2007–08 season with the Wolves. He was selected by the Phoenix Coyotes in the second-round of the 2008 NHL Entry Draft, 49th overall. He is the only member of the Staal brothers not to be taken in the first round of the NHL Entry Draft and the only one not to have been drafted by an Eastern Conference team. He is the only right-handed shooter of all four brothers.

On April 3, 2009, Staal signed an amateur tryout contract with the San Antonio Rampage, the AHL affiliate of the Coyotes. He appeared in five games for the Rampage in 2009, however he was sent back to the Sudbury Wolves for the remainder of the season.

On May 13, 2010, the Carolina Hurricanes acquired his rights from the Phoenix Coyotes in exchange for a fifth-round draft pick. On May 14, 2010, the Hurricanes signed Staal to a three-year entry-level contract. To start the 2010–11 season, he was assigned to the Hurricanes AHL affiliate, the Charlotte Checkers of the AHL. Struggling to gain ice time after 12 games, on November 19, 2010, Staal was reassigned to their ECHL affiliate, the Florida Everblades, but was later recalled. For the 2011–12 season, Staal returned to the Charlotte Checkers. On March 12, 2012, the Hurricanes loaned him to the Boston Bruins' affiliate Providence Bruins of the AHL for the remainder of the 2011–12 season.

After scoring 3 goals and 4 assists in 52 games with Charlotte in 2012–13, Staal made his NHL debut with the Hurricanes on April 25, 2013 against the New York Rangers. He was in the Hurricanes' starting line-up for the game, starting on a forward line with brothers Eric and Jordan.

After five seasons within the Hurricanes organization, Staal was released as a free agent in the summer. With limited NHL or AHL interest, Staal signed a one-year deal with the Florida Everblades of the ECHL on October 7, 2015. Prior to the 2015–16 season, he was traded by the Everblades to the South Carolina Stingrays on October 15, 2015.

On July 4, 2016, Staal signed abroad to a one-year contract with the Edinburgh Capitals of the EIHL.

In June 2018, Staal retired from playing and signed a contract to become an assistant coach with OHA Edmonton of the Canadian Sport School Hockey League.

Staal was named the fifth assistant coach in Orlando Solar Bears history on August 8, 2019. He took on the title of associate coach for the 2021–22 ECHL season, remaining with the team until 2022 when Orlando head coach Drake Berehowsky left his position.

In August 2022, Staal was named an assistant coach at AHL side Charlotte Checkers. Staal had spent five seasons as a player with the Checkers between 2010 and 2015.

Jared's Stats

S	TEAM	LEAGUE	GP	G	A	TP	PIM	+/-	POST	GP	G	A	TP	PIM	+/-
2004-05	🇨🇦 Thunder Bay Kings U15 AAA	WAAA U15	17	4	7	11	8	-							
2005-06	🇨🇦 Thunder Bay Kings U16 AAA	U16 AAA	64	24	25	49	72	-							
2006-07	🇨🇦 Sudbury Wolves	OHL	63	2	1	3	18	-7	Playoffs	21	1	0	1	2	-1
2007-08	🇨🇦 Sudbury Wolves	OHL	60	21	28	49	44	-11							
2008-09	🇨🇦 Sudbury Wolves	OHL	67	19	33	52	38	-17	Playoffs	6	0	1	1	2	-3
	San Antonio Rampage	AHL	5	0	0	0	0	0							
2009-10	🇨🇦 Sudbury Wolves	OHL	59	12	37	49	57	-10	Playoffs	3	0	0	0	4	-5
	San Antonio Rampage	AHL	5	0	1	1	2	1							
2010-11	Charlotte Checkers	AHL	13	1	1	2	2	-3							
	Florida Everblades	ECHL	33	6	5	11	6	-3							
2011-12	Charlotte Checkers	AHL	37	3	3	6	18	-5							
	Providence Bruins Loan	AHL	7	0	2	2	2	-1							
2012-13	Carolina Hurricanes	NHL	2	0	0	0	2	-2							
	Charlotte Checkers	AHL	52	4	3	7	25	-12	Playoffs	3	0	0	0	0	0
2013-14	Charlotte Checkers	AHL	50	2	5	7	23	-2							
2014-15	Charlotte Checkers	AHL	63	7	4	11	27	-23							
2015-16	South Carolina Stingrays	ECHL	64	12	12	24	23	-1	Playoffs	6	1	0	1	2	1
2016-17	🏴󠁧󠁢󠁳󠁣󠁴󠁿 Edinburgh Capitals "A"	EIHL	44	12	21	33	14	-							

S	TEAM	LEAGUE	GP	G	A	TP	PIM	+/-	POST	GP	G	A	TP	PIM	+/-
2005-06	🇨🇦 Thunder Bay Kings U16 AAA	OHL Cup	3	1	0	1	4	-							
2016-17	🏴󠁧󠁢󠁳󠁣󠁴󠁿 Edinburgh Capitals	EIHL Cup	10	3	5	8	6	-							

TEAM STAFF HISTORY

S	TEAM	LEAGUE	ROLE ON TEAM	NOTES
2018-19	🇨🇦 OHA Edmonton U15 Prep	CSSHL U15	Asst. Coach	
	🇨🇦 OHA Edmonton Prep	CSSHL U18	Asst. Coach	
2019-20	Orlando Solar Bears	ECHL	Asst. Coach	
2020-21	Orlando Solar Bears	ECHL	Asst. Coach	
2021-22	Orlando Solar Bears	ECHL	Assoc. Coach	
2022-23	Charlotte Checkers	AHL	Asst. Coach	

Jared Aulin

1. Having played for many clubs what is your favourite memory on the ice?

My favourite memory would be my time playing for Team Canada at the World Jr. Championships. Even though I have great memories from my short time in the NHL, the proud feeling of playing with the support of your entire country behind you is amazing. The pain of losing to Russia in the finals is still there, but the memories made and the experiences I had, are unbeatable.

2. How did it feel to play in the NHL for LA Kings?

Playing my first NHL game was a dream come true. I remember it distinctly and there were mixed emotions. Warming up and getting my first shift against the St. Louis Blues was exhilarating. I remember rushing over the blue line, beating the defenceman wide, dropping the puck to Mathieu Schneider and then hip ripping one off of the crossbar and me getting hit from behind to draw a penalty. To almost get an assist and then draw a penalty was very exciting. After that first shift, I saw limited ice time and that excited feeling goes away and you start to wonder why you weren't given more of an opportunity after a great first shift. That's the life of a rookie hockey player though.

3. Would you class your NHL goals against Carolina Hurricanes in the 8-2 victory on 7th Feb 2003 as your most memorable? If not, what was your most memorable goal?

Those two goals are definitely the most memorable. I remember finally listening to my parents and coaches and using my shot. I ripped it short side shelf on Kevin Weekes and before I had time to celebrate, I was mauled by my teammates in pure excitement. There was a very thoughtful and generous fan who had Kevin Weekes sign a picture of my 1st NHL goal and they gave it to me. I have the utmost respect for him for doing that for me and to Kevin Weekes for signing it.

4. **How did your shoulder injury effect your career?**

My shoulder injury basically ended my time in North America. I tried to continue playing with it after the rehab was done, but the opportunity I was being given just wasn't there anymore. I took a step back and questioned if it was worth pursuing my dream anymore, while playing through extreme pain. My shoulder has very limited mobility and is full of arthritis, so I am in pain 24/7 but I have learned how to deal with it.

5. **What made you leave North America for Sweden?**

I actually missed three years of hockey and then found a passion for it again. I made my way back to the AHL and felt I had a great comeback season but being on a try out agreement for most of the year, you take a backseat to the players who are signed, no matter what kind of numbers you put up. I was told to stay in NA after that season by certain NHL teams to be their call up guy, but I had heard that story before and even if it was coming from an honest place, I felt it was best to take my talents to Europe.

6. **After 3 seasons in the Swedish Hockey League, what tempted you to leave mid-season to join Straubing Tigers in the German League?**

I played 5 seasons in Sweden where I had lots of individual and team success. My years in Sweden was the highlight of my career. I've never played for such an amazing organization with fans who truly cared about the players as people and not just as a hockey player. The connection between the city, players and fans is something I will cherish for the rest of my life.

I then spent 4 great years in Switzerland, where I also made great memories due to team and individual success. We accomplished an amazing feat in winning 3 titles in one year. We had a great group of players and a solid following from passionate fans. I experienced two knee injuries in my final two seasons there and with the limited amount of imports allowed to play, the team did not want to take a risk on me, so I was bought out and went to Straubing.

7. **Was it your Brother in law, Layne Ulmer, that convinced you to join Storm?**

Coach Finnerty and I chatted a lot and I really wanted to go to Manchester. Once I found out I had the opportunity to play with Layne, it was a no brainer and I am forever grateful to the Storm organization for making it happen.

8. What did you like about playing in Altrincham?

I loved the city of Altrincham. It's such a beautiful area. Walking into the Shelter and experiencing the character and excitement from the fans, with 20 of my new buddies is what I loved most.

Outside of hockey, my fiancé and I loved going to the market with our dog to eat and people watch. It's a place we definitely want to go back to.

9. How would you compare the Altrincham rink to others you have played in?

Obviously, it's not the biggest or most beautiful arena in the world, but it has character. When I played in Straubing we had what was considered to be the "worst rink" in the league as well, but I'd rather take an older arena filled with loud and passionate fans over a beautiful, big and empty arena any day of the week.

10. What was the worst rink you have played in?

The worst rink I ever played in was in an exhibition game against a 2nd league team in Germany. The arena was open so there were people smoking, the boards were all wood and the corners had chain link fence where there was supposed to be glass. It was very interesting to say the least.

11. What was you highlight of playing for the Storm?

The highlight was definitely getting to play alongside my brother in law Layne. Setting him up for a goal was something I had always pictured but never got to experience, until Finnerty and Jamie allowed us that opportunity. Our first shift together was pretty darn cool.

Outside of the rink it was nice to spend time with my fiancé, our dog and my sister Kirsten (Layne's wife), Layne and the kids, Bodhi and Cove. We spent a lot of time together and we were fortunate that the Storm put us up in the same apartment complex. Both of us having played pro hockey all over Europe, we never got to enjoy that kind of quality family time.

12. What was the lowest point of playing for Storm?

The lowest point would be when we were in the midst of a great practice and Finner got the call that the season was cancelled. We were feeling great and in the hunt for a playoff spot and then all of a sudden, the season gets cancelled in the middle of practice. It was a super odd feeling and one way to get over it was to ice the hurt from the inside with a few cold beers on the ice with the fellas.

13. Do you think you have a few seasons left in you? Where would you like to see out your playing career?

I believe I have a few more good seasons left in me, but unfortunately at my age and this pandemic, teams are looking for more youthful players. Whatever happens, I will always look back on my career and appreciate all of the memories made, friendships gained, and unbelievable life experiences provided to me from the game of hockey.

14. What do you plan doing after your career on the ice ends?

I've always been told I'd make a great coach based on how I am in the dressing room. I see myself as a guy who is able to bring out the best in people, no matter what situation I am in. I love to build people up and I somehow know how to do it without knocking someone's character. Life is about being positive and the easiest way to do that is to provide a fun and confident atmosphere. I do know it's not an easy gig to get into, but whatever opportunity life after hockey presents me, I'll be doing my best at it.

15. Do you have any message for the Storm fans who are reading this?

First off, I know the pain of not having hockey for a season. It sucks and it's hard to get over, but the reality is, the game will be back. The important thing is for the fans to continue supporting the team and the EIHL. The league was at a point where it was gaining major respect from the top leagues in Europe. It's up to the league, the organizations and the fans to continue building the league up to greatness.

To the Storm fans, THANK YOU! My time in Manchester will be remembered because of your passion, your friendships, your support and your ability to remind us all that we are more than just hockey players, we are human. That in itself is something amazing and I can't thank you enough. Thank you for your support, your applause, your encouragement and your passion! Thank you for the memories! WE ARE STORM!!

16. Who was the biggest influence in your career?

My parents have always been the biggest influences in my life and my career. They loved me unconditionally, supported me through everything and they taught me to always be kind. They showed myself and my siblings how important it is to be known as a good person first. Not just to be identified as a good person, but to actually be one. If I turn out to be half the people they are, I'll be more than proud of myself.

CAREER HIGHLIGHTS	
SEASON	AWARDS BY SEASON
1997-1998	• AEHL U15 Most Valuable Player
1999-2000	• CHL Top Prospects Game
2000-2001	• WHL (West) First All-Star Team • WHL Most Assists (77)
2001-2002	• U20 WJC Silver Medal • WHL (West) First All-Star Team
2002-2003	• AHL All-Star Game
2005-2006	• AHL Calder Cup Champion
2012-2013	• Allsvenskan Most Assists (34) • Allsvenskan Most Points (50) • Allsvenskan to Elitserien Promotion (Örebro)
2017-2018	• NLB Champion (Rapperswil) • Swiss Cup Winner (Rapperswil)

S	TEAM	LEAGUE	GP	G	A	TP	PIM	+/-	POST	GP	G	A	TP	PIM	+/-
1996-97	Airdrie Xtreme U15 AAA	AEHL U15	33	30	25	55	28								
1997-98	Airdrie Xtreme U15 AAA	AEHL U15	36	42	61	103	76								
	Kamloops Blazers	WHL	2	0	0	0	0	1							
1998-99	Kamloops Blazers	WHL	55	7	19	26	23	5	Playoffs	13	1	3	4	2	4
1999-00	Kamloops Blazers	WHL	57	17	38	55	70	4	Playoffs	4	0	1	1	6	-3
2000-01	Kamloops Blazers	WHL	70	31	77	108	62	1	Playoffs	4	0	2	2	0	-5
2001-02	Kamloops Blazers	WHL	46	33	34	67	80	30	Playoffs	4	1	2	3	2	-4
	Canada U20	WJC-20	7	4	5	9	4	8							
2002-03	Los Angeles Kings	NHL	17	2	2	4	0	-3							
	Manchester Monarchs	AHL	44	12	32	44	21	-2	Playoffs	3	0	4	4	0	0
2003-04	Portland Pirates	AHL	10	2	1	3	4	0	Playoffs	6	1	1	2	4	0
2004-05	Portland Pirates	AHL	65	11	28	39	30	-9							
2005-06	Hershey Bears	AHL	61	11	28	39	38	-14	Playoffs	5	0	0	0	6	0
2006-07	Springfield Falcons	AHL	13	2	2	4	2	-12							
2007-08	Univ. of Calgary	USports	16	14	20	34	22								
2008-09	Did not play		-							-					
2009-10	Syracuse Crunch	AHL	64	16	21	37	36	-2							
2010-11	Leksands IF	Allsvenskan	36	10	20	30	28	3	Qualification	5	3	0	3	6	2
2011-12	Örebro HK	Allsvenskan	49	25	33	58	24	23	Kvalserien SHL	9	0	4	4	6	-3
2012-13	Örebro HK	Allsvenskan	48	16	34	50	34	8							
2013-14	Örebro HK "A"	SHL	50	7	20	27	36	7	Kvalserien SHL	7	2	7	9	2	7
2014-15	Örebro HK	SHL	47	7	17	24	6	2	Playoffs	3	0	2	2	2	-1
2015-16	SC Rapperswil-Jona Lakers "A"	NLB	45	11	34	45	22	4	Playoffs	12	3	6	9	0	1
2016-17	SC Rapperswil-Jona Lakers	NLB	47	19	35	54	24	14	Playoffs	14	2	6	8	14	3
2017-18	SC Rapperswil-Jona Lakers "A"	NLB	39	11	35	46	18	14	Playoffs	13	4	10	14	2	2
2018-19	SC Rapperswil-Jona Lakers	NLA	19	0	4	4	8	-12							
	Straubing Tigers	DEL	19	1	9	10	0	-3	Playoffs	2	0	0	0	0	-1
2019-20	Manchester Storm "A"	EIHL	48	10	35	45	26	-12							

S	TEAM	LEAGUE	GP	G	A	TP	PIM	+/-	POST	GP	G	A	TP	PIM	+/-
1995-96	Calgary Flames Peewee	QC Int PW	-	-	-	-	-								
1998-99	Team Alberta	CWG	6	6	2	8	6								
1999-00	Canada U18	Nations Cup	3	1	2	3	2								
2014-15	Team Canada	International	3	0	1	1	2	-1							
	Team Canada	Deutschland Cup	3	0	1	1	2	-1							
2015-16	SC Rapperswil-Jona Lakers	Swiss Cup	3	0	2	2	2								
2016-17	SC Rapperswil-Jona Lakers	Swiss Cup	2	1	2	3	0								
2017-18	SC Rapperswil-Jona Lakers	Swiss Cup	5	2	2	4	0								
2018-19	SC Rapperswil-Jona Lakers	Swiss Cup	2	0	0	0	2								
2019-20	Manchester Storm	EIHL Cup	11	2	2	4	0	-11							

Mike Torchia

Mike Torchia was born on February 23, 1972 and is a Canadian former professional ice hockey goaltender.

Torchia was born in Toronto, Ontario. As a youth, he played in the 1985 Quebec International Pee-Wee Hockey Tournament with the Toronto Marlboros minor ice hockey team. He played on the same backyard rink with Eric Lindros growing up as a kid in Toronto.

Torchia was named to the Memorial Cup All-Star Team in 1990, and won the Hap Emms Memorial Trophy at the 1990 Memorial Cup. He was also named an Ontario Hockey League first team all-star in 1991.

Torchia was drafted 74th overall by the Minnesota North Stars in the 1991 NHL Entry Draft. In his six career National Hockey League games for the Dallas Stars during the 1994–95 NHL season, he registered a record of three wins, two losses, and one tie with a GAA of 3.30 and an .895 save percentage.

Torchia was named to the ISL Second All-Star team in 2001.

Torchia was later a colour commentator for the Kitchener Rangers on 570 News.

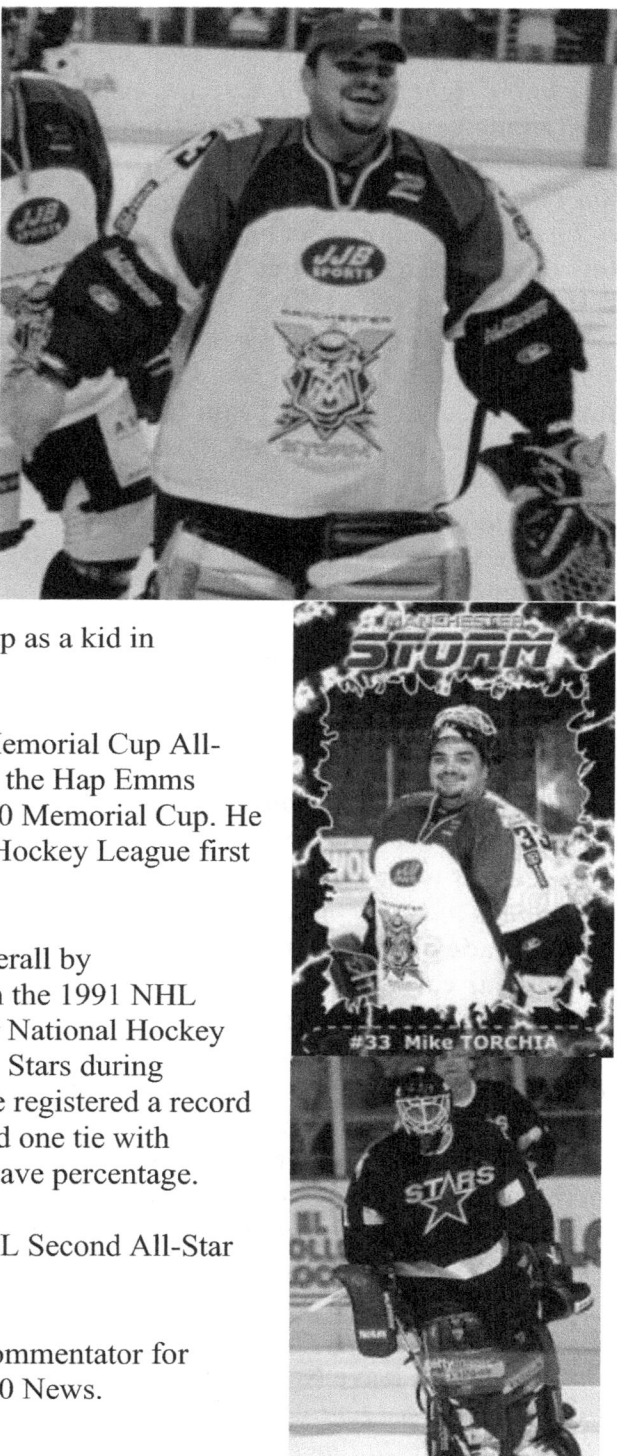

What made you decide on a career in hockey?
You don't decide, it chooses you. That's if you are fortunate to be in the right place at the right time. Your hard work makes it happen.

What made you decide to be a netminder?
This happened by accident, when I was- really young in Toronto a goalie didn't turn up for a game. The coach asked everyone if they wanted to have a go. I tried it as a 7 year old and loved it. I raised my hand at the right time.

How did it feel to be drafted by the Minnesota North Stars in 1991 in the 4th Round?
It was surreal, I never pictured myself being drafted. Seeing the likes of Bobby Clark in front of you, people you loved to watch play!

How did it feel to play for Team Canada?
My time there was very special. We didn't play a lot, mostly it was training, but it was still very special. Pulling on the Canada shirt was wonderful and I wore it with great pride.

You made your NHL debut in 1994 for the Dallas Stars, can you remember it?
I remember it like yesterday and very fondly. I was in Detroit the night before. We had an afternoon game the following day- and nothing had been said. At 10am on the matchday Bob Gainey- came down for a team meeting and announced 4 hours before the game that I was playing. I had no time to worry about it. I simply got my stuff from my hotel room and got into a cab and went off to the rink. Both teams had played earlier in the year and there was rivalry between the clubs as well as animosity. We won 2-1. The goal I conceded was when Joe Murphy cut across and that thew me off and I miss timed things to let the puck passed me.

Having made 6 appearances for the Stars in 1994/95, what happened next in your career?
Dallas had goalies coming up from the Czech Republic as well as Marty Turko, it was a numbers game and I was traded. I blew my knee and missed most of the season. Then I was traded to Anaheim, but ended up being traded again and ended up in Italy.

Having played OHL, AHL, IHL and ECHL, what was your favourite North American League (apert from the NHL)?
That is a tough question, all were great. The IHL and AHL are a step down from the NHL and filled with players all trying to make that step up. The East Coast was fun but not a league that I wanted to spend much time in. The OHL was full of kids so all had positives and negatives.

What made you leave North America in 1998 and head for Italy?
Opportunities were really what was behind the move to Italy. When it comes to injuries the North American schedule is a grind. European leagues have a maximum of 50 to 60 games a season, whilst in North America its nearer 80,

not including the play offs, so in a single season you could end up playing around 106 games in a year. Long seasons are tough on the body!

Your experience in Italy only lasted a season, what happened?
What persuaded you to come to the UK in 2000 and sign for the Sheffield Steelers?

The year I played in Italy saw great changes in its structure and rules. When I played there each team could ice 10 Canadians and 2 Americans. They changed the rules to allow only 2 imports. The UK did something similar a few years later I seem to recall. But with these changes to the league it would have been a terrible league to play in and not something I wanted to do. Mike Blaisdell called me, I liked the guy and as a result of his call I came over. They were a great team and it was special at Sheffield and a fun place to come and play.

2001 Saw the move to Manchester, what influenced you to make the move to the MEN Arena?

The opportunity to be number one goalie at the Storm. Trevor Gallant was there and was a good friend of mine. Then I had a good chat with Lipper (Daryl Lipsey). I had issues with getting funds at Sheffield which further helped make the decision. I had fun at the Storm and we found our form just at the right time before Manchester made the play offs. We ended up losing in the final to Sheffield.

You left the Storm to drop down to the Guildford Flames, what was the reason for dropping down a league?

It wasn't my choice, I was not getting paid at Manchester. The guys ended up all over the place. It was tough as a goalie to find a spot, so I accepted the offer from Guildford.

You headed back to Canada in 2003 to end your career, what was the highlight of your career?

Lots of different highs and lows. My 1ˢᵗ NHL game was a highlight as well as winning the Memorial Cup with Kitchener.

Did you enjoy your time in the UK?

I talk about it all the time. I loved my time in the UK. It was the closest thing to being in North America. It was a great time and very enjoyable.

What was your favourite memory on or off the ice whilst in the UK?

The run we had in Manchester, and the Grand slam we won in Sheffield despite the adversity suffered at Sheffield. It brought out true leadership in David Longstaff and David Allison. The way they conducted themselves. It was hard times that year but as a team we stuck together. I still talk a lot about my times in the UK and id love to come back and visit the many friends I made there.

Mike's Stats

S	TEAM	LEAGUE	GP	GAA	SV%	SO	WLT	POST	GP	GAA	SV%	SO	WLT
1987-88	Toronto Red Wings U18 AAA	GTHL U18	40	3.10	-	-	-						
	Henry Carr Crusaders	MetJBHL	1	30.00	-	-	-						
1988-89	Kitchener Rangers	OHL	30	4.02	-	-	-	Playoffs	2	3.81	-	-	-
1989-90	Kitchener Rangers	OHL	40	3.58	.875	-	-	Playoffs	17	3.52	-	-	-
1990-91	Kitchener Rangers	OHL	57	3.96	.891	-	-	Playoffs	6	4.71	-	-	-
1991-92	Kitchener Rangers	OHL	55	4.00	.881	-	-	Playoffs	14	3.13	-	-	-
1992-93	Kalamazoo Wings	IHL	48	3.80	.892	0	-						
	Team Canada	International	5	2.20	-	-	-						
1993-94	Kalamazoo Wings	IHL	43	3.68	.889	0	-	Playoffs	4	3.80	.905	1	-
1994-95	Dallas Stars	NHL	6	3.30	.895	0	3-2-1						
	Kalamazoo Wings	IHL	41	2.97	.904	3	-	Playoffs	6	3.97	.851	0	-
1995-96	Portland Pirates	AHL	12	4.79	.855	-	-						
	Michigan K-Wings	IHL	1	1.00	.966	-	-						
	Orlando Solar Bears	IHL	7	2.99	.909	-	-						
	Baltimore Bandits	AHL	5	4.21	.902	-	-	Playoffs	1	0.00	1.000	-	-
	Hampton Roads Admirals	ECHL	5	3.92	.904	0	2-2-0						
1996-97	Fort Wayne Komets	IHL	57	3.47	.893	-	-						
	Baltimore Bandits	AHL	0	-	-	-	-	Playoffs	1	6.00	.871	-	-
1997-98	Milwaukee Admirals	IHL	34	3.09	.886	-	-						
	San Antonio Dragons	IHL	2	6.10	.833	-	-						
	Peoria Rivermen	ECHL	5	3.21	.889	0	4-1-0	Playoffs	1	7.00	-	-	-
1998-99	Asiago	Italy	13	4.10	-	-	-						
	Asiago	Alpenliga	30	4.37	-	-	-						
1999-00	Mohawk Valley Prowlers	UHL	23	3.85	.883	0	8-9-4						
	Birmingham Bulls	ECHL	14	4.43	.866	0	4-10-0						
2000-01	Sheffield Steelers	BISL	23	2.06	.917	-	-	Playoffs	1	5.00	.815	-	-
2001-02	Manchester Storm	BISL	23	2.82	.916	-	-	Playoffs	5	3.15	.897	-	-
2002-03	Manchester Storm	BISL	3	4.50	.865	-	-						
	Guildford Flames	BNL	24	3.42	.881	-	-	Playoffs	8	2.88	.902	-	-
2003-04	Cambridge Hornets	OHA Sr.	10	4.00	-	-	-						
2004-05	Cambridge Hornets	MLH	11	4.42	-	-	-						
2005-06	Cambridge Hornets	MLH	8	5.54	.875	0	3-5-0						

S	TEAM	LEAGUE	GP	GAA	SV%	SO	WLT	POST	GP	GAA	SV%	SO	WLT
1984-85	Toronto Marlboros Peewee	QC Int PW	-	-	-	-	-						
1989-90	Kitchener Rangers	M-Cup	5	3.90	-	-	-						
2000-01	Sheffield Steelers	Autumn Cup	4	2.00	.918	-	-						
	Sheffield Steelers	BISL Cup	1	2.00	.909	-	-						

Jay Rosehill

What made you choose ice hockey as a profession?
It was just what we did in Canada. My older brother played hockey so I just followed suit. As I got older it became a dream of mine to play professionally. Specifically in the NHL

How did it feel to be drafted by Tampa Bay in 2003?
It was pretty wild. It was around that time I started to garner attention at that level. Seeing my name beside an NHL logo and in The Hockey News was surreal for me. It seemed so unattainable but here it was happening. It was pretty special

You had to wait until 2009 before appearing in the NHL with Toronto did you think your chance had gone of playing in the NHL?
I never did. I always just kept going. I ran into some coaches who didn't believe in me and had some tough years but I k we it was all about opportunity so I just kept on going

Do you remember your NHL debut? Who was it against?
I do. It was Hockey Night in Canada on CBC which is a a legendary Saturday night broadcast in Canada. I was playing for the Toronto Maple Leafs and against their rivals the Montreal Canadiens. My Dad flew in on the red eye when he found out I was playing because he wanted to be there. It was amazing afterward to finally say I did it.

Do you remember your first goal?
Ya I was lucky enough to score my 3rd game against Marc Andre Fleury who was playing for the Pittsburgh and they were the Stanley Cup champions. Scoring isn't what I'm known for so it was special to score in that league so quickly on the season

Did you choose to go to the Philadelphia Flyers or where you traded by the Leafs?
I was traded there after the 2012 lockout

What made you leave North America and head for Scotland to play for Braehead Clan in 2016?
The North American game had changed so much in a matter of years. My role was diminished and I k ew my time in the NHL was no longer. I wanted to go to a new country and play a different role. I was ready for a new experience and The UK seemed to fit that bill

What expectations did you have of playing in the UK?
I really didn't come with any. I just thought I would come and do what I was capable of and see where the chips fell

Were the expectations met?
They were. I really enjoyed the crowds and the type of hockey they still played. I would love to see all the teams have the same amount of fan support in the league. The ones that have it are fantastic. I also think the officiating needs a lot of development!

Having played 117 games over 5 seasons in the NHL what was your most memorable occasion in the NHL and why?
Probably my first game for the Flyers.
It happened to be against my old Team the Maple Leafs. I got in a fight with Colton Orr and scored the game winner and got a star of the game. Couldn't have gone better

Who was the best player that you had played against and why?
Sidney Crosby and Alex Ovechkin we're both a level above everyone else. Aid for his awareness and poise, Alex for his power and extreme skill level

What are you doing now for a living?
I'm a rode sip all firefighter now in Calgary. I love it

What is the best rink that you have played in and why?
Madison Square Garden in New York City is pretty special. It's so iconic in the middle of Manhattan and when you think Muhammad Ali has fought there and the countless other legends it's pretty neat

Which team has the best fans and why?
Most of the Canadian teams have the most passionate fans but Chicago in probably the loudest building

What was your most memorable occasion whilst in the UK on or off the ice?
Winning our conference in Braehead was pretty special. Also unexpectedly being one of the top teams in Manchester was a fun time as well.
Playing the Old Course at St Andrews with my brother was a lifetime bucket list thing for me as well. I love golf and golf history so There's no better place than Scotland for that.

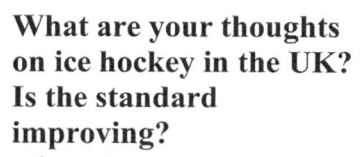

What are your thoughts on ice hockey in the UK? Is the standard improving?
I found the UK players were more advanced than most people would think. There is quality in the system and I think they've started to show that on the world stage recently which is great!

Would you recommend playing in the UK to players in North America?
I already have. It's a great place to play. The country is great to live in, the people are great and I enjoyed my time there. I will continue to recommend it to players looking to head overseas

Jay's Stats

S	TEAM	LEAGUE	GP	G	A	TP	PIM	+/-	POST	GP	G	A	TP	PIM	+/-
2001-02	Red Deer Chiefs U18 AAA	AMHL	30	3	9	12	116	-							
2002-03	Olds Grizzlys	AJHL	49	4	1	5	204	-							
2003-04	Olds Grizzlys	AJHL	42	4	12	16	172	-	Playoffs	14	2	2	4	-	
2004-05	Univ. of Minnesota-Duluth	NCAA	34	0	5	5	103	-							
2005-06	Springfield Falcons	AHL	45	1	1	2	68	-27							
	Johnstown Chiefs	ECHL	5	0	0	0	13	-2	Playoffs	5	0	0	0	4	
2006-07	Springfield Falcons	AHL	64	0	6	6	85	-11							
2007-08	Norfolk Admirals	AHL	66	3	4	7	194	-2							
	Mississippi Sea Wolves	ECHL	2	0	0	0	6	0							
2008-09	Norfolk Admirals	AHL	57	5	7	12	221	5							
	Toronto Marlies	AHL	13	2	1	3	54	-1	Playoffs	6	0	0	0	4	-1
2009-10	Toronto Maple Leafs	NHL	15	1	1	2	67	-2							
	Toronto Marlies	AHL	46	1	2	3	172	-12							
2010-11	Toronto Maple Leafs	NHL	26	1	2	3	71	-6							
	Toronto Marlies	AHL	32	7	6	13	114	7							
2011-12	Toronto Maple Leafs	NHL	31	0	0	0	60	-4							
	Toronto Marlies	AHL	4	0	0	0	20	0	Playoffs	13	0	0	0	44	-1
2012-13	Norfolk Admirals	AHL	33	4	4	8	90	-1							
	Philadelphia Flyers	NHL	11	1	0	1	64	-4							
2013-14	Philadelphia Flyers	NHL	34	2	0	2	90	-8							
2014-15	Lehigh Valley Phantoms	AHL	65	5	7	12	219	-15							
2015-16	Lehigh Valley Phantoms	AHL	23	1	2	3	33	1							
2016-17	Braehead Clan "A"	EIHL	40	4	18	22	176	-	Playoffs	2	0	0	0	8	-
2017-18	Manchester Storm "C"	EIHL	42	6	11	17	186	-	Playoffs	2	0	0	0	2	-

S	TEAM	LEAGUE	GP	G	A	TP	PIM	+/-	POST	GP	G	A	TP	PIM	+/-
2016-17	Braehead Clan	EIHL Cup	10	0	1	1	35	-							
2017-18	Manchester Storm	EIHL Cup	5	1	1	2	10	-							

Sean McMorrow

What made you choose Ice Hockey as a career?

The best way to answer that is to say I was blessed enough to be at the top level of the sport since I was 9 years old. The earliest age where they have the AAA level, which is the highest level for the kids that are 9 years old. From that point on I played triple A until I was drafted into the OHL. Before that I played a year in tier 2 Junior A which is a feeder league into the OHL. I was drafted into the OHL and was then drafted into the National Hockey League. Once that happened their was no doubt in my mind that I was going to pick hockey as a career because I was lucky enough to be selected in a worldwide NHL draft. The door had been opened and I had to try to make the most of it. From the NHL draft when I was 18 years old, I knew that I would be making a career in ice hockey.

How did it feel to make your OHL debut with Sarnia Sting in 1999?

Sarnia was the beginning of Pro Style hockey, a sort of NHL for teenagers. Very professional and the highest level. The teams act the same as the pro teams as far as taking care of the players was concerned and it was a dream come true to make my debut. It was the first time I had moved away from home and was about a 3 hours drive away from Toronto. I was living in billets with a lovely family in charge of all the land parents. I was 17, playing away from home and proud to be making my debut and playing for Sarnia and Mark Hunter who was my GM and Coach, who drafted me into the league and later ended up trading for me to go to join the London Knights.

Buffalo Sabres drafted you in 2000 in round 8 but it took 2 years for you to make an appearance. Did you think your chance had gone?

I had no idea that the process was like this until I had to go through it and live it as a personal experience. How it works is when a player gets drafted into the games NHL they are 18 years old. Its not really about the first game, its more about signing the contracts and the games would then follow after to make it possible. If a player makes the team as an 18 year old like a Sidney Crosby etc, the guys who are the top picks or top 5 picks in the 1st round they will play. But for everybody else they are too young. You have to be 20 years old to play in the NHL. An NHL side isn't going to sign you *unless you are making the team as an 18 or 19 year old, because you have to go back to Junior to carry on your career, so its completely normal for 1st overall picks to play, but for 2nd, 3rd, 4th round picks to return to Junior to play your 19th and 20th year old seasons and then there is a deadline of June 1st after the 20 year old season, or for some their 19th season depending on when your 19th birthday7is. I have a January birthday so I was 20 and into my 3rd year. 2 years from when you get drafted on 1st June, the deadline that the NHL team needs to decide whether to sign you to an entry level or not. Then you can become a free agent again. So for me, luckily I signed the entry level contract for Buffalo and then I was lucky enough to be called up in the first year of that contract. I was blessed being an 8th rounder and able to play an NHL game in the 1st year of my entry level contract., which if you come from Junior like the OHL, the entry level is always 3 years, but if you are a college guy from the NCAA, your first contract is 2 years long.*

You only made 1 appearance for Buffalo, can you remember the match?

I remember the match very clearly. I'm asked about it quite a bit and the reason for that is because with me playing the 1 regular season game in the NHL was a special story because of where I am from and who it was against. I often tell the story that I grew up watching a cultural show called "Hockey Night in Canada", where the Toronto Maple Leafs would have a home game every Saturday night and the BBC of Canada is CBC and so CBC would be the channel and "Hockey night in Canada", was the show and it would be the Toronto Maple Leafs against whoever. So I grew up with it as my culture and its what I did every Saturday night at my Grandfather's house with hot chocolate and raisin bread toast, watching "Hockey Night in Canada". So the game I got called up for, for Buffalo was against the Toronto Maple Leafs on a Saturday night, and it was on "Hockey Night in Canada", the same thing in the same way that I grew up with. That was my experience of the NHL, so I was up against my home team, the

Toronto Maple Leafs in Toronto. Because of all those reasons I remember it very clearly. It was quite an experience and ill never forget that one.

What happened at Buffalo, did they push you out to the AHL and play for the Rochester Americans?

Usually with the smaller market teams like Buffalo, they really embrace their system where even their 1st, 2nd or 3rd rounders, they all did a couple of years in Rochester so pretty much when you are in a situation like that, the goal is to be able to keep that spot in Rochester. Because it is a normal part of that process, so guys that get sent down to the level below the AHL, they need to keep up their level of games. I was proud that I never got sent down and was able to keep my spot and then obviously I got my call up to the NHL, so I was proud to play in Rochester as it was part of the process.

Your first senior goal was for Oshawa Generals in the OHL in 2002, can you remember it?

My first OHL goal I remember very well as ive talked about it a couple of times in interviews over the last couple of months because of the funny story behind it. Its actually on youtube and you can search for it by typing "Sean McMorrows 1st OHL goal". I was playing for the Oshawa Generals in Windsor. It had been about 137 games that I had played in the OHL as a defenseman that I hadn't scored. It was the 3rd year and I was looking for that goal and now playing as a forward and I scored in Windsor, big body in front of the net, I did my job and the puck went off me, but mostly off my stick so it was legit. I did the Teemu Selanne celebration and I told everybody that I was going to do it. When I actually did it, I caught my glove, it was pretty cool. I definitely remember it and it was cool. I definitely remember and it was great.

After 10 seasons playing in North America what made you decide to head to the UK and play for Belfast?

The decision to go overseas, its usually the same for the other guys that are playing in the American Hockey League, that's one level below the NHL. What happens is guys will get into their 2nd or 3rd contract, be in the AHL for the 7th or 8th season and you are ready to see something else. So you make that decision. Others make that decision that they are ready when they are *about 30 years old and they make that decision that they have hit that ceiling in America and a lot of guys make the right choice and go across and they have a lot of success and actually make a lot more money and have more fun, and other guys end up coming back, it just depends on what your journey was meant for. For me, I was ready to see something different. I thought that my type of player was capped out in North America and I had this opportunity to sign for the Belfast Giants and their General Manager was Mark Bernard who was a former goal tender in the Super League and played with the London Knights when they had a team in London and he brokered the deal with Todd Kelman. He negotiated for me and it was pretty lucky for me!*

Why did you leave Belfast in 2020 and sign for Dundee?

My decision to go to Dundee after my season in Belfast was not mine. Because of personal issues, the Belfast Giants had notified me that I must get those issues resolved before I could return and unfortunately I was unable to do that. So I signed for the team that really wanted me, and I had a great experience in Dundee and got to see the country of Scotland and have no regrets. I loved it!

Who gave you the nickname of Sheriff and why?

The first time I heard it was actually in the notorious league, the LNAH in Quebec and my owner, it was after a game and the owner who owned the bar we were in, in our after game hangout. He called me over and I had had a really good game, so I knew he was going to say something to me. The words that came out of his mouth was: "From now on, we call you Le Sheriff!"

Did you enjoy your time in the UK?
Absolutely, my time in the UK, I usually refer it as the "funnest" time of my life. When I came to the UK I was able to experience what being a star in the league was really like. I was the leading all-star goal getter with my play for the Giants, so most people voted for me to play in the all-star game and I actually got to score in the game. And just experiences like that really boosted my confidence and I had an incredible time in the UK.

What do you remember most about it?
What I remember most is probably the people and how great they are and how great their personalities are and how great the way of life is in the UK and Ireland. I just had such a good time there. The colour of the green for a Canadian will do it for you alone. The uniqueness, the fact that it is in Ireland. The sun showers, the umbrellas, the fact that the rain is going to stop in a minute so don't worry. Where as in Canada it would rain for hours. And just little things like that I really enjoyed. I really enjoyed the culture. I'm a big history and geography cultural guy, so you cant get a better place than Northern Ireland for stuff like that, for all of the UK for that matter. It's probably what I remember the most.

Dody Wood

Darin Michael "Dody" Wood was born on March 18, 1972 and is a Canadian former professional ice hockey left winger drafted by the San Jose Sharks in the third round, 45th overall, in the 1991 NHL Entry Draft. He dressed for 106 NHL games with the San Jose Sharks before being traded to the New Jersey Devils on December 7, 1997. He was later assigned to the Albany River Rats for the remainder of the 97-98 season. In September 2000, he signed as a free agent with the Vancouver Canucks.

Wood also played with the IHL's Kansas City Blades, where he was voted most popular player two times as well as winning community service awards. He wore number 16 in his first stint with the team (1992–1995), and 13 when he returned (1998) because someone else already had 16, but returned to 16 later on. He also suited up for a few games with the Memphis RiverKings of the CHL as well as the Dayton Bombers in the 2003-2004 season.

In his time with San Jose, Wood went toe-to-toe with popular enforcer Tie Domi. The fight occurred in Domi's final season with the Winnipeg Jets. Wood was considered a strong opponent against Domi. In fact, the brawl between the two was one of the few fights Domi had lost. Wood was considered an enforcer as well. He participated in several fights throughout his professional career, these include fights with: Jim Paek (1993), Donald Brashear (1997), and Scott Walker (1997).

The NHL in the UK

Wood continued his hockey career after the NHL by playing for a senior league, the Horse Lake Thunder of the North Peace Hockey League and eventually playing for the Allan Cup. The league included many players that played with Wood in his NHL career including former Vancouver Canuck and Montreal Canadien Gino Odjick, former Calgary Flames fighter Sasha [The Masha] Lakovic and his brother Greg Lakovic, and Theo Fleury's cousin Todd Holt".Here, Dody Wood was referred to as the "former San Jose tough guy". Several articles note the irony of "Odjick, Lakovic and Wood banding together in a league with the word *peace* in its title"

Dody's Stats

S	TEAM	LEAGUE	GP	G	A	TP	PIM	+/-	POST	GP	G	A	TP	PIM	+/-
1989-90	Fort St. John Huskies	PCJHL	44	51	73	124	270	-							
	Seattle Thunderbirds	WHL	0	0	0	0	0	-	Playoffs	5	0	0	0	2	-
1990-91	Seattle Thunderbirds	WHL	69	28	37	65	272	-	Playoffs	6	0	1	1	32	-
1991-92	Seattle Thunderbirds	WHL	37	13	19	32	232	-							
	Swift Current Broncos	WHL	3	0	2	2	14	-	Playoffs	7	2	1	3	37	-
1992-93	San Jose Sharks	NHL	13	1	1	2	71	-5							
	Kansas City Blades	IHL	36	3	2	5	216	-4	Playoffs	6	0	1	1	15	0
1993-94	Kansas City Blades	IHL	48	5	15	20	320	0							
1994-95	San Jose Sharks	NHL	9	1	1	2	29	-							
	Kansas City Blades	IHL	44	5	13	18	255	0	Playoffs	21	7	10	17	87	10
1995-96	San Jose Sharks	NHL	32	3	6	9	138	-							
1996-97	San Jose Sharks	NHL	44	3	2	5	193	-3							
	Kansas City Blades	IHL	6	3	6	9	35	8							
1997-98	San Jose Sharks	NHL	8	0	0	0	40	-3							
	Albany River Rats	AHL	34	4	13	17	185	1	Playoffs	13	2	0	2	55	-3
	Kansas City Blades	IHL	2	0	1	1	31	0							
1998-99	Kansas City Blades	IHL	60	11	16	27	286	-8	Playoffs	3	0	1	1	25	2
1999-00	Kansas City Blades	IHL	77	13	28	41	341	1							
2000-01	Kansas City Blades	IHL	45	9	14	23	211	3							
2001-02	Ayr Scottish Eagles	BISL	42	16	15	31	171	-	Playoffs	7	3	4	7	11	-
2002-03	Nottingham Panthers	BISL	27	2	8	10	105	-	Playoffs	16	2	3	5	98	-
2003-04	Dayton Bombers	ECHL	13	1	1	2	87	-3							
	Memphis RiverKings	CHL	10	1	1	2	32	-5							
	Saint-Georges-de-Beauce	QSMHL	18	4	4	8	116	-							
2004-05	Horse Lake Thunder	NorthPHL	9	2	7	9	71	-							
S	TEAM	LEAGUE	GP	G	A	TP	PIM	+/-	POST	GP	G	A	TP	PIM	+/-
2004-05	Horse Lake Thunder	Allan Cup	-	-	-	-	-	-							

1. **What made you choose ice hockey as a profession?**
   I really had no thought as a young kid to play in the NHL, until about 16 when I was being scouted for WHL, even that was an old age for that
2. **How did it feel to be drafted by San Jose?**
   I watched the draft on TV first 2 rounds were televised and I had to be selected in the first 3 rounds, I waited a hour after the 2nd round and received no call so I went and played in a softball tourney. My dad got the call and when he told me it was a very special moment between me and my dad
3. **Do you remember your debut in the NHL?**
   My debut was in New York against the Rangers and I was nervous excited and pumped up, it was a huge and unforgettable moment
4. **Do you remember scoring your first goal in the NHL in 1992-93 season?**
   My first goal, I almost didn't want credit for it, Jeff Odgers told me what if that's the only goal or chance you have, last game of season. It was a shot that hit my backside for the tip
5. **You played 106 games in the NHL over 5 seasons what was your best memory of playing in the NHL and why?**
   The best moment I have about the NHL will be the long days and hours with my team mates when we could sit back and talk about careers and memories.
6. **You spent a lot of seasons between San Jose and the Kansas City Blades, did you prefer playing in the NHL or the IHL?**
   That is an easy one everyone wants to play in the NHL but it's a close second in KC because I played a regular shift and contributed to winning.
7. **What made you leave Kansas to come to the UK in 2001 and sign for Ayr?**
   Signing in the UK was difficult, the IHL merged with the AHL and I wasn't actively searching for a team due to shoulder surgery and wasn't sure if I was done. I went to Ayr because of a good friend Ed Courtney
8. **Did you have any expectations of playing in the UK?**

It was really a last minute decision and had zero time to look at the league, but I did not expect the year I had, All star team point per game and stilling playing my style of hockey

9. **Where they met?**
   The league had a lot of former players from the leagues in America but we were older players, but the teams were equal in talent so made it a very competitive league

10. **How did you find the game in the UK when comparing it to what you had experienced in North America?**
    I think with the success the GB national team is having has definitely helped the league get better with my ex coach Peter Russell

11. **What was your best memory of playing ice hockey?**
    Best memory I have is probably scoring a playoff hat trick to send our team to next round of playoffs

12. **Who was the best player that you have played with and why?**
    I have played with a few great players, Patrick Marleau, record for games played , Owen Nolan just a brute force and goal scorer, Jeff Friesen all around offensive player at 18 when he debuted

13. **Who was the best player that you have played against?**
    I played against Wayne Gretzky, Mario Lemieux Pavel Bure ranked probably 1,2,3

14. **What was the best goal that you have scored?**
    I think the best goal I scored was off the faceoff in Nottingham when the ref dropped and I shot from draw,

15. **What was the best rink that you have played in and why?**
    I think the best rink was Madison Square Garden for the fact its world famous

16. **Which team has the best fans and why?**
    The best fans are the ones that support your team, for many reasons different teams stand out but KC fans are the best

17. **What are you doing now for a job?**
    My job now is with Shell Canada and field operator

18. **Do you miss playing ice hockey?**
    Do I miss playing ice hockey, toughest question, no I don't I miss the hockey family in the dressing room

Justin Hodgman

Justin Hodgman was born on June 27, 1988 and is a retired Canadian professional ice hockey player who last played for UK Elite Ice Hockey League (EIHL) side Sheffield Steelers. Hodgman was most recently with Ferencvárosi TC of the Erste Liga.

Hodgman was a three-time Turner Cup champion with the Fort Wayne Komets in the IHL. He is the youngest player in IHL history to win the Turner Cup playoff MVP award at the age of 19. He played junior hockey for the Erie Otters of the OHL. While playing for the Erie Otters he led the team in scoring three of his four seasons 2007, 2008, 2009. After going undrafted by NHL clubs, he signed as a free agent with the Rockford IceHogs of the American Hockey League in 2009. In his first full professional season in 2009–10, Hodgman was loaned to the ECHL team Toledo Walleye before he was traded by the IceHogs to the Toronto Marlies to play out the year on January 21, 2010.

After three seasons abroad in Finnish Liiga and the Russian Kontinental Hockey League , Hodgman returned to North America signing a one-year two way contract with the Arizona Coyotes on July 1, 2014. Despite a strong training camp, Hodgman was assigned to begin the year with the Portland Pirates. On October 25, 2015, Hodgman was recalled by Arizona and in his first NHL game, he scored his first career goal on the powerplay against Roberto Luongo of the Florida Panthers. Hodgman was unable to secure a regular role with the Coyotes, appearing in 5 games.

On July 8, 2015, Hodgman continued in North America, signing a one-year two-way contract with the St. Louis Blues. In the 2015–16 season, Hodgman was reassigned to add depth to AHL affiliate, the Chicago Wolves. He appeared in 15 games with the Wolves, producing 6 assists, before opting to return to Europe. After clearing unconditional waivers and accepting a mutual termination of his contract with the Blues, Hodgman signed an optional two-year deal with Swedish club, Örebro HK of the top tier SHL on January 4, 2016.

Hodgman split the 2016–17 season, between HC Dynamo Pardubice of the Czech Extraliga and Pelicans of the Liiga. In scoring 20 points in 26 games in his second stint with the Pelicans.

Hodgman opted to return in the offseason to his first professional club, the Fort Wayne Komets of the ECHL on July 18, 2017. Hodgman played two further seasons in Fort Wayne, before returning to Europe following the 2018–19 campaign in signing a one-year contract with German club, Krefeld Pinguine of the DEL, on May 29, 2019.

Hodgman continued his career abroad in the 2020–21 season moving to Ferencvárosi TC of the Erste Liga in Budapest, Hungary.

In June 2021, UK EIHL side Sheffield Steelers announced Hodgman had signed terms ahead of the 2021–22 season. Hodgman retired from hockey in April 2022 following Sheffield's play-off quarter-final defeat to the Dundee Stars.

Justin's Stats

S	TEAM	LEAGUE	GP	G	A	TP	PIM	+/-	POST	GP	G	A	TP	PIM	+/-
2002-03	Mississauga Rebels U15 AAA	GTHL U15	-	-	-	-	-	-							
2003-04	Brampton Battalion U16 AAA	SCTA U16	30	19	29	48	34	-							
2004-05	Huntsville-Muskoka Otters	OPJHL	44	10	10	20	36	-							
2005-06	Erie Otters	OHL	57	7	13	20	55	-7							
2006-07	Erie Otters	OHL	67	19	32	51	63	-29							
2007-08	Erie Otters	OHL	64	37	43	80	75	-10							
	Fort Wayne Komets	IHL	11	4	4	8	7	0	Playoffs	13	7	7	14	12	11
2008-09	Erie Otters	OHL	66	24	42	66	71	-5	Playoffs	5	0	1	1	4	-7
	Fort Wayne Komets	IHL	6	2	3	5	20	4	Playoffs	11	7	5	12	16	8

Season	Team	League	GP	G	A	Pts	PIM	+/-		Playoffs GP	G	A	Pts	PIM	+/-
2009-10	Toledo Walleye	ECHL	33	9	12	21	35	-9							
	Toronto Marlies	AHL	38	7	5	12	23	-7							
	Fort Wayne Komets	IHL	3	1	2	3	0	-	Playoffs	10	4	13	17	8	-
2010-11	Toronto Marlies	AHL	42	12	17	29	44	7							
	Reading Royals	ECHL	3	0	1	1	4	0							
2011-12	Pelicans	SM-liiga	59	14	39	53	123	12	Playoffs	17	3	8	11	42	-2
2012-13	Metallurg Magnitogorsk	KHL	51	11	20	31	46	5	Playoffs	7	1	1	2	18	0
2013-14	Metallurg Magnitogorsk	KHL	18	3	6	9	12	1							
	Torpedo Nizhny Novgorod	KHL	14	1	6	7	6	2							
	Admiral Vladivostok	KHL	17	7	3	10	12	6	Playoffs	5	1	3	4	2	1
2014-15	Arizona Coyotes	NHL	5	1	0	1	2	-2							
	Portland Pirates	AHL	62	11	24	35	55	-11							
2015-16	Chicago Wolves	AHL	15	0	6	6	21	3							
	Örebro HK	SHL	11	1	3	4	2	-6							
2016-17	HC Dynamo Pardubice	Czechia	5	0	2	2	0	-4							
	Pelicans	Liiga	26	10	10	20	80	1	Playoffs	4	1	1	2	4	-2
2017-18	Fort Wayne Komets	ECHL	30	9	16	25	26	8	Playoffs	1	0	0	0	0	0
2018-19	Fort Wayne Komets	ECHL	50	15	42	57	53	7	Playoffs	4	0	1	1	17	-2
2019-20	Krefeld Pinguine	DEL	33	2	14	16	12	-3							
2020-21	Ferencvárosi TC	Erste Liga	33	14	26	40	99	14	Playoffs	8	3	3	6	-	-1
2021-22	Sheffield Steelers	EIHL	51	10	24	34	24	10	Playoffs	2	0	0	0	0	1

1. **What made you take up the sport of Ice Hockey?**
   Being Canadian it's something that is ingrained in our everyday life. Pretty much my whole family played, uncles, cousins and my dad. It is in the Canadian blood. I started when I was 3 and never looked back. I played in my 1st team when I was 6, the Brampton Maroons, it was my first love from day 1.

2. **Your career has involved many clubs in many countries, what made you take up the sport professionally?**
   At a young age I decided that hockey was what I wanted to do and all I have ever wanted to do with my life and I was going to do whatever I took to have as long a career as I could and I had a career that spanned over 15 years of playing professionally and I'm proud of that. I hope to get back into the rinks as a professional coach in the near future.

3. **After playing in Canada and the USA, why did you leave north America to play in Finland with Pelicans in 2011?**
   That's a tough one. I just wasn't getting the contracts offered that I thought I deserved after my play. I had just come off a pretty serious knee and leg injury where I had fractures up and down my left leg

after getting knee on kneed in an overtime period in Toronto so I asked for help and the outcome of my search was discovering a side in Finland needed a centre for their team. It worked out great and I had a great year scoring which propelled me toward the KHL. We ended up losing in a final, but I had a phenomenal season. It was one of the best career moves I could have made. I didn't think that way at the time, but it was!

4. **You left Finland to play in the KHL, having played for 3 clubs in the KHL how do you view the standard of playing in the KHL when comparing it to the NHL?**
   The KHL is unbelievable. A lot of people ask me what my favourite country was to play in. obviously apart from the NHL, the KHL was my favourite. The standard of hockey was just unbelievable. I was there for the lockout year. It was very special for all, as we travelled through all those countries and the experience of that was great. It was not quite the NHL which everyone knows, but a very close 2nd and it was well run and coached.

5. **Having enjoyed the delights of Eastern Europe what made you decide to head to the States?**
   After playing in the KHL, I had been away from my family for 2 years and I wanted to come home if I could. I had offers to go back to the KHL, but I also had an American agent working for me and he thought I could get some NHL interest with a contract offer from the Coyotes which was my 1st NHL contract offer and I hadn't had one before and by now I was 26 and I thought it was an ideal opportunity, so I took that contract with the Coyotes.

6. **How did it feel to sign for the Arizona Coyotes?**
   It was a dream come true, especially as most NHL contracts are signed with 18 to 20 year olds. I knew there was a lot of hard work ahead. I never even thought it was possible to make the team, but I made the Coyotes out of training camp and I was on their opening day roster but I got sent down to get some playing time.

7. **How did you feel when you scored a goal in the NHL?**
   It was fairy-tale stuff, in the 3rd period on a powerplay, down by a goal. I was put on the powerplay when I wasn't supposed to be on the powerplay team. I tied up the game and we went on to win in overtime. I was interviewed with the fans after the game. It was magical stuff. I felt very privileged and honoured to be part of such a prestigious league, and I'm just thankful to everyone who had helped me to get to that point.

8. **Can you remember it?**
   Yes I remember it well. The puck was down at the point, a shot was made on the net, it rebounded in front of me, I had a wide open goal and I made sure I put it in and celebrated as it was my 1st ever NHL goal.
9. **In 2016 you headed back to play in Europe once more and play in 3 countries which country do you prefer playing in?**
   I think Russia was my favourite. I had great experiences in Finland, Sweden and the Czech Republic, but Russia was definitely my favourite. Hungary was great. England was also awesome and I wish I could have played there longer. I am so very thankful for the experiences I had in all of the countries, but, if I were to pick just one to go back to and play in right now it would be Russia and the KHL.
10. **In 2016 you returned to play for the Pelicans, do you have happy memories in Finland with them?**
    Yes of course, Finland, the city of Lahti. The Pelicans organisation was great for me, my career and my family for life and hockey experiences. Making friends and lifelong connections and lifelong memories. Obviously the first go round and going to the finals after the team the year before nearly got relegated and we had a really special run and then when the opportunity came to go back after things didn't go well in the Czech Republic. I jumped all over it. It was just a 6 month contract and unfortunately the team success wasn't good. I also had some injury issues with a broken hand. I'm still very thankful for both my stints with the Pelicans.
11. **2017 saw you return to the States and again return to a former club (Fort Wayne Komets) you seem to leave clubs in a positive way so they are happy for you to return. Which club was your favourite club to play for and why?**
    Oh man, that's tough. Yes I'm thankful that there was a club that was willing to take me back into the organisation. I think that's always a positive. There are so many reasons why there are multiple clubs, for this reason, obviously Fort Wayne is now home for me. I won 3 championships here and my family is here and the Komets organisation and fans are also a very special group to play in front of and I'm very lucky to call here home. I always love to go and watch the boys play, so the Komets are definitely up there. I absolutely

loved my time in Sheffield and really wished I had come over earlier in my career and played more years, so Sheffield is definitely up there in my top clubs. The Erie Otters deserve a shout out, although they weren't a professional club, they played in the OHL, where you were learning to be a pro. I had 4 amazing seasons there with again great friends and making new connections and memories. The Pelicans, again a great organisation that I am thankful for. Those are definitely the ones of note!

12. **Back to Europe once more for the past 3 seasons ending up in the UK, which country do you prefer to play hockey in and why?**
The hockey in Finland was great. The hockey in Germany was really, really good. Unfortunately my time there wasn't as enjoyable with my injury issues and an organisation with issues, we were dead last and we weren't sure we were going to get our pay cheques. It made life difficult, struggling on and off the ice there, but the hockey was great. It's a great league! The hockey in Hungary was getting much, much better. I was very much impressed! As everyone knows, I think the hockey in the UK is getting better and better as well, and continuing to raise the standard and level of play. I think that has happened for the length of my career and I'm sure its only going to get higher and higher I'm sure! Its tough to say which one I would prefer to play in. I think the hockey in Finland would have been the best in my 2nd stint year, but they were all definitely enjoyable to play in!

13. **What made you come to the UK and sign for the Sheffield Steelers?**
That was something that was in the works for a while. For the previous 2 seasons I had been "kicking the tires" with England with former players, my agent and friends. It always seemed I was going to end up there. There were a few organisations to target and Sheffield always came pup as a top one for me. I would have been there in the covid year, but was very thankful to make something work the following year which was last season and my last season and it was good to end it with a good organisation. A trophy or two would have been nice. I should be thankful for everything I went through in Sheffield as it was my final season.

14. **Did you have any preconceptions of playing in the UK?**
Only that I knew that I wasn't going to underestimate it as their games were getting better and better. I treated it with the respect it deserved. I was very satisfied with the overall experience.

15. **Having arrived in Sheffield were all of your expectations met?**
They really were. Everything I was told and everything I studied and told to prepare for was really met. A top organisation, passionate

fans. It would be cool to travel the UK and play in different countries, see different cities and different styles of play. Absolutely every expectation had been met in Sheffield. We had a trophy capable team and weren't able to bring any of these home, but we were right there and we battled through a lot last year so I was proud of my season.

16. **How do you rate the British Elite League against the other leagues that you have played in?**

    Its really good and getting better. I cant stress enough a lot of the leagues I played in were top 5 leagues in Europe until the end of my career. So it's really tough to compare completely to these, but all I can say is that its getting more and more respect as the years go on, and it's a great league.

17. **Who was the best player that you have played with over the years and why?**

    A few stand out. When I was in Russia that was probably the top. We had Ryan O'Reilly; Evgei Malkin; Mats Zuccarello, Sergi Gonchar and Nikolai Kulyomin, that was pretty special to have played with over the years. I was playing in the NHL and my linemates in my first game were Sam Gagner and Martin Eirat. I was getting to be around Shane Doan, Keith Yandle, Oliver Ekman Larsson and Mike Smith. All these great players, playing with them with the Coyotes was very cool. I think that would be the top 2 leagues I've played in and a handful of players that it was pretty cool to be around every day.

18. **What was the best goal that you have scored?**

    The NHL goal was probably the best I've ever scored and probably the most special goal. Besides that was the triple overtime goal as a 19 year old for Fort Wayne to win the cup which was pretty cool. We were down 3-1 in the series and one that stands out across this as the nicest goal that I've ever scored was in my rookie year against Binghamton Senators. I remember distinctly as I was talking about it last year. It was end to end with a toe drag, so a little bit of everything there.

19. **In all of the games you have played in, what was your favourite game and why?**

    Well obviously my first NHL game, playing in front of my kids for the first time is always special, especially when they came over to Europe. Another one that really sticks out for me was my 1st game back after coming

back from my mental health issues in Sheffield. I had extreme anxiety and didn't know what to expect when I put myself out there, but the support I had was unbelievable. They called my name and I came out to great support from the Sheffield fans. It gave me goosebumps and brought tears to my eyes. It was overwhelming and something ill never forget.

20. **What was the best rink that you have played in and why?**
    There's a lot of cool rinks with some history the ones in Moscow like CSKA and St Petersburg which regularly sees 18000 fans in attendance. Other than that arenas in the NHL that I got to play in like Washington Capitals, that was very special and probably the best one I played in on the road in the NHL. I'm probably forgetting some, but its usually the history or the level of competition that you are playing. Again, I know this will sound silly, but as a teenager, I did play in the arena where they filmed "Slapshot", so I guess that was pretty cool as well!

21. **In your opinion which club had the best fans and why?**
    Oh wow, I could get myself into trouble here but, going back to Erie, those fans are passionate, Fort Wayne was great even when I was there in the IHL, we had 12,000 fans multiple times that was special, they were very engaged! In Lahti again they loved their hockey and were very passionate, chanting your name. playing in Krefeld although it wasn't a great season playing and seeing that yellow wall and the way they treat their games its like football games with the cheering. It was pretty cool. I will always come back to Sheffield, I feel its one of the best fan bases invested in the game and their players and in the club. That will always stay with me and it was just a great way to finish my career.

22. **Any thoughts on how you see your future? Will you remain in Europe of do you see you ending your career back in north America?**
    Now I'm happily retired of course I miss playing, but I do not regret my decision. I am very happy at home working on the next chapter of my life and my future for me and my family. I'm loving coaching and I plan on coaching professionally in the future which I'm sure will include stints in Europe and I can't wait to see what comes next!

CHRONOLOGICAL LIST

(Note: NHL Lockouts 04/05 and 12/13)

PLAYER	NAT	NHL Teams	UK TEAMS	PERIOD IN UK	Seasons
The Old Days					
Farrand Gillie		Detroit Cougars 1 28/29	BRI	38-39	1
Gordon Poirier		MON	BRI, HAR	46-51	5
London Lions					
Terry Clancy		Calif Seals, TOR	LONL	73-74	1
Mike Korney		DET	LONL	73-74	1
Tord Lundstrom	SWE	DET	LONL	73-74	1
Rick McCann		DET	LONL	73-74	1
Bill McKenzie		DET	LONL	73-74	1
Thomas Mellor		DET	LONL	73-74	1
Rick Newell		DET	LONL	73-74	1
Nelson Pyatt		DET	LONL	73-74	1
Terry Richardson		DET	LONL	73-74	1
Ulf Sterner	SWE	NYR	LONL	73-74	1
Murray Wing		DET 1	LONL	73-74	1
HBL Period					
Ron Plumb		HAR	FIF	84-86	2
Todd Bidner		WAS	FIF, PET, TEL, NOT, BRA, HUM, TEE, DUR, GUI, BLB	85-00	15
Garry Unger		TOR, DET, STL, ATL, LAK, EDM	DUNR, PET	85-88	3
Mark Pavelich	USA	NYR, MNS	DUNR 1	86-87	1
Al Sims		BOS, HAR, LAK	FIF	86-88	2
Fred Perlini		TOR	NOT, FIF, DEE, TRA, BLB, STR, BAS, LVL, GUI	86-96	10
Jim McTaggart		WAS	PET	87-88	1
Rocky Saganiuk		TOR, PIT	AYB, PET, MUR, DUR	87-95	8
Jere Gillis	USA	VAN. NYR, QUE, BUF, PHI	SOL, PET	88-91	3
Mike Rowe		PIT	WHI, FIF, BAS	88-95	7

The NHL in the UK

Name	NHL Teams	UK Teams	Years	Games
Mike Blaisdell	DET, NYR, PIT, TOR	DUR, NOT, SHE	90-01	11
Ron Shudra	EDM	SOL, SHE, HUL, EDI, COV, SHE, SCI	90-08	18
Daryl Evans	LAK, WAS, TOR	WHI	90-91	1
Jim McGeough	WAS, PIT	BRA	91-92	1
Mike Ware	EDM	MUR, EDI, CAR, SHE, LONK, CAR	92-04	12
Len Hachborn	PHI, LAK	AYRR	92-93	1
Kevin LaVallee	CAL, LAK, STL, PIT	AYRR	92-93	1
Selmar Odelein	EDM	NOT, SHE	92-94	2
Mark Morrison	NYR	FIF	93-05	12
Gary Yaremchuk	TOR	DUR	93-94	1
Doug Smail	WIN, MNS, QUE, OTT	FIF, CAR	93-96	3
Shawn Byram	NYI, CHI	BRA 1, MAN 2, AYR 5	94-02	8
Ken Priestlay	BUF, PIT	SHE 94-99, DUN 02/03	94-03	9
Laurie Boschman	TOR, EDM, WIN, NJ, OTT	FIF	94-95	1
Tony Cimellaro	OTT	DUR, BLA	94-95	1
Derek Laxdal	TOR, NYI	HUM, NOT, SHE	95-00	5
Wayne Cowley	EDM (1 93/94)	SHE (95-96), NEW (97-99)	95-99	4

ISL Period

Name	NHL Teams	UK Teams	Years	Games
Jim Mathieson	WAS 2- 89/90	NEW, NOT, AYR	96-00	4
Jamie Leach	PIT, HAR, FLO	SHE, NOT	96-01	5
Glenn Mulvenna	PIT 1 PHI 1	SHE 96/97, NEW 97-01	96-01	5
Jason Lafreniere	QUE, NYR, TAM	SHE 96/97 EDI GUI 01-03	96-03	7
Eric Calder	WAS	MAN	96-97	1
Darryl Olsen	CAL 1	NOT	96-97	1
Brad Zavisha	EDM	MAN	96-97	1
Marty Dallman	TOR (6)	NOT	96-98	2
Ken Hodge Jr	MNS, BOS, TAM	CAR	96-98	2
Brad Turner	NYI	MAN	96-98	2
Frank Caprice	VAN	CAR 96-98, AYR 98-99	96-99	3
Ed Courtenay	SAN,	SHE, AYR 97-02 / 05-10, BEL,	97-10	5

		NEW, MPX 05-10		
Jim Hrivnak	WAS, WIN, STL	MAN	97-98	1
Mike MacWilliam	NYI	CAR	97-99	2
Denis Chasse	STL, WAS, WIN, OTT	BRA, CAR	98-01	3
Frank Pietrangelo	PIT, HAR	MAN	98-01	3
Pierre Claude Drouin	BOS 3 96/97	BRA, NOT 98-02	98-02	4
Mark Kolesar	TOR	NOT, LONK	98-03	5
Paxton Schulte	QUE, CAL	BRA, BEL	98-04	6
Darcy Loewen	BUF, OTT	NOT	98-99	3
Vincent Riendeau	MON, STL, DET, BOS	AYR	98-99	1
Mike Zanier	EDM	NOT	98-99	1
Shayne Stephenson	BOS, TAM	AYR	99/00	1
Darren Banks	BOS	LON	99-00	1
Geoff Sarjeant	STL, SAN	AYR	99-00	1
Claudio Scremin	SAN	LONK	99-00	1
Dale Craigwell	SAN	SHE	99-01	2
Dennis Vial	NYR, DET, OTT	SHE	99-01	2
Jordan Willis	DAL 1	NOT	99-01	2
Barry Nieckar	HAR, CAL, ANA	LONK, NOT	99-03	4
Shayne Toporowski	TOR	BEL	00/01	1
Paul Beraldo	BOS	SHE	00-01	1
Kevin Brown	LAK, HAR, CAR, EDM,	MAN	00-01	1
Bobby Halkidis	BUF, LAK, TOR, DET, TAM, NYI	NEW J 2 games	00-01	1
Bill Huard	BOS, OTT, QUE, DAL, EDM, LAK	LONK -1	00-01	1
Scott Metcalfe	EDM, BUF	SHE	00-01	1
Dave Morissette	MON	LONK	00-01	1
Mike O'Neill	WIN, ANA	SHE	00-01	1
Derek Wilkinson	TAM	BEL	00-01	1
Lee Sorochan	CAL	LONK 00/01, BELO 02/03	00-03	3
Corey Spring	TAM	MAN 00/01, BRA 20/03	00-03	3
Mike Torchia	DAL	SHE, MAN, GUI	00-03	3

David Struch	CAL	NOT, LONK, BRA,	00-04	4
Jason Bowen	PHI, EDM	BEL, AYR, GUI, BEL	00-06	6
Philippe De Rouville	PIT 3 94-97	AYR 8- 00/01, BEL 3- 06/07	00-07	7
Barrie Moore	BUF, EDM, WAS	MAN 00/01, COV 05-09	00-09	9
Mike Bales	BOS, OTT	BEL	01-02	1
Phil Crowe	LAK, PHI, OTT, NAS	AYR	01-02	1
Joaquin Gage	EDM	AYR	01-02	1
Justin Hocking	LAK 1 93/94	MAN	01-02	1
Brad Lauer	NYI. CHI, OTT, PIT	SHE	01-02	1
Peter Leboutillier	ANA,	SHE	01-02	1
Kevin Miehm	STL	SHE	01-02	1
Terry Sandwith	EDM	BEL	01-02	1
Ryan Bach	LAK	SHE, BEL	01-03	2
Ian Herbers	EDM , TAM, NYI	AYR 01/02, GUI 02/03	01-03	2
Paul Kruse	CAL, NYI, BUF, SAN	SHE, BEL	01-03	2
Mike McBain	TAM	BRA	01-03	2
Jim Paek	PIT, LAK, OTT	NOT	01-03	2
Dody Wood	SAN	AYR, NOT	01-03	2
Daniel Goneau	NYR 96-00	BRA 01/02, FIF 03/04	01-04	3
Russ Romaniuk	WIN, PHI	MAN, CAR	01-05	4
Jason Ruff	STL, TAM	BELO 01/02, 03/04, 05=-07	01-07	6
Eric Charron	MON, TAM, WAS, CAL	NOT	02-03	1
Jonathan Delisle	MON 1 98/99	BRA	02-03	1
Doug MacDonald	BUF	BEL	02-03	1
Iain Fraser	NYI, QUE, DAL, EDM, WIN, SAN	SHE 02/03 NEW 06/07	02-07	5
Ed Patterson	PIT	LONK, CAR	02-07	5
EIHL Period				
John Craighead	TOR (5 96/97)	NOT, CAR	03-05	2
Jeff Ulmer	NYR	Car 03/04 3, BRAE 16/17 6	03-17	2
Scott Nichol	BUF, CAL, CHI	LONR	04-05	1
Derek Bekar	STL, LAK, NYI	DUN	04-05	1

Name		NHL Teams	UK Teams	Season	#
Wade Belak		COOL, CAL, TOR	COV	04-05	1
Nick Boynton		BOS	NOT	04-05	1
Eric Cairns		NYI, NYR,		04-05	1
Jeff Christian		NJD, PIT, PHO	SHE	04-05	1
Rob Davison		SAN, NYI, VAN,	CAR	04-05	1
Steve McKenna		LAK, MIN, PIT, NYR	NOT	04-05	1
Jamie McLennan		NYI, STL, MIN, CAL, NYR	GUI	04-05	1
David Oliver		EDM, NYR, OTT, DAL	GUI	04-05	1
Brendan Witt		WAS	BRA 3	04-05	1
Mel Angelstad		WAS	BEL NEW	04-06	2
Chris McAllister		VAN, TOR, PHI, COL, NYR	NEW 04/05, 08/09	04-09	5
Eric Beaudoin		FLO	NEW	05-06	1
Theo Fleury		CAL, COL, NYR, CHI	BEL	05-06	1
Mike Minard		EDM 1 -99/00	BEL	05-07	2
Radoslav Hecl	SLO	BUF	MPX	06-07	1
Brantt Myhres		TAM, PHI, SAN, NAS, WAS, BOS	NEW	06-07	1
Rumun Ndur		BUF, NYR, ATL	COV, NOT	06-09	3
Sylvain Cloutier		CHI	COV, HUL	06-14	8
Jeff MacMillan		DAL	MPX	07-08	1
Dean Melanson		BUF, WAS	BAS	07-08	1
Mike Stutzel		PHO	EDI	07-08	1
Matt Elich	USA	TAM	CAR	08-09	1
Jay Henderson		BOS	NOT	09-10	1
Cameron Mann		BOS, NAS	NOT	09-10	1
Cody Rukowski		STL 1 02/03	EDI	09-10	1
Sean McMorrow		BUF 1 02/03	BEL, DUN	09-11	2
Chris Allen		FLO	EDI, COV, TEL, PET, SOL, NOL	09-14	5
Mario Laroque		TAM	NOT 9/10 BRAE 13/14	09-14	5
Owen Fussey		WAS 4 03/04	EDI, COV, GUI	09-15	6
Brad Smyth		FLO, LAK, NYR, NAS, OTT	BEL	10-11	1
Craig Weller		PHO, MIN	CAR	10-11	1
Drew Bannister		TAM, EDM, ANA, NYR	HUL, BRAE	10-12	2
Jordan Krestanovich		COL	BRAE	10-13	3
Dan Tkaczuk		CAL	NOT	11-12	1

Name		Teams	UK Teams	Years	Seasons
Matt Beleskey		ANA	COV	12-13	1
Paul Bissonette		PIT, PHO	CAR	12-13	1
Tom Sestito	USA	CBJ, PHI	SHE	12-13	1
Anthony Stewart		FLO, ATL, CAR	NOT	12-13	1
Greg Stewart		MON	BEL	12-13	1
Drew Fata		NYI	SHE	12-14	2
David Ling		MON, CBJ,	NOT 12/13 15/16	12-16	4
Phil Oreskovic		TOR	NOT	13-14	1
Bob Wren		ANA, TOR	NOT	13-14	1
Greg Jacina		FLO	NOT	13-15	2
Dustin Kohn		NYI	SHE	13-15	2
Stefan Meyer		FLO, CAL	SHE, BRAE	13-16	3
Danny Bois		OTT	SHE	14-15	1
Ryan O'Marra		EDM, ANA	COV	14-15	1
Nathan Robinson		DET, BOS	NOT, BEL	14-15	1
Kevin Westgarth		LAK, CAR, CAL	BEL	14-15	1
Matt Keith		CHI, NYI	BRAE	14-17	3
Kris Beech		PIT, NAS, WAS, COL, VAN	BEL	15-16	1
Mike Duco		FLO, VAN	SHE	15-16	1
Chris Holt		NYR 1 STL 1	BRAE	15-16	1
Cam Janssen	USA	NJD, STL	NOT	15-16	1
Nathan McIver		VAN, ANA	BRAE	15-16	1
Guillaume Desbiens		VAN, CAL	SHE 15-17	15-17	2
Ric Jackman		DAL, BOS, TOR, PIT, FLO, ANA	BRAE, FIF	15-17	2
Brad Moran		CBJ, VAN	NOT	15-17	2
Derrick Walser		CBJ	BEL	15-17	2
Jim Vandermeer		PHI, CHI, CAL, PHO, EDM, SAN	BEL	15-19	4
Patrick Bordeleau		COL	CAR	16-17	1
David Brine		FLO	CAR	16-17	1
Brian McGrattan		OTT, PHO, CAL, NAS	NOT	16-17	1
Jesse Schultz		VAN	SHE	16-17	1
Jared Staal		CARolina Hurricanes	EDI	16-17	1
Jason Williams		DET, CHI, ATL, CBJ, DAL, PIT	NOT	16-17	1
Jay Rosehill		TOR, PHI	BRAE, MAN	16-18	2
Pavel Vorobyev	UKR	CHI	EDI	16-18	2
Stefan Della Rovere		STL	BRAE 16/17, SHE 18/19	16-19	3

Name	Nat	NHL Teams	UK/Other	Years	#
Layne Ulmer		NYR	CAR 16-18 MAN 19/20	16-20	4
Tyson Strachan		STL, FLO, WAS, BUF, MIN	CAR	17-18	1
Andre Devaux		TOR, NYR	SHE 17/18	17-18	1
Cole Jarrett		NYI 1 05/06	BEL	17-18	1
Peter LeBlanc		WAS 1	FIF	17-18	1
Yann Sauve		VAN	NOT	17-18	1
Jonathan Ferland		MON 7 05/06	BEL	17-19	2
Michael Garnett		ATL 24 05/06	NOT	17-19	2
Tim Wallace	USA	PIT, NYI, TAM, CAR	SHE, MKL	17-19	2
Kyle Baun		CHI	BEL	18-19	1
Patrick Dwyer	USA	CAR	BEL	18-19	1
Josh Gratton		PHI, PHO	GLA	18-19	1
Kevin Henderson		NAS 4-12/13	NOT	18-19	1
Dylan Olsen	USA	CHI, FLO	NOT	18-19	1
Chris Stewart		COL, STL, BUF, MIN, ANA, CAL	NOT	18-19	1
Brett Bulmer		MIN	FIF, NOT	18-20	2
Aaron Johnson		CBJ, NYI, CAL, CHI, EDM, BOS	SHE	18-20	2
Charles Linglet		EDM	CAR	18-20	2
Keaton Ellerby	USA	FLO, LAK, WIN	SHE	21-22	1
Justin Hodgman		ARI	SHE	21-22	1

NHL LOCKOUTS
2004/05 NHL Lockout
A number of NHL players went to Great Britain.
In the Elite Ice Hockey League, Coventry Blaze signed Wade Belak,
Cardiff Devils signed Rob Davison,
London Racers signed Eric Cairns and Scott Nichol, and
Nottingham Panthers signed Nick Boynton, Ian Moran, Steve McKenna.

McKenna also used that season to play for the Adelaide Avalanche in the Australian Ice Hockey League.
In the British National League, Guildford Flames signed Jamie McLennan and David Oliver,
Bracknell Bees signed Brendan Witt while
Newcastle Vipers signed Chris McAllister. In 2008, McCallister signed for the Vipers for a second time.

London Racers incident
During the lockout, Cairns played for the London Racers. On March 23, 2005, he was involved in a notorious fight with Wade Belak (playing for Coventry Blaze), during which he punched a linesman. Cairns was called initially for a slashing major against Andre Payette and then threw a punch at an official who was escorting him to the penalty box. Cairns skated around the rink for about a minute threatening the officials, unable to lose his teammates who were attempting to ensure he did not further escalate the incident. Instead of leaving the ice, Cairns instead skated to the Coventry bench where he threw a punch which resulted in a bench-clearing brawl. He was suspended for the remainder of the season and the entire next season in all IIHF tournaments, although the NHL allowed him to return the following year.[1]

2012/13 NHL Lock Out

Matt Beleskey	Anaheim Ducks	Coventry Blaze	EIHL
Anthony Stewart	Carolina Hurricanes	Nottingham Panthers	EIHL
Drew Miller	Detroit Red Wings	Braehead Clan	EIHL
Tom Sestito	Philadelphia Flyers	Sheffield Steelers	EIHL

ICE COLD MURDER
a book by
Michael A Chambers

A murder mystery story Centred around a game of Ice Hockey

The town of Merrivale is of average size and population that contains the usual; housing and amenities it warrants and Saturday afternoons are strictly reserved for the weekly game of football, hockey and rugby as well as a shopping spree for the locals.

When a body is found within hockey owner Mark Atkin's establishment, Inspector Dilley has to unravel this terrible scene in order to find out what happened. Amongst a complexity of doors, keys and camera pictures which have much to do with it all.

Many people are involved with the events that occur this day which puts them 'in the frame' within this much troubled club.

WHO DID IT?

132 pages, a royal size paperback
Scores of pictures, *save* this for your bookshelf.

£8.00p includes postage (via Paypal -using** email, leave your address for postage)

Or by cheque - call 07848915159)
Contact spikc2004@yahoo.co.uk** for any info.

DROP THE PUCK
6 SEASONS
128 GAMES
INCLUDES NIHL PLAYOFF FINALS
BASN
You Tube
@BASN TV
BASN
BRITISH AMERICAN SPORTS NETWORK